RENASCENT PRAGMATISM

For Manuela Romero,
thankfully for what is ... and in anticipation of what is to come
and
for Cruz Romero Morales
and our life of love.

Renascent Pragmatism

Studies in Law and Social Science

Edited by

ALFONSO MORALES
University of Texas at El Paso

ASHGATE

Published by
Ashgate Publishing Limited
Gower House
Croft Road
Aldershot
Hants GU11 3HR
England

Ashgate Publishing Company
Suite 420
101 Cherry Street
Burlington, VT 05401-4405
USA

Ashgate website: http://www.ashgate.com

British Library Cataloguing in Publication Data
Renascent pragmatism : studies in law and social science. -
(Law, justice and power)
1.Sociological jurisprudence 2.Pragmatism
I.Morales, Alfonso
340.1'15

Library of Congress Cataloging-in-Publication Data
Renascent pragmatism : studies in law and social science / [edited by] Alfonso Morales.
p. cm. -- (Law, justice and power)
Includes bibliographical references and index.
ISBN 0-7546-2180-4
1. Sociological jurisprudence. 2. Pragmatism. I. Morales, Alfonso, 1961- II. Series.

K370 .R46 2003
340'.115--dc21

2002028169

ISBN 0 7546 2180 4

Printed and bound in Great Britain by MPG Books Ltd, Bodmin, Cornwall

Contents

List of Contributors

Cary Coglianese J.D., Ph.D. is Associate Professor of Public Policy at Harvard University's John F. Kennedy School of Government and Chair of the Regulatory Policy Program at the School's Center for Business and Government. His interdisciplinary research focuses on issues of regulation and administrative law. In particular, he has examined alternative means of designing regulatory processes and the role of disputing in regulatory policy making, with his published work including: "Litigating Within Relationships: Disputes and Disturbance in the Regulatory Process", Law and Society Review (1996); "Assessing Consensus: The Promise and Performance of Negotiated Rulemaking", Duke Law Journal (1997); and "Assessing the Advocacy of Negotiated Rulemaking", New York University Environmental Law Journal (2001). His recently-published book, *Regulating from the Inside: Can Environmental Management Systems Achieve Policy Goals?* (2001), is the first to examine the public policy implications of emerging trends in private environmental management. In other research, Coglianese has written on international regulation, federalism, interest groups, and regulatory politics. An affiliated scholar at the Harvard Law School and the director of the Kennedy School's Politics Research Group, Coglianese teaches public law, environmental policy, and professional ethics. He is a member of the editorial advisory board of the Law and Society Review, coordinator of the Law and Society Association's international collaborative research network on regulatory governance, and a recipient of the American Political Science Association's Edward S. Corwin Award. Coglianese received his J.D., M.P.P. (public policy), and Ph.D. in political science from the University of Michigan.

William P. Fisher Jr., Ph.D. completed the University of Chicago's Social Sciences Divisional Master's degree in 1984, then was a Spencer Foundation Dissertation Fellow, and earned a Ph.D. in Chicago's Department of Education in 1988, concentrating in Measurement, Evaluation, and Statistical Analysis (MESA). Dr. Fisher is a member of the Institute for Objective Measurement's Board of Directors, and Chair of its Program Committee. He hosted the 10th International Objective Measurement Workshops at LSU Health Sciences Center in April 2000, measurement theory to the quantification of quality of health care; serving on the LSU Health Care Services Division's Health Care Effectiveness Team, supervising outcome measurement projects relevant to disease management programs in the Louisiana statewide public hospital system; and exploring the possibility of a poetics of quantification.

Helen Ingram Ph.D is Warmington Chair of Social Ecology at the University of California at Irvine. She has authored or coauthored nine books and over 90 book chapters and articles. Most of her work is in the area of the relationship of public policy to democracy and the politics of natural resources, especially water.

Robert R. Jimenez MA is a doctoral student in sociology at the University of Michigan with an emphasis on power, history, and social change. Jimenez's research interests include the intersection of community-based organizations, gangs, and government agencies.

Murray J. Leaf Ph.D is Professor of Anthropology and Political Economy at the University of Texas at Dallas. He has conducted ethnological field research in India and has served on development projects sponsored by USAID and the Government of India, USAID and the Government of Bangladesh, and the United Nations Centre for Regional Development, Nagoya Japan. His publications include: *Man, Mind and Science, a History of Anthropology*, Columbia, 1978, *Song of Hope*: *The Green Revolution in a Punjab Village*, Rutgers, 1984, "Local Control Versus Technocracy: The Bangladesh Flood Response Study", Journal of International Affairs, Summer 1997, and *Pragmatism and Development: the Prospect for Pluralist Transformation in the Third World*, Bergen and Garvey, 1998.

Peter Margulies Ph.D is Professor of Law at Roger Williams University School of Law, where he directs the Family and Disability Law Clinic and teaches Professional Responsibility. He has written almost twenty articles on lawyering and legal education, including *Representation of Domestic Violence Survivors as a New Paradigm of Poverty Law: In Search of Access, Connection, and Voice*, 63 Geo. Wash. L. Rev. 1071 (1995); *Identity on Trial: Subordination, Social Science Evidence, and Criminal Defense*, 51 Rutgers L. Rev. 45 (1998); and *The Virtues and Vices of Solidarity: Regulating the Roles of Lawyers Representing Persons Accused of Terrorist Activity*, which will appear shortly in the Maryland Law Review.

Alfonso Morales Ph.D. is Assistant Professor of Sociology at the University of Texas at El Paso. His Ph.D. is from Northwestern and his research has been supported by the American Bar Foundation and the Ford Foundation. He is affiliated with the Center for Law and Border Studies at UTEP. Recent publications include, “Income Tax Compliance and Alternative Views of Ethics and Human Nature” in *The Ethics of Tax Evasion* edited by Robert McGee; “Policy from Theory: A Critical Reconstruction of Theory on the ‘Informal’ Economy” in *Sociological Imagination*, and “Epistemic Foundations for a Practicing Socio-legal Science”, in the *Law and Society Review*. He is currently working on a book on Chicago’s Maxwell Street Market and lawyering in the U.S.-Mexico borderlands.

Anne Larason Schneider Ph.D. is Dean of the College of Public Programs at Arizona State University and Professor, School of Justice Studies. She earned her B.S. and M.S. degrees in political science from Oklahoma State University and her Ph.D. in political science from Indiana University. Dr. Schneider’s primary academic interests are in public policy and in the elusive quest for understanding how and why we get the kinds of policy that characterize the United States at this time. One of her primary concerns is that public policy often does not serve society as well as it should, even though democracy seems to be the best form of governance that human beings have devised. She is the author of Policy Design for Democracy (co-authored with Helen Ingram and published by the University Press of Kansas in 1997), Deterrence and Juvenile Crime (Springer-Verlag in 1989). Her best-known article (again, with Helen Ingram) is “The Social Construction of Target Populations” that appeared in the *American Political Science Review* in 1993.

Charlene Haddock Seigfried Ph.D. is a professor of Philosophy and American Studies and a member of the Women’s Studies committee at Purdue University. She is a former president of the Society for the Advancement of American Philosophy, was the John Dewey Lecturer for 1998, and is currently on the executive board of the Society for the Study of Women Philosophers. Among her publications are, *Chaos and Context, William James’s Radical Reconstruction of Philosophy*, an *Pragmatism and Feminism*. She is currently editing *Feminist Interpretations of John Dewey*.

Brian Z. Tamanaha J.D. is a Professor at St. John’s University School of Law. He earned a Doctorate of Juridical Science at Harvard Law School, and has written two dozen articles and three books in the field of socio-legal studies, including *Realistic Socio-Legal Theory: Pragmatism and a Social Theory of Law* (Oxford University Press 1997) and *A General Jurisprudence of Law and Society* (Oxford University Press, 2001).

William G. Weaver J.D., Ph.D. is Associate Professor of Political Science at the University of Texas at El Paso. He writes about issues in political theory and law and is currently working on a book on tort liability.

Foreword - Pragmatism as a Discipline: (Re)Introducing Pragmatist Philosophy to Law and Social Science

Alfonso Morales

> For philosophical problems arise when language *goes on holiday*.
>
> Ludwig Wittgenstein

> Everything rests, so far as I can see, on a condition, obvious to the eye, which may be called, if one care to, the pluralism of experience.
>
> William Carlos Williams

Scholarship is produced by people in ongoing relationships over time and in particular places. In brief, scholarship is anchored to social context. Of this we have little doubt. People we have met and those we will meet; places we inhabit and those we would like to visit all claim some of the attention we dedicate to scholarship. For example, if you know I desire a Fulbright fellowship in Mexico almost as much for my son's proficiency in Spanish as for my intellectual interests, then you have a concrete example of how our many plans and aspirations overlap with the variety of our needs and wants. Intellectual problems are matters of personal perspective as well as aspects of public matters and activities. Our interests are rooted in relationships with people, places, and ideas.

The chapters of this book combine each author's interests in people, places, and ideas. Indeed, part of the impetus for this book stemmed from the observation that much recent scholarship has been generated on pragmatism, but frequently only elaborating one element of the position to the exclusion of the relationship between that element and social life. Since pragmatism is an *operative* and *instrumental* philosophy, engagement with its ideas should make some difference to the engaged, even if it is only to find that pragmatism has nothing to offer the thinker on a problem

(Tamanaha 1997, chapter 2). No less than ten recent books develop connections between some precipitating concerns of "classical" pragmatists and our contemporary interests and needs (please see the reference section at the end of this Foreword). Why the renascent interest in pragmatism? The ideas have never gone away, but our interest in them seems to be increasing. My answer is pragmatic: there is a small but fairly constant number of scholars, mostly philosophers and social theorists, interested in preserving or updating the 'revolt against dualism' in their particular contexts. To these have been added scholars (mostly social scientists and legal scholars) interested in public problems, and in theory; but who embrace consequentialist approaches to both. The latter embrace theories and approaches to science rooted in behavioral assumptions and implications premised on the *active* control of ourselves and our environment.

Our interests and needs are a river plain into which courses have been cut by social life. In the most direct way possible, pragmatism urges that we consider our needs and interests and the context in which these flow. But in this process, pragmatists also urge us to understand and transform ourselves and the context experimentally in order to develop solutions to the problem at hand. Experimentation privileges understanding systems of ideas in practice rathen that conceptual description of these systems. Science is understood to have a role, but one limited by other meaning-making activities. Pragmatist inspired work also acknowledges that the habits and practices which we have inherited are hard to change. We desire to address social problems, but we can only access the strata of past and present exposed to us by the streams of activities of social life. Durability is limited and circumstances are obstinate, and never permit a total understanding. However, life gives willingly what the pragmatist desires, which is the understanding of problems from perspectives. It is up to a community, inclusive of scholars or policy makers, to do the work of understanding situations. Engaging in understanding means that the community inquires by developing an actionable understanding of a situation using linked experiments that employ the ideas-in-practice. The process is continuous, one can never step in the same river twice, and it is incremental, the broad courses do not change much even if individuals occasionally undergo radical change.

The chapters in this book can be seen as efforts of understanding tools, ideas, and situations. Each chapter makes connections with important contributions from pragmatism and recent pragmatist thought. *Because* the authors consider recent social, legal and policy research, and seek to bridge toward possible futures for socio-legal practice, the chapters convey some informed reflections on what we know and what use the tools will be in navigating life's streams of activity.

In this Foreword I take up three purposes. First, I will sketch pragmatist method and ideas, with ocassional comparison to essentialist thought. Second, I will briefly describe some of pragmatism's recent manifestations in legal scholarship and the social sciences. Third, I will sketch the organization of the rest of the book. The dominant metaphor of the chapter is hydrological. In the same way that James described the formation of habits in terms of channels in the brain, scholarly traditions provide tools for understanding the courses of social life. In this respect, pragmatist scholarship can be no different from other streams of thought. However, pragmatism differs from other ways of knowing in two significant ways. First, it is profoundly democratic in that it welcomes a flood of participation. In turn, participation remakes the plain of our experience, opening channels to flow through, and inviting inquiry about the strata exposed. Secondly, pragmatist thought is self-correcting for the same reasons as science, as it is constantly reminding us of the limits and possibilities of human practices, both generally and specifically in scholarship.

A Pragmatist View of Knowing: Sketching How, By Whom, and For What

To many, pragmatism is a politically conservative 'going concern' To others, it is a source of political and personal innovation (Seigfried 1996, Shusterman 1997). Finally, others see it as neutral and empty of prescription for social life (Tamanaha 1997). Regardless, the corpus is diverse and large, and contemporary users of pragmatist writings are urged to begin their understanding by examining a history or two (I recommend Lovejoy's *The Revolt Against Dualism* and Rucker's *The Chicago Pragmatists*); by looking at thematically edited collections of Dewey, James, and others (I use those by McDermott). Also, when looking at recent collections, view them both with an eye to the purposes intended by the editor(s), how each chapter's contents is geneolgized, and for one's particular needs. For instance, this volume is intended for legal scholars or social scientists of an empirical bent who are interested in working on empirical and policy related problems. In other words, those who are employers of science, but remain skeptical of its power. Theorists, philosophers, and others may find it of interest (as they are represented herein), but my interest is primarily in showing how the pragmatist's view of science as a democratic and skeptical practice can be formulated as methodological practices and extended to empirical problems in order to eventually bear fruit in social policy.

Pragmatism uses an operative theory of knowledge, such a theory regards knowledge as something to use to help resolve human problems. This knowledge is produced by science, the disinterested inquiry into things which we are interested in, by a community of people whose methods and findings are constantly refined. Science is democratic, admitting all to a community of inquirers. As Putnam puts it, "the model is a group of inquirers trying to produce good ideas and trying to test them to see which ones have value" (1995: 70-71). Winch (1958) contributed to the philosophy of a democratic and problem oriented philosophy by showing that our understanding of behavior is incomplete if we have not understood the rules, or system of rules, which produce the behavior. Pragmatists seek to understand the rules from the perspective of the participants. For Winch, social relations exist in ideas capable of being learned and described in their own right without a need for analyst composed categories.

The contrasting positivist or essentialist positions are treated elsewhere in more detail by authors represented here (Leaf 1979 and Tamanaha 1997 are among the interlocutors). The most common concerns pragmatists have of positivist or essentialist science is that it repeats old names or invents new ones for old ideas that have previously been shown to be both self-contradictory and unproductive. Pragmatism eschews name creation for its own sake in favor of developing tools to understand the world we observe and the rules which produce it. These tools are available in a variety of forms (see a limited discussion in the methodological chapters), but there are many sources for understanding conceptual and methodological tools, some more genealogical (Leaf 1979) and some more theoretical (Tamanaha 1997, Leaf 1984, Morales 1998b).

How a scholar acquires these tools for understanding is not necessarily unimportant (some atmospheres of learning are friendlier to particular positions than others. Baron and Hannan 1994 compate economics and sociologists in terms of tools acquired). However, those of the pragmatist tradition and attitude are far more concerned with the subsequent problem of employing those tools to understand social life and the further questions of discovering what has worked in addressing social problems, followed by experimenting to solve the problems of our contemporary circumstances. William James was not speaking idly when he called pragmatism a new name for some old ways of thinking but he was speaking modestly. His project, like that of other pragmatists since, has been to extend prior insights about our condition and contemporary life. Trepidation is one outcome of the ongoing need for individuals to reconstruct their own and social life, and only by combining will and emotional energy are people able to alternate between the tough and tender habits of mind required to achieve their ends. In this regard pragmatism is democratic, admitting all to the practice of inquiry and transformative action.

Pragmatic ways of thinking lie at the core of our traditions of science and liberal democracy. Prescriptions for truth and method underlie the pragmatist approach. James, like the other pragmatists, was concerned with the difference ideas could make in behavior. What difference is made in the world from true or false beliefs? James' concern with this question led him to understand truth as part of a network of self-implying conceptions. He wrote: "The true is the name for whatever proves itself to be good in the way of belief, and good, too, for definite and assignable reasons" This notion of truth shares with Holmes' "prediction" theory of law the idea of an interest in reasons or the ends sought, and Holmes' concern is also with "the reasons for desiring particular ends" Both authors trust an experimental vision of policy practice, a vision contingent on context as well as cognizant of power and politics but a vision not cynical regarding the possibilities for dialogue and the transformative potentials of public participation.

However, irrespective of this vision and practice, social scientific thought in the last five decades has been, generally speaking, more interested in new names for seemingly new topics or perspectives than fundamental debates about the ideas of science and human nature that lie behind the debates. It is not hard to see why. There are great incentives to be able to claim originality, and it is much easier to do this by becoming identified with something that seems radically new than by trying to articulate the subtle changes that have to be made to truly powerful but long-standing approaches and assumptions as they generate new results and are applied in new circumstances. As mentioned, pragmatism eschews labeling for the analyst's sake, privileging instead a concern for understanding behavior in its many perspectives.

The heart of pragmatism is not a set of deductive first principles to impose on experience, but a self-discipline to avoid such imposition. By examining analysts assumptions, pragmatism renders the complexity of labeling schemes and competing traditions of social theory more intelligible and presents these schemes and traditions as a byproduct of those assumptions. By comprehending the connection between philosophical assumptions, problem formulation, data collection, theory, and problem solving, pragmatist inspired scholars bring a scepticism to analysis, one tempered by the desire to address human problems; they address them *as economically as possible* which is itself only possible by stripping methods and theories to what work. Pragmatic currents remind us that the theoretical and methodological choices we make have implications beyond our disciplinary concerns and debates. Furthermore, employing pragmatic devices to navigate troubled waters can produce a tempered optimism about the application of science to social problems. Thus, pragmatism provides a corrective for the academics socialized impulse toward proliferating theoretical or conceptual labels in a way that obscures our understanding of behavior (Morales 1998a and b; 2001), admonishing those who think that science is only for describing social problems.

Thus, pragmatism has two sides closely interrelated and grounded in a common understanding of knowledge: (a) knowledge is contextual and social, but also that (b) knowledge is produced in the reconciliation of perceptions which cannot be separated from the reconciliation of purposes. On the one hand, pragmatism is what James called radical empiricism, by which he meant a conception of knowledge as wholly based upon and contextualized within experience. Pragmatism makes no appeals to such supposed absolutes as laws of logic, concepts of pure mind or pure matter, or the rest of the armamentarium of distinctions that enlightenment materialism and idealism depended on and that, however disguised, carry on into modern positivism and deconstructivist postmodernism. On the other hand, pragmatism was and is broadly acknowledged as the guiding impulse behind many progressive era reforms; for example, the legislative and socio-economic programs of the New Deal (Irons 1982, but see Shamir 1995 chapter 6), and the post-war democratic reconstruction of Western Europe and Japan (Leaf 1998). In these, pragmatic arguments for social policy consistently displaced enlightenment concerns with foundationalist or essentialist arguments about free markets, absolute rights in property, utilitarian actors and the like with concerns about reconciling observable interests, solving observable problems with available means, and constructing social institutions that would allow people with interests and values in conflict to negotiate solutions from below rather than have them imposed from above.

Yet, despite pragmatism's world-shaping practical success, since the middle of the 20th century, academic interest in pragmatism as a basis and source of public policy was largely replaced by a preoccupation with a return to the kinds of arguments that were dominant in the enlightenment. This shift in the social sciences has only one basis in social life, the effort to distinguish one's work from that of predecessors and contemporaries and so be valued by one's peers. On the other hand, actual lawyering, judicial practice, and other elements of legal behavior have not swayed much from pragmatist foundations since the law could not be anchored on any foundation except that which anchors pragmatism: the flux of social life. Ever-changing behavior has constrained and compelled the jurisprudential concern with long-evolved ways of thinking that have been bottled as legal precedent and judicial interpretation understood best with Holmes' prediction theory of law, and this is well recognized. So, while in the mid-20th century many policy and social science analysts could turn to foundationalist concerns, the law could not because the law had to be anchored in a relatively unclouded view of social life. Meanwhile policy makers, like social scientists, could make superficially sound arguments in the face of ambiguous empirical evidence and blame the ambiguity on error terms in an analysis or anything but their logically erected self-referential theories. The result was an accelerated alienation of what many take to be social or policy theory from what is actually done in the world. This sort of remove mirrors the alienation within the academy between postmodernist claims that empirical science is impossible and the empirical scientists persistence in doing it anyway in order to get some sort of results. For some social scientists, particularly for pragmatists, the positivist and deconstructivist's problem is the absence of self-implied connections between branches of theory, empirical work, method and policy. Pragmatism is a river that as it reaches the sea, branches out, producing distributaries infused with elements of all four.

Pragmatism's resurgence is partly due to grassroots concerns with policies that work and partly due to social scientists dissatisfaction with general theory or middle-range and all other such types of theory or labels for theory that do not make theory relevant to real life. For scholars of law and social science, pragmatism provides a consistent, comprehensive, and productive understanding of social life. We know that this understanding will be socially constructed and contextual. That is not a weakness but its strength. It is precisely what makes it verifiable, shareable, applicable, and productive. But contexts are of many kinds and what those are cannot be in anyway predetermined, nor will they stay the same. Contexts exist now that have never existed before. Others that were once experienced by virtually everyone on a daily basis can now be reconstructed only with the greatest difficulty if at all. Pragmatism is a progressive tradition in every sense. To restore it, we must advance it; to advance it, we must restore it.

Currents in the Flood Plain: Pragmatist Projects in History and Social and Legal Science

The restorative/progressive project has adherents in many disciplines. They draw on the rich soil of ideas in which the present inquiries are rooted. I will sketch some of these developments in order to locate the present project in the broader context.

Historically speaking it is noted that pragmatism was the reining historiography until the 1950s (Feffer 1993, Kloppenberg 1998). Recently, a variety of scholars have taken up the task of producing a nuanced view of pragmatism, its emergence, its relation to various political and economic problems of the first half of the 20th century, and its ongoing importance. Feffer (1993) charts the initial congruence between pragmatism and progressivism, its successes and failures, and eventual divergence. Ross' (1991) award winning book on the history of American social science carefully attends to competing people and ideas between 1865 and 1930. Her work locates pragmatism as central to social science in the U.S. and makes clear that choices for how to practice social science are rooted in history, in the interests and purposes people pursued, that are not necessarily foreordained. In doing so she offers a classically pragmatic point, prior choices can become open to re-examination. Wilshire (2000) makes an argument for the connection between pragmatist and Native American thought. Finally, Leaf (1979), has produced a history of anthropology (writ very broadly) in which he makes eminently clear the implications for theory, method, and empirical research of the choice between pragmatist and positivist epistemic positions on science.

Among feminists, pragmatism is proving an insightful tool (Seigfried 1996, Nussbaum 2000) with broad implications for ethics and theories of the subject. Dewey, Mead, Holmes, and other pragmatists are again the subject of critical interest (Campbell 1995, Joas 1985) and of new compilations (Posner 1992). Other work is reflective about the intellectual history and trajectory of pragmatism (Diggins 1995) and pragmatism as social theory (Joas 1993). Finally, some scholars have, as we have here, compiled essays on pragmatism, some previously published while others are original contributions (Dickstein 1998, Goodman 1995, Menand 1997, Hollinger and Depew 1995). Few, however, have dedicated themselves to the concerns of public policy, methods, and empirical research as we do here. Our interest in these historical efforts and compilations is tied to our recognition that the contemporary context invites reflection on the understandings and concerns of earlier scholars as well as what we might chart for our projects.

Disciplinary examples are many, but I will review here only a few, either for their centrality or how they indicate connections between pragmatism and disciplinary based work. In political science and policy analysis, the work of Kaufman-Osborn (1982) is notable for his recovery of Dewey from "technophile" interpretations while Shields (1996) locates public administration in pragmatic roots. Also important for policy work are the writings of Helen Ingram and Anne Schneider (1990, 1993) who also have an original essay in this volume. In political science an entire issue of the *American Journal of Political Science* (1999 v. 43 no. 2) was devoted to reviewing essays reviving pragmatism. In sociology, Rochberg-Halton (1986), Emirbayer (1997), Shalin (1986, 1992) and Joas (1993, 1996) exemplify the long term interest in pragmatism, even as apart from the growth of symbolic interactionism. In economics, particularly in the school of institutional economics we see a deep commitment to pragmatist ideas as represented by sociological symbolic interactionism, (Harvey and Kantovich 1992, Biddle 1990, Brown 1985, Mayhew 1987, Neale 1990). Among scholars of law the tradition is equally old, but Tamanaha's work (1997) and that of Peter Margulies (both represented herein) and Patterson (1990) is reinfusing various areas of legal scholarship with the pragmatist attitude. In anthropology, Leaf (1972, 1984, 1998) is a primary example of the pragmatist analysis of social life. Also Falk-Moore (1986), Turner (1986), and others pursue analysis and produce understandings of social life otherwise recognizable as pragmatist.

The preceding review is brief, but to it we must indicate one last piece of evidence of pragmatism's renewed vigor and that is the webpage http://www.pragmatism.org/. One can find much of interest on this site mostly representing philosophy, but the site is open to contributions from scholars of law and social science. We can see that the chapters presented here are but a few examples of the many works demonstrating the practice of pragmatic thought and attitude.

How This Book is Organized

The chapters in this book seek to demarcate social science in the pragmatist tradition as a constructive position in clear distinction to positivist and postpositivist thought as well as equally distinct from deconstructive postmodern thought. The chapters are of a 'tough-minded' optimism. Authors take on difficult problems of power and knowledge in social life as well as developing critiques of theory, method, and policy practice. Instead of attempting to summarize the rich arguments of each chapter I will sketch, for each section some of the catalyzing ideas and trends which argue for organizing the book in *these* four sections.

The social sciences, like all human endeavors, have a complex history of many schools of thought. The contemporary positions social scientists take are rooted in philosophical schools and the debates in these are one important source of pragmatism and other contemporary manifestations of old traditions. Consequently, philosophical traditions are also an important source of information on the limits and possibilities for different sorts of social scientific practice. In the first section of this book, authors take up pragmatist notions of theory, action, and decision-making as well as how those ideas are part and parcel of social rules constructing behavior and our ideas about how we understand behavior. People think with the ideas they learn in experiences which represent social institutions. Our most intimate experiences reflect one or another social institution. So, in differentiating the pragmatist tradition as a constructive postmodern position from positivist and postpositivist thought and from deconstructive postmodern thought, authors focus on the difference which is in relation to the ends pragmatists have in mind. Pragmatists, postmodernists, and some positivists generally agree that the conceptual construction of a situation reflects the ends of the conceptualizer, and that such ends are the product of interaction. The difference is that in the positivist and postmodernist view the interaction is essentially esoteric while in the pragmatic view it is essentially public. In the pragmatic view, it is not just an interaction among the analysts as a self-recognizing elect, but an interaction between scientists and those they would understand or whose problems they would assist in resolving. Pragmatists assume that interaction is generative of more interaction, but it is also self-limiting since we live many roles related to several institutions. So, whether we think about leadership, about how judges make decisions, or about the desirability for consensus decision-making, we will find in these essays that the possibilities and limits of action are grounded in local meaning and behavior representative of larger, yet learned and therefore amenable institutions and ideas.

The second section of the book contains chapters on social scientific method. Peirce's concerns with conceptual clarity, Dewey's interest in problem oriented inquiry, and Mead's focus on language are central to pragmatist positions on method. Pragmatism cannot say to have inspired a particular methodology (although it can claim important influence on versions of Sociological Symbolic Interactionism, Institutionalist Economics and field methods in the social sciences), but we can say that some research methods, even some quantitative methods, are closer in spirit to the pragmatist problem/solution oriented attitude than are other methods whose development and uses are based on different philosophical foundations. The chapters in this section are *methodological* in the sense that they are reflections on some of the philosophy upon which methodological *procedures* are based. Systematic methods are one important way for people to create useful knowledge from what they observe. Improvement of methods can come from technical developments, but also from reflection on the problems from which techniques emerged. The chapters in this section are of the latter sort. Instead of a concern with detailing a particular technique, the authors engage the problem of method from its emergence in history and philosophy and the transformation of those concerns into useful techniques (although the chapters and bibliographies detail examples).

The pragmatist position on inquiry is radically democratic because it is inclusive, and it is inclusive because it is skeptical, contingent, and experimental. Here, chapters explore methodological choices which produce a contingent predictability of observed behavior to develop, in Dewey's terms, "the controlled or directed transformation of an indeterminate situation into one that is so determinate in its constituent distinctions and relations as to convert the elements of the original situation into a unified whole".

Ideas are tools of explanation. The difference ideas make in concrete policy-making processes is the subject of the third section of the book. Pragmatism makes no attempt to reify ideas, only to ensure that they can make a difference. Once the character and use of ideas is understood, predictions can be made about policy interventions in the ideas-in-practice. The scientists concepts, "norms", "capacities", or whatever, are not regarded as magical invocations that add to our understanding or have the desired policy impact. Rather, these or any concepts used in doing science, designing institutions or creating policies, must understand the way the people involved make sense of their situation and convince themselves and others of what they see and how they should act. However, this is more than understanding the subjects behavior from the subjects viewpoint because it is the same view we have of science. Concepts or ideas, inquiry and resultant policy prescriptions are all organized by the ends we have in mind and our efforts to convince ourselves and others that what we are doing should be done, and perhaps even rewarded. Given that the ends we have in mind are also subject to revision, it should be clear that the policy prescriptions one expects from a pragmatist are experimental and contingent.

As for an ethical position, Tamanaha notes that pragmatism is empty of normative prescription, but this view is not universally held (see Seigfried and Nussbaum). We can say that Tamanaha is correct in noting that pragmatism does not provide any single or fixed scale of evaluation of the sort one finds in positivists, some postmodernists, and some Critical Legal Studies scholars who are willing to impose some single way to see all situations. But it is not the case that pragmatism provides no prescriptions at all. In fact, in a most general way pragmatism contains a very clear set of prescriptions on what one should look at and on how one should go about using the results. The pragmatic position is that imposition is fundamentally a two-way street. It is reciprocal, not unilateral. The model is not Plato's prisoner speculating about shadows, but rather two or more people talking about making something or doing something. Of course an analyst can impose a view of a situation that has no saliency for those actually in it, but this is unlikely to be of use. Alternatively, however, analysts can be receptive to a situation's participants. They can suppress their impulse to impose their own ends and work instead to see what those concerned are trying to impose on each other; it is here that one finds both the most stable description of a situation and a rudimentary understanding of ethical positions and dilemmas therein.

In the fourth section, authors engage empirical research with the pragmatist attitude. In these chapters problems are posed, theories are critiqued, and methods are deployed to understand problems found in the 'real' world. Whether it be how lawyers negotiate relationships with clients, or how community leaders deal with their community and local government, these chapters seek to provide insights about how people build meaning from interaction and how the force of that meaning on future interaction is manifested.

Taken together, these chapters (and the resurgence of pragmatism) will be of interest to social scientists concerned with policy processes and with methodological choices as well as those reflecting on theoretical explanations for behavior. It is also of consequence to legal scholars, critical and otherwise, for its close connection to jurisprudence and so, to understanding judge-made law.

Many of our colleagues in the physical sciences make poetic references about the inspiration of their work, inspiration similar to that found in Darwin as he ended his paradigm changing book with the observation that there is "a grandeur in this view of life". A similarly generative appreciation of life is supplied at least in part by pragmatism. Using pragmatism to navigate our streams of thought and practice can move us to embrace life for all its facets and in all of its inspiring and perplexing moments, knowing well, as did William Carlos Williams, the limits and possibilities of science and poetry.

Acknowledgements

Thanks to Karla Hernandez for her help compiling the reference list and for editorial assistance on this foreword. Thanks also to Murray Leaf, Michael Topp, Ken Holzman and Bill Weaver for comments on prior drafts.

References

Campbell, James, (1995) *Understanding John Dewey: Nature and Cooperative Intelligence.* Chicago: Open Court.

Dickstein, Morris., ed. (1998). *The Revival of Pragmatism; New Essays on Social Thought, Law, and Culture.* London: Duke University Press.

Diggins, John Patrick, (1994). *The Promise of Pragmatism: Modernism and the Crisis of Knowledge and Authority.* Chicago: The University of Chicago Press.

Emirbayer, Mustafa, (1997). "Manifesto for a Relational Sociology". *American Journal of Sociology* 103, 2 (September): 281-317.

Goodman, Russell B., ed. (1995). *Pragmatism: A Contemporary Reader.* New York: Routledge.

Halton-Rochberg, Eugene. *Meaning and Modernity: Social Theory in the Pragmatic Attitude.* Chicago: The University of Chicago Press.

Joas, Hans. 1985. *G.H. Mead; A Contemporary Re-examination of His Thought.* Cambridge, Mass: The MIT Press.

Joas, Hans. 1993. *Pragmatism and Social Theory.* Chicago: The University of Chicago Press.

Joas, Hans. 1996. *The Creativity of Action.* Chicago: The University of Chicago Press.

Kaufman-Osborn, Timothy V. 1982. "Pragmatism, Policy Science, and the State", *American Journal of Political Science*, 29, 4: 827-849.

Leaf, Murray. 1979. *Man, Mind, and Science: A History of Anthropology.* New York: Columbia University Press.

Leaf, Murray. 1984. *Song of Hope: The Green Revolution in a Panjab Village*. New Brunswick, New Jersey: Rutgers University Press.

Leaf, Murray. 1998. *Pragmatism and Development; The Prospect for Pluralist Transformation in the Third World*. Westport, Connecticut: Bergin and Garvey.

Lovejoy, Arthur O. 1996. *The Revolt Against Dualism: An Inquiry Concerning the Existence of Ideas*. New Brunswick, U.S.A.: Transaction Publishers.

Menand, Louis. 1997. *Pragmatism: A Reader*. New York: Vintage Books.

Menand, Louis. 2001. *The Metaphysical Club*. New York: Farrar, Straus and Giroux.

Moore-Falk, Sally. 1986. *Social Facts and Fabrications*. Cambridge, Massachusetts: Cambridge University Press.

Morales, Alfonso. 1998a. "Pragmatism's Mundanity: Epistemic Foundations for Practicing Sociolegal Science", *Law and Society Review* 32, 2: 493-514.

Morales, Alfonso. 1998b. "Income Tax Compliance and Alternative Views of Ethics and Human Nature", *The Ethics of Tax Evasion*, edited by Robert W. McGee. South Orange, NJ: The Dumont Institute for Public Policy Research.

Morales, Alfonso. 2001. "Policy from Theory: A Critical Reconstruction of Theory on the 'Informal' Economy", *Sociological Imagination*.

Patterson, Dennis M. 1990. "Law's Pragmatism: Law as Practice and Narrative", *Virginia Law Review* 76: 937-998.

Posner, Richard A., ed. 1992. *The Essential Holmes*. Chicago: The University of Chicago Press.

Ross, Dorothy. 1991. *The Origins of American Social Science*. Cambridge: Cambridge University Press.

Rucker, Darnell. 1969. *The Chicago Pragmatists*. Minneapolis: University of Minnesota Press.

Schneider, Anne, and Helen Ingram. 1990. "Behavioral Assumptions of Policy Tools", *Journal of Politics* 52, 2: 510-529.

Schneider, Anne, and Helen Ingram. 1993. "Social Construction of Target Populations: Implications for Politics and Policy", *American Political Science Review* 87, 2 (June): 334-347.

Seigfried, Charlene Haddock. 1996. *Pragmatism and Feminism: Reweaving the Social Fabric*. Chicago: The University of Chicago Press.

Shalin, Dmitri N. 1986. "Pragmatism and Social Interactionism", *American Sociological Review* 51, 1 (February): 9-29.

Shalin, Dmitri N. 1992. "Critical Theory and the Pragmatist Challenge", *American Journal of Sociology* 98, 2 (September): 237-279.

Shamir, Ronen. 1995. *Managing Legal Uncertainty: Elite Lawyers in the New Deal*. Durham, NC: Duke University Press.

Shields, Patricia M. 1996. "Pragmatism: Exploring Public Administration's Policy Imprint", *Administration and Society* 28, 3: 390-411.

Shusterman, Richard. 1997. *Practicing Philosophy: Pragmatism and the Philosophical life*. New York: Routledge.

Tamanaha, Brian Z. 1997. *Realistic Socio-Legal Theory: Pragmatism and a Social Theory of Law*. Oxford: Clarendon Press.

Turner, Frederick. 1986. "Ch.4: Reflexivity as Evolution in Thoreau's Walden", pp. 73-96 in *The Anthropology of Experience*, Victor W.

Winch, Peter. 1958, 1988. *The Idea of a Social Science and Its Relation to Philosophy*. 2nd ed. London: Routledge.

Acknowledgements

My first thanks must go to Austin Sarat who in 1998 in the midst of a Law and Society Association Summer Institute helped rekindle my energy with his interest in this book. Also, I would not have been at that Summer Institute and, indeed, this book would not have been completed without the loving support of my spouse (and colleague) Manuela Romero. Any words I share here cannot embrace my feelings for her. And thanks to our son Cruz my most valued distraction. I have benefitted from a ten-year relationship with the Law and Society Association. The LSA has been a fruitful academic home, and for three years I organized panels on pragmatism each year with growing interest from attendees. Some of the chapters of this book come from papers presented at the 2000 annual meeting in Miami.

My interest in pragmatism can be tied to my family, nuclear and extended and especially my parents, my mother whom I thank for her exemplary excitement for embracing experience, and my father who exemplifies a healthy scepticism and experimental attitude. Intellectually, besides my parents, I thank Murray Leaf for introducing me to pragmatism, and again, I cannot find words to fully acknowledge my debt to him. I've always wanted the chance to acknowledge people whose support and example are persistent in my life and are particularly present to me now: *mil gracias* to Art McEvoy, Beth Mertz, Brian Tamanaha, Paul Hirsch, Hector Delgado, Gloria Rodriguez, Ismael Guerrero, Jim Williams, Kip Bobroff, Margaret Montoya, Melvin Oliver, Howie Erlanger, Lisa Frohman, Nancy Mathews, Laurie Edelman, Liz Boyle, Jerry Van Hoy, Michael Padilla, Neil Foley, H. Mark Ellis, Rick Lempert, Cesar Rodriguez, Jonathan Simon, Bob Nelson, Wendy Espeland, Charles Ragin, Laura Gomez, Bill Weaver, Art Stinchcombe, Susan Silbey, Bryant Garth and the many colleagues who have encouraged my work over the years. I would like to thank Bob Webking, who when director of the Center for Law and Border Studies consistently support my scholarship. Connie Dominguez the administrative assistant and students Karla Hernandez and Lydia Saenz who assisted in the preparation of this manuscript. As well, I would like to thank Lucero Vasquez-Radonic who was a gem during the editing process. John Bauer and his staff at PDX printing in El Paso TX were also timely in that regard. I hope that some of the many students with whom I have worked will find something of use in these pages. Finally, I would like to embrace the authors who have contributed here, *un abrazo fuerte*, thanks very much and let us all get to work.

PART I

PRAGMATIC PHILOSOPHY ON SOCIAL, LEGAL, AND SCHOLARLY PRACTICE

1 The "Democracy of Self Devotion":[1] Oliver Wendell Holmes, Jr., and Pragmatism

William G. Weaver

Frogs need storks.

Martin Luther

Introduction

During the 1940s, journalist Westbrook Pegler frequently attacked Oliver Wendell Holmes, Jr., referring to him as a "cynical and senile brutalitarian" with the "morals ... [of] a pig", and "the god of an evil cult"[2]. This was just the beginning in a growing crescendo of criticism of Holmes increasingly made by writers on the political Left.[3] Strangely, the people who attack him now with such vigor are politically of the same mind as those who turned him into "The Yankee From Olympus". These attacks are frequently *ad hominem*, but when compared to attacks on other leading pragmatists we can see remarkable similarity between them. What makes this seem odd at first is that many of these critics specifically and admittedly share the same epistemological views as Holmes and other pragmatists.

Most of the critics on the Left would have little trouble with the epistemology of Wittgenstein, Dewey, Donald Davidson, and W.V.O. Quine. The work of these antifoundationalist[4] thinkers explains and gives sophistication to pragmatism's original claims that truth is what is "good in the way of belief"[5], and that efforts to "think outside of space and time" are "churning the void in the hope of making cheese"[6] . The peculiar style of organic metaphor made available by Darwin's thought, which gave birth to pragmatism, seemed ready made for legal theorists. Increasing disaffection with formalism, the conception of law as something which is better and purer when segregated from the banal events and language of the everyday world, found its home in pragmatism. Since its beginnings with William James and Charles Peirce, pragmatism found sympathetic teachers and practitioners in the law. Now it can be said that "pragmatism is the implicit working theory of most good lawyers"[7], and "[n]obody wants to talk about a 'science of law' any longer"[8]. Nevertheless, both the Left and the Right attack pragmatism for moral insufficiency.

To the Left, the pragmatist is an apologist for the status quo who refuses to come to the aid of the oppressed. For the Right, the pragmatist is a nihilist whose main concern is with sophistry. Left wing critics of Holmes and other pragmatists often refer to themselves as "postmodernists"[9], and accuse pragmatists of indifference toward the suffering and the oppressed. On this view, postmodernism takes over where pragmatism stops and shows that antifoundationalist thought leads to a politics of liberation. This politics excludes market-based economic structures and holds the oppressed to comprise a special reservoir of untapped insight into justice. As discussed below, it seems that the main complaint with Holmes and his kindred is that they peel politics away from epistemology. Indeed they believe that politics and theory come apart. This violates the faith of many on the Left that theory is the source of justice and that political institutions are only as legitimate as the theories that underlie them. However, this is not what the pragmatist thinks. The pragmatist thinks that devotion to theory may be just as damaging and unfruitful as devotion to traditional legal formalism. An institution is not made just or unjust through the strength of the best theory possible to justify it. Rather, justice is a communal delineation of the practices of elected officials, those populating our courts, prosecutors, and bar associations. This makes pragmatism more dangerous to the theory-enamored Left than its ideological opponents. Pragmatism harks to the same epistemological origins as postmodernists, yet it denies the link between epistemology and politics. Perhaps another generalization is that postmodernists see the main work of thinking to be done after an epistemology has been established. In other words, the epistemology one adopts determines the political trajectory of one's beliefs. Antifoundationalists who reject the postmodernist label do not think that epistemology and political belief have much to do with each other. As Rorty once pointed out, Quine was an unreconstructed Nixonite, Donald Davidson is a New Deal liberal, Wittgenstein was nearly apolitical, and Heidegger was a Nazi.[10] Postmodernists frequently view this apparent discord between epistemology and politics as a moral failing of the thinker. Pragmatists do not see it as a moral failing to not hook up epistemology with politics, though they are certainly willing and prepared to argue that political postures may be evil. But this evil is not because these postures are in discord with truth, but because they cause cruelty and suffering

The adulation of Holmes chagrins these critics and they are often at a loss to understand why he is so widely esteemed. In recent years, many have concluded that Holmes' popularity was achieved through fraud, that his friends and admirers created a myth about the man that led to the public perception of him as the avuncular, kindly gray-headed judge. By this argument, the real Holmes is almost the opposite of that perception. Contemporary critics are "left with the question how a man in many ways so illiberal could have become a patron saint of liberal reform"[11]. On this account, Holmes is a hoax, and not worthy of admiration. There is nothing in his work that will provide a basis for retooling the legal system; he gives no means with which to move toward justice. Pragmatism is wedded to a belief in incrementalism that runs counter to the beliefs of many on the Left. In this sense, it more closely resembles the thought of Edmund Burke than that of Thomas Paine. This incrementalist outlook is more suited to law than its more theoretically driven cousins, and so became attractive to lawyers and judges. In what follows we look at the relationship between Holmes and some of the criticisms he suffers and what that relationship has to say about how pragmatism is viewed by the Left.

Pragmatism and the Law

The Enlightenment transformed the common law from merely an auxiliary service with a spotty record, mainly available to the privileged and the wealthy, into an ideal of universal justice which could work for the poor as well as the rich. Under 18th and 19th century humanist ideals, the law became a primary means through which the lowly, as well as the wealthy, could seek haven from abusive governments, recoup losses from injurious neighbors, and obtain orders against government officials to perform their mandated duties. Never mind that the practice strayed far from these ideals, for if justice had any potential forum at all it would be the courts. Even in the common person's utter distrust of the business-controlled courts there remained the indignation that the ideal of the law had been perverted, that there was a natural function for the law that was being subverted to the interests of the venal. It was not that the law was unworkable, but that it was not being allowed a chance to work. In some cases, though, the law was allowed to "work". In Holmes' own state of Massachusetts, for example, pre-revolutionary juries decided not only issues of fact, but issues of law. And even when juries ignored judicial instructions in reaching their decisions, Massachusetts judges had no power to set aside those decisions.[12] As William Nelson notes, "In a legal system in which juries have the power to find the law, whatever disputes arise cannot be resolved by mere majoritarian fiat, but must be resolved by a process of consensus building that produces legal rules acceptable to a broad base of society as a whole"[13].

Post-revolutionary Americans saw "liberty as the very 'object' of law"[14]. Surely, some groups abandoned any hope that the legal system could reform, as was the case with the voluntarist movement among labor in the latter part of the 19th century.[15] But most people, even battered labor leaders, saw the courts as the eventual place where justice would become available. Reform of the legal profession, and especially the appointment and election of judges, became the crucial issue for many activists. But at the core of the legal profession, even after the reform movements were largely successful, there remained the Enlightenment ideal that the law was one of the main aids in helping society progress toward ever-more just conditions.

The idea of progress in law is one that has been much debated, and is still integral to the thinking of some of our best known legal theorists. Two major theoretical traditions, positivism and natural law, revolve around the importance of refinement. Progress in the law is a matter of honing and refining practice to some standard, which though objective only reveals itself partially at various times under different circumstances. For the natural law theorist, the refinement required is in the application of rules in accordance with catholic principles of individual rights. Ronald Dworkin, in a variation of this type, in his 1986 *tour de force*, *Law's Empire*, ends his work with a discussion of the idea of law "working itself pure"; a condition where "present law gropes toward pure law when modes of decision appear that seem to satisfy fairness and process and bring law closer to its own ambition"[16]. For Dworkin, decisions of communities must be delimited by fundamental rights of individuals. These rights are not granted by the majority, but are requirements of justice. Progress means ever-refined application of rules around the contours of individual rights. This position relies on a standard for evaluating justice that is not generated by the group to which it will apply.[17] Indeed, the legitimacy of a government is determined not by the cultural judgment of its behavior by its citizens, but by its conformance to external standards.

Positivism is also dedicated to a concept of refinement, though here the refinement is in the ever-more accurate analysis and description of pedigrees of legitimacy for rules and their applications.[18] While the positivist generally allows that refinement of pedigree and meaning cannot eliminate all uncertainty about the application of rules, those circumstances where the judge must use what Dworkin terms "strong" discretion are few. Indeed, one of the main differences between thinkers such as Dworkin and positivists such as H.L.A. Hart is that Dworkin sees the need for broad and pervasive "weak" discretion in judging while Hart sees only the need for the occasional use of "strong" discretion. This just highlights the importance of the idea of law as refinement even among disparate thinkers in the opposed traditions of natural law and positivism; law is an edge that needs to be made ever sharper through the grinding of cases and analysis of principles and rules. This idea of refinement owes a lot to an Enlightenment hangover, and this is where pragmatism sharply diverges from these theories of law.

In the second half of the 19th Century, after the appearance of *The Origin of Species*, the main Enlightenment considerations that vivified views of the law needed to be replaced. Darwin showed that we can think of humans as collections of contingencies, moving assemblages of accidental mutations and phenotypical variations that turned out more or less to be helpful in adapting to the environments at hand. Darwin's work challenged the mythic history of what it meant to be a human and so closed the distance between us and the "brutes". More pointedly, Darwin's work led to the conclusion that there is nothing which stands to the law like the law stands to the individual. There is no overarching rational story under the name of Nature or God or Reason that the language of law must tell in order to be legitimate. And if this is the case, the idea of progress is one that can only be determined through internal referents; nothing outside of the human community will do as guideposts on our journey. But internal referents are inherently unstable from the Enlightenment perspective, for they are fixed in the matter of the moments in which they arise. They are unfit for planning the trajectory of law; they are unfit to plan progress. But the implications of Darwin's thought let people see that a story about what humans are is one that can be narrated by humans, not one that is sanctified by an external power we ignore at our peril. This was at once both terrifying and exhilarating. It cut us loose from traditional theoretical support for our moral and ethical schemes, but also freed us to experiment with new practices and new justifications for those practices. Darwin showed us that humans are not central to the universe, but are the result of the same inexorable process that produced koala bears and cockroaches. Daniel Dennett, in his remarkable *Darwin's Dangerous Idea*, makes the point this way:

> By taking tiny – the tiniest possible – steps, this process can gradually, over eons, traverse these huge distances ... At no point would anything miraculous – from on high – be needed. Each step has been accomplished by brute, mechanical, algorithmic climbing, from the base already built by the efforts of earlier climbing.[19]

Before Darwin it was literally inconceivable that sentience could arise without the existence of some prior mind, some designer that purposefully caused the creation of thinking animals. Only out of mind could mind arise, or as John Locke makes the point: It is "impossible to conceive that ever bare incogitative matter should produce a thinking intelligent being as that nothing should of itself produce matter ... [I]t is as impossible that, incogitative matter should produce a cogitative being, as that nothing, or the negation of all being, should produce a positive being or matter"[20]. This is the Enlightenment.

Prejudice in favor of humans, the idea that people are different in kind from the "brutes", that we are obviously blessed divine contrivances and constitute a different and superior category altogether. What makes us human, supposedly, is the ineluctability and ineffability of Mind, the impossibility of describing the mental in causal terms. The Mind represented the eternal and the essential and contained a special unchanging ingredient that linked all humans together across time and space. This fixed ingredient gave us special powers and was the essence of being human. Our Mind gave us a meta-tool that made it "man's essence ... to be a knower of essences"[21]. As Dewey describes it,

> The conceptions that had reigned in the philosophy of nature and knowledge for two thousand years, the conceptions that had become the familiar furniture of the mind, rested on the assumption of the superiority of the fixed and final; they rested upon treating change and origin as signs of defect and unreality.[22]

Darwin gave us a causal explanation for the human mind, and it did not distinguish in kind between the "brutes" and people. There is no division between essential and accidental features. The human phenotype was created through the same process as was the weasel. Once we began to realize the accidents that led up to the consciousness of humans it became difficult to see people as something that occupied the attention of a benevolent creator: The "idea that one species of organism is, unlike all the others, oriented not just toward its own increased prosperity but toward Truth, is as un-Darwinian as the idea that every human being has a built-in moral compass – a conscience that swings free of both social history and individual luck".[23]

But our special adaptive tool, language, allowed us to characterize our species as part god or, in the alternative, the creation of deities. As Donald Davidson says, our grammar conspired to help us tell a divine story about our origins. Dennett gives an example of how this impulse works. Suppose there are a thousand people in a coin-flipping contest and the winner of each coin flip moves on while the loser is eliminated. There will eventually be a single winner, a person who has won every coin toss. Such a person may not easily attribute the results to chance, or "beating the odds". The winner may think she is divinely deserving or favored by God. Now, the human species is the result of not a thousand winning coin-flips, but millions of "coin-flips" over millions of years. Is it unusual, then, that people are inclined to see themselves as central players in a grand narrative of the divine? What we lose sight of, Dennett says, is that in this "game" someone or some species has to be the winner. Whatever species ended up with the tool of language would have used that tool to separate it in kind from other species, to divinize itself and its origins. On this view, religion and the less helpful tendencies of the Enlightenment are efforts to legitimate the belief that humans are of special origin, efforts to mask our contingent origins with divine narratives.

Another fear of recognizing our contingency is seen in efforts to stop the decentering effects that began with Copernicus and were continued by physicists and psychologists. The people fighting this decentering argue that the mind is fundamentally resistant to scientific and causal explanation. They understand that they can lose all other battles except for the assault on the *élan vital* of mind and still win the war. But Freud dealt this defense a serious and nearly fatal blow by redescribing the mind as a centerless mass of swirling events and varied "voices".[24] Freud did for the inside of the head what Darwin had done for the outside. Between Freud and Darwin the "Enlightenment prejudice" was put to attack by telling the story, from the molecular to the molar levels, of how cognition and personality came about without the aid of any preexisting cognition. To see the evidence of this twisted trail from protein soup to Einstein we need look no further than our own bodies. Within us is the trace evidence of millions of years of associated bundles of matter looking for niches to occupy and use as launching points for replication. Is it possible that these nonconscious bundles of matter could come together in some contingently arrived at designs and associations that yield a conscious item such as a person? What else, asks Dennett, is a plausible explanatory candidate? "Can it be", Dennett asks, "if you put enough of these dumb homunculi together you make a real conscious person?". These "homunculi" or "robots" are the proteins, viruses, bacterium, cells of various classifications, and all the other nonconscious matter making up our bodies.

Dennett notes that, "it certainly does not follow from the fact that you are descended from robots that you are a robot. After all, you are also a descendant of some bacteria, and you are not a bacterium ... [But] you are *made of* robots — or what comes to the same thing, a collection of trillions of macromolecular machines. And all of these are ultimately descended from the original macros. So something made of robots *can* exhibit genuine consciousness, or genuine intentionality, because you do if anything does".[25]

Darwin's reorganized concept of "human" threatened the law with a sea change of understanding of law's goals and origins. The de-divinized account of law and the human species that came available with the advent of Darwinist thought, and its adaptation by jurists such as Holmes, nevertheless, did not result in a radical break with the Enlightenment optimism that attached to law and the idea of progress. The optimism of American legal realism derived from the notion that Darwinism liberated people from the oppression of thinking they are constrained by external cannons of justice, or of the will of God, or similar ineffable and insurmountable limits to what humans may naturally and justly think and do.

Barely a century before Goethe's *Faust*, Milton rejected all that Faust stands for. For Milton, Faust would be an abomination, a devotion to self rather than to God. In *Paradise Lost*, Adam, after being lectured by the Archangel Michael, makes a similar point:

> Greatly instructed I shall hence depart
> Greatly in peace of thought, and have my fill
> Of knowledge, what this vessel can contain;
> Beyond which was my folly to aspire
> Henceforth I learn, that to obey is best,

And love with fear the only God, to walk
As in his presence, ever to observe
His providence, and on him sole depend,
Merciful over all his works, with good
Still overcoming evil, and by small
Accomplishing great things, by things deemed weak
Subverting worldly strong, and worldly wise
By simply meek; that suffering for truth's sake
It is fortitude to highest victory,
And to the faithful death the gate of life.[26]

Here, vision, excess, dynamic appropriation of nature, is abhorred and portrayed as the feeble yearnings of a weak creature. But in the time between Milton and Goethe there is wedged the rising science, the new faith and God of Europe. Dynamic, rather than pastoral or gentle, appropriation tore through society and complicated economic systems that followed the newly created wealth. In this world, Faust is king and the Adams are plowed under. Appropriation of nature or the items in the environment to fulfil desire is divine, and repose and worship are sinful. Appropriation, turning "nature" into "value" is the primary good in this world. This transformation of striving from devotion to God into devotion to self and acquisition has its counterparts in the law. With Darwin, what began several centuries earlier, the conversion of humans as creatures of God to humans as candidates for godhood, was complete: "[m]an has become ... a kind of prosthetic God".[27] Once it became possible to see the person as a thoroughly accidental creation owing no deference to a realm of perfection or unchanging truths, the fields of vision of humans as great adaptors, creators, and appropriators opened up before adherents to the Darwinian explanation of diversity of life.

Positivism and Kantianism banks on the concept of refinement, but pragmatism rejects this approach. Pragmatists adopted the Darwinian metaphors of organic change, mutation and niche finding. Progress in law is not found in narrowing and refining, but in multiplying distinctions and finding new ways of thinking and talking about our problems and dilemmas. Through this multiplicity we have a greater capacity to adapt law to the vagaries of society and to use it as a tool for social experimentation. But the post-Darwinian optimism of the legal realists was not to last. The optimism of the American legal realists, of the adaptors of Darwinian thought to law, originated from two wings. First, legal realists, like their Enlightenment-molded brothers and sisters placed great faith in the power of science to aid law in its effort to help society progress. Specifically, legal realists were excited about the possibilities of social science and the apparent hope that in the future legal decisions could be based on the unequivocal results of behavioral studies. Second, legal realists felt that they had been freed from the classic image of the judge as a person of repose, a passive instrument of the law, a person not affected by the eddies of political pressure. Now judges could be seen as active participants in the reshaping of society, and perhaps the best placed public officials to engage in experiments to improve the lot of the average person in our culture.

Holmes shared the optimism in science, but he did not share the belief that judges should experiment with social machinery. In this respect, Holmes is closer to Felix Frankfurter than Jerome Frank, even though Frankfurter is often not thought of as a legal realist. It is Holmes' refusal to be optimistic that frequently leads to his vilification. As Holmes says, "I am neither optimist nor pessimist. There are half a dozen futures (I mean for our civilization) that seem to me equally probable and among them is the possibility of civilization cutting its own throat or of one going down hill in some way".[28] As with Holmes, sometimes the notion that the judiciary had been freed from self-imposed prejudices merely took the form of a judge feeling compelled *not* to act in the face of experimental behavior on the part of the state or federal legislatures. Even though Holmes did not see himself as a social engineer, he vehemently argued that legislatures should be free to so act. Then two events occurred to strip the optimism from the legal realists. The first of these was the realization that social science was not going to be able to deliver the unequivocal descriptions and evaluations of human behavior as hoped for. Such studies took far longer than had ever been anticipated, and rather than settling issues about the direction of progress, these studies merely became the launching point for new battles. The idea that neutral studies of human behavior could produce data that would force conclusions in conformance with some demonstrated brute fact faded away. There was no such thing as a brute fact to force the law to any particular conclusion about how to decide cases at hand. The second event was World War II. If the new understanding of the person set us free to create without guilt, it also set us free to perpetrate evil. Dostoevsky's aphorism, "Without God everything is permitted", seemed to underlay both the constructive and destructive aspects of Darwinism, both the Roosevelts and the Hitlers.

With the collapse of the legal realists' optimism, their epistemology came more to the fore and more starkly displayed against the Enlightenment beliefs that a preceding era of law relied upon. Darwinism buttressed the disillusionment of many in the law, and as Roberto Unger has quipped, some lawyers and judges "lost their faith but kept their jobs".[29]

On some accounts, the new story of the origins of our species laid open by Darwin lead to despair, to hopelessness, to anomie. Holmes is now viewed by many as an icon of despair. These people now see him as a studied relativist, a person who uses statutes and precedent merely as props in a stage show of law. This seems to be the opinion of Ronald Dworkin, Lon Fuller, Henry Hart, and Grant Gilmore.[30] Though, as Stanley Fish succinctly comments, "relativism is a position one can entertain but never occupy", many on both the Left and the Right believe that it is a position Holmes aspired to.

Attacks on Holmes

Political theorist Harvey Mansfield once referred to John Dewey as a "medium-size malefactor", as a potential talent ultimately of no consequence because of his quest to take the jurisdiction for truth away from philosophers and deliver it into the hands of the community. Dewey thought that the effort to hook up truth, power, righteousness, and certainty to extra-communal items had failed both as a matter of practicality and as a matter of evidence. Dewey, in thinking that truth comes in human-sized packages, denuded the heroic tradition of a greatness external to the human community, a greatness which transmitted a moral telemetry to the inhabitants of earth and could be glimpsed by the properly trained and the staunchly faithful. He tried to make our existence completely human, without the addition of a nonhuman, dimly perceived and understood power as the source of rationality, morality, or truth.

Pragmatists and antifoundationalists, people who like Dewey see the human enterprise as human all the way through, have often been subjected to derogatory metaphors of stature. Dewey is "medium-size", while Wittgenstein cuts the universe down to human size,[31] and Richard Rorty condemns us to the judgments, vanities, and desires of the group in which we happen to find ourselves. Professor Louise Weinberg, in continuing this metaphor, proclaims Oliver Wendell Holmes, Jr., a "failure" because of his "littleness". Holmes was the chief inspiration of the reformist Left in the early part of this century, many members of which took hold of power in the 1930s with the election of Roosevelt. But more recently, echoing the 1940s attacks of Pegler, Holmes' thought is viewed by the left with disdain and loathing. Indeed, Holmes' worth as a lawyer and judge and figure in history has been called into account, and Weinberg claims that Holmes' greatness was womped up by Felix Frankfurter and Harold Laski. According to Weinberg, Holmes is actually a failure in law and life and does not deserve to be studied, much less venerated.

Weinberg relates an anecdote alluding to this misplaced reverence. She says that the "late Charles E. Wyzanski, Jr. once told me a story. Felix Frankfurter had remarked to Holmes that he, Holmes, always looked so tall. Holmes had replied, 'That is because, Felix, you always approach me on your knees'".[32] Weinberg thinks we should get off our knees and see Holmes for the "almost wholly irrelevant" and "ruthless" person that he was.[33] These opinions are a variation on a criticism famously leveled at Holmes by Grant Gilmore in his *The Ages of American Law*. There, Gilmore called Holmes, "savage, harsh, and cruel, a bitter and lifelong pessimist who saw in the course of human life nothing but a continuing struggle in which the rich and powerful impose their will on the poor and weak".[34] Gilmore's view has been generally taken over by the Left, and it is vulgar now in those quarters to openly praise Holmes. But it seems that the accusation of cold-heartedness is not really the main impetus for these attacks on Holmes. The more forceful reason for the denigration of Holmes is found in the way he is seen to make life two-dimensional. And the most vicious thing Holmes does is to remove hope from the landscape of law. He has no room in his jurisprudence for the ideal, for hope, for the notion that justice may beat the venal in the end. Once the optimism of American legal realism evaporated, the Left needed a replacement that would yield the sort of power it perceived it had lost. Darwin, Holmes, and pragmatists caused the Left discomfort, for they were now seen as devoid of the power to effect change and do the work necessary to put us in touch with justice. But the Left's past was intimately connected with these thinkers, and so these thinkers needed to be marginalized.

The primary means to hope, as Holmes' critics see it, is through the power of theory, the power to remake our world through the intellect. Holmes is indicted for trying to expunge the possibility of radically different futures; in de-divinizing the law he casts out not only formalism but hope. He reduces justice to merely retail operations in the everyday to and fro between lawyers, judges, and juries, and makes it impossible to provide a wholesale account of how society should change to attain justice. The only way such a wholesale change can be structured and proffered is through theory. This turns out not to be a criticism of Holmes' character or even of his manner of judging, but a criticism of Holmes' failure to provide a place for theory as a tool for change. What is really being criticized is pragmatism.

Weinberg's treatment of Holmes is similar to how other pragmatists have been criticized. Pragmatism and pragmatists have been attacked for fuzzy-headedness, lacking rigorous methodology, and amoralism for over a century. More recent attacks focus on pragmatism's resistance to subordination to a particular political slant. Pragmatism is deplored by the Right as amoralist sophistic manipulation of opinion and by the Left as country club dilettantism that proffers radical epistemology, but helps to maintain the political status quo. To the Right it is relativistic intellectualism devoid of moral standards, and to the Left it refuses to acknowledge the connection between epistemology and politics.

Holmes, so long embraced by the reformist Left and disaffected Marxists of the middle decades of the last century, is now criticized for his harshness, his alleged shallowness, and the passing into obscurity of most of his legal opinions. By these lights Holmes' frailties and mean-spiritedness make him ineligible for adulation, and indeed make it incumbent on us to minimize his stature and delimit his influence on current thinking. Holmes' beliefs and decisions have been asserted to be conducive to fascism and "[i]f totalitarianism ever becomes the form of American government, its leaders, no doubt, will canonize as one of the patron saints Mr. Justice Holmes".[35] As David Seipp notes, "For these critics, [Holmes'] views were better suited to Nazi Germany than to American law".[36]

Ben Palmer's inaugural article in a famous 1940s series attacking Holmes in the American Bar Association Journal is unsubtly titled "Hobbes, Holmes, and Hitler".[37] Many theories of law depend upon law's insulation from the society in which it operates. Dworkin's "law working itself pure" requires that the law be its own creation separated from other means of social judgment. According to Dworkin, "principles" (standards to be observed not because they get you something, but because they are requirements of justice) are placed over and against societal decisions. H.L.A. Hart, as do all positivists, believes in the segregation of law and the most important of communal evaluations, moral judgment. Holmes is often referred to as a positivist, but he does not share the search for a purity of authority and pedigree in rules that Hart and Hans Kelsen advocate. Darwin and the horrors of his service in the Civil War caused Holmes to not only reject the refinement view of law, but to also adopt an amoral approach to judging. From Holmes' perspective, the real immoralists in the law are those that would marry the legal profession to moral consideration. This union would yield judges who made decisions based on personal predilection in the guise of "principles". The result of the marriage of law and morality is the substitution of a judge's opinion for the opinion of the community.

Much of the admiration for Holmes is based on his apparent ability to make his own moral beliefs opaque to his judging. This is frequently referred to as the "maturity" of Holmes, a maturity born of a studied aloofness from the emotional aspects of cases at bar. Jerome Frank, for example, referred to Holmes as the "completely adult jurist"[38] for his ability to set himself aside in deciding cases. But it is not that Holmes thought morality had no place in law, it is that the judge's morality had no place in law. Morality of a different sort, a second level morality and, the morality of the community did indeed have important sway in his decisions. Holmes said time and again that one of the surest ways of figuring out what the community desires is to look at what its representatives have done. It is certainly arguable that this makes Holmes more of an adherent to the moral implications of community desire for law than his critics. Much of what the critics fear is precisely the impulses of the community.

More radical[39] brands of legal theory require broad judicial deviation from legislative expression as a means of achieving justice. Roberto Unger and critical legal studies habitues, for example, would use the judiciary to help dismantle the liberalism that he claims is so isolating and denuding of the capacity of the individual. Similarly, critical race theory would rewire the connections of communication in the societal switchboard so that those without power will be plugged into power when distribution of scarce resources is made.

It is the substitution of a personal predilection for the desires of the community that Holmes abhorred. Holmes was instrumental in breaking down the view of law as an insular item, one that operates more efficiently the more it is removed from the common and everyday tasks and opinions of the citizens. That this deference to the desires of the community created lamentable consequences is clear, but pragmatism is nothing if not committed to truth and morality as judgements of the group.

Many people, when attacking Holmes for his lack of feeling for the consequences of law, point to United Zinc and Chemical Co. v. Britt, 258 U.S. 268, 42 S. Ct. 299 (1922), and Buck v. Bell, 274 U.S. 200 (1927). These cases are cruel in their results and substantively are almost universally considered bad decisions. In *United Zinc*, two children trespassed onto defendant's property and went swimming in an apparently clean and clear pool of water. The pool in fact was poisoned with sulphuric acid and zinc sulphate. The children died; one almost immediately and the other after languishing for a day or so. Other children present summoned help, and two men were severely poisoned trying to save the swimmers. In an awful display of the cruelty of the contemporary rule governing landowners' duty to trespassers, Holmes wrote the opinion of the Court reversing judgment for the plaintiffs.

The opinion is indefensible under current law and was unnecessary and harsh even when handed down. However, the attacks on Holmes for this ruling often focus on his lack of emotion in dealing with the facts of the case as much as on the substantive legal problems with the ruling. Holmes did not relate the facts in any detail and is excoriated for this because it appears that he is trying to keep the accident obscure in the mind of readers so they will not realize the full horror of what occurred. As one commentator writes, "Holmes presented the facts in a brief, matter-of-fact way: 'On July 27, 1916, the children, who were eight and eleven years old, came upon the petitioner's land, went into the water, were poisoned and died.' Holmes' language here is passive. The children did not dive, swim, or jump; they 'went' into the water'".[40] Furthermore, "Holmes makes it difficult to picture the children and their actions. We can only guess at the conditions of their death".[41] Ignoring the odd complaint that Holmes presented facts in a "matter-of-fact" way, an obvious explanation for Holmes' account is that the embellishments that the critic thinks are necessary are in fact irrelevant to the issue at law. It does not matter if the children dove or jumped in the water, or, unless deciding damages, what the "conditions of their death" were. Another commentator writes, "[i]t is difficult, even today, to read this tragic case without horror, and to wonder how Holmes could have decided as he did: one sees the two children wandering from their camp site; the hot summer day; the cool clear water, looking like an inviting swimming pool; the deadly poison".[42] The issue at law concerned the duty landowners owe to trespassers in maintaining alleged attractive nuisances or latent defects on their property. The deaths were indeed horrible, but judges who succumb to emotionalism in their opinion writing are seldom treated well by history or their contemporaries.

Those who criticize Holmes would be outraged by a Richard Posner or a Frank Easterbrook who wrote emotional opinions based in generalized considerations of justice, rather than identifiable features of law, bemoaning the destruction of contractual limitation of liability and damages by advancing "liberal" doctrines in tort law. In *United Zinc*, there was no evidence to indicate the dead children entered upon defendant's property because of the deadly pools of water. Rather, the evidence indicates that the children were not regular trespassers of the property, and that they came upon the pools and decided impulsively to go for a swim. This point is not unimportant to the development of law in the 1920s. Holmes' main reason for reversing the judgment for plaintiffs was his concern that the "turntable" decisions needed defined limits.[43]

Five years after *United Zinc*, Holmes gave his most infamous opinion, Buck v. Bell, 274 U.S. 200, 71 L. Ed. 1000 (1927). In this case, the state of Virginia wished to sterilize Carrie Buck against her will in conformance with a eugenics statute. Holmes incorrectly termed Carrie Buck an "imbecile" and declared that "[i]t is better for all the world, if instead of waiting to execute degenerate offspring for crime, or to let them starve for their imbecility, society can prevent those who are manifestly unfit from continuing their kind. The principle that sustains compulsory vaccination is broad enough to cover cutting the Fallopian tubes. Three generations of imbeciles are enough".[44]

Holmes notes one critic, "certainly understood the power in evoking visual images. He used this tactic to his advantage in Buck v. Bell, and was careful to avoid it in United Zinc and Chem. Co. v. Britt ... where it would have prejudiced readers against his holding".[45] Even if we accept the claim that Holmes was cruel and unfeeling, it does not seem to explain the sustained attacks on the reputation of a man who has been dead for almost seventy years.

A more recent strategy of attack points to underlying reasons for this drawn out animosity. This strategy seeks to strip Holmes (and Posner and Rorty as well) of his pragmatist credentials, as in the following statement by Albert Alschuler: "In my view, because Holmes was indifferent to the flourishing or happiness of all members of society, he should not be regarded as a utilitarian or a pragmatist".[46] Rather than seeing pragmatism as the epistemological outgrowth of Darwin as described by Dewey, these critics add moral requirements for the mantle of pragmatist.

And on this score, they believe Holmes is profoundly deficient. But it seems strange to close the pragmatist club to all but cheery optimists, or those that wish their fellow citizens well, or who are advocates of flourishing and happiness. These really are not even moral requirements, but more akin to required "moods". It is no moral failing in our society to be indifferent to the flourishing of others, so long as we do not act to obstruct that flourishing in ways that are proscribed by the community. After all, we all obstruct the flourishing of others in many ways. We may take the last seats to see *Hamlet*, causing a person who has never seen Shakespeare to miss an opportunity that might change her life. We push for pay raises for ourselves even though we know that our raise will mean less for someone else. We tolerate all sorts of conditions that prey upon our fellow citizens without lifting a finger to help. Of course, it is good to defer one's own needs and wants to those of others, but no one is expected to do this even more than a small percentage of the time. These sorts of complaints about Holmes, especially when put forward as arguments against his legitimacy as a pragmatist, are too vague and undefined to be of any use. We need to get to the motivations for these complaints.

It is telling that over time Holmes receives more aid from so-called "conservative" scholars, lawyers, and judges than he does from "liberals". Richard Posner, a prolific writer, bane to feminist and critical race theory legal scholars, and associate judge on the U.S. Seventh Circuit Court of Appeals, begins his introduction of Holmes in his edited volume of his writings claiming that Holmes "is the most illustrious figure in the history of American law".[47] In the next sentence he notes, somewhat dryly, that Holmes is "to an extent no longer fully appreciated".[48] It certainly does not help Holmes' image with the Left that he is championed by Posner. Posner, who takes a comprehensive law and economics approach to jurisprudence, is seen by the Left as a racist and misogynist who uses the cover of economic calculation to hide the injustice of his opinions. Statements such as "Rape parallels theft in being a coerced taking in a setting of low transaction costs"[49] do little to endear Posner to the Left. Some claim that he occupies these positions consciously to thwart justice while others see him as much a victim of our legal heritage as the groups he allegedly obstructs in the struggle for justice. The general consensus among the Left, though, is that Posner's work is "nothing more than thinly veiled ideology to legitimate the inequalities wrought by the market systems".[50]

Arguably, Posner is as much misunderstood as Holmes is, and his attraction to Holmes is based in a kinship of spirit in two main practices: a restrained approach to judicial decision making and the effort to divorce oneself from one's own opinions when acting as a judge. Since it is fundamental to the Left's recent theoretical writings that one can never escape one's self, it sees Posner and Holmes as implementing their desires under cover of objectivity. On this ground, one's politics are *always* acted out in one's decisions. Criticisms of Holmes are echoed in the treatment of Posner. For example, writers have claimed: "Too often ... Posner's thought is glib and shallow. His presentations cascade trippingly from issue to issue, seldom pausing to develop the complexities of any topic, or even the ramifications of his own best insights";[51] "[Posner's] economic approach to law [is] cold, colorless, and distorting [and] *is woefully insensitive to human suffering*";[52] Posner's writings ennobling consent as the basis of freedom reflect a "thirst for pain, surrender, and humiliation".[53] The inability of many thinkers to unhitch politics from epistemology causes them to denigrate Holmes and his intellectual descendants. Holmes did think that politics and epistemology came apart, that one's epistemological views need not lead to a particular political position. The effort to disassociate Holmes from the pragmatist tradition is a play to recoup pragmatism to the Left, to make it a "prophetic pragmatism"[54] which recovers the hope that Holmes allegedly disposed of.

The Power of Theory

Contemporary philosopher Richard Rorty once said there is something alluringly romantic about destroying one world to get to another. There is something both glorious and horrible in the impulse to leave our past behind, to eradicate tradition and so be free of what G.K. Chesterton called the "democracy of the dead", or what Jefferson termed the "dead hand of the past". From the thought that a little revolution now and then is a good thing, to Plato's expulsion of adults in search of the just society, to Christine de Pizan's world without men, political theorists have always looked for reagents to dissolve the past's ties to the present. The past, or tradition, somehow was always getting in the way of justice. The perfect society was also the new society, the one without a past, one unconstrained in molding itself around the contours of justice.

To be sure, not all political theorists thought this way, but for every sober Burkian history seems to be littered with a dozen thinkers who think we need to dispose of this world to reach one where justice prevails. And though there are many theorists who use the new world motif to create dystopias rather than utopias, these people, just like their counterparts, see something powerful in the imagery of the new society. William Golding, for example, in *Lord of the Flies*, erases one past in order to reveal another, or alternative past. Plato gets rid of tradition in a way similar to that of Golding's. Complaining that human association and government as it formed in Athens were distorted by misperception of truth and reality, Plato started his perfect world by ordering the adults out. Malformed by miscategorized and misunderstood experience, adults in Plato's *Republic* were a blight to the unformed minds of the young, and nothing less than the excision of the entire learned culture was needed to give spring to justice.

Hobbes, Locke, Hegel, and Rousseau dispose of the past by imagining a past that has no past. They take us to a precultural, prelinguistic, pretradition void where time wafts around unaccounted for and unrecognized by the inhabitants. In *The Book of the City of Ladies*, Christine de Pizan sloughs off men and their traditions, traditions forced on women who have a superior capacity for harmonic community. Thomas More and Jonathan Swift had their travelers stumble on fully developed worlds and contrasted these with the world encapsulated in the minds of their wandering protagonists. And before being accused of leaving United States thinkers off of this list, we should note that Thoreau in "Paradise (to be) Regained", saw that if only love could overtake tradition, we could save ourselves.

Of course many people have attempted to create new societies, to eradicate tradition even while remaining within the midst of the tradition they would destroy. Such efforts range from Albert Brisbane's numerous settlements to Robert Owens' *New Harmony* to Thomas Jefferson's "academical village" at the University of Virginia. Planning and theory seem to be indispensable requirements when pursuing paradise; requirements brought to their theoretical apogee in the new society of B.F. Skinner in *Walden II*.

For pragmatists, in a sense all we have is our history, our complex of traditions. We can no more get rid of our pasts than we can get rid of our renal system. I admit that this view puts pragmatism on the anti-radical side of things. This is not a political conclusion, but a claim that while we can remake ourselves over time, we cannot remake ourselves immediately by identifying and jettisoning the "bad stuff" in our minds or souls. We can only change the world and ourselves one sentence at a time. This does not mean that one cannot be a pragmatist and still have visions of a perfect or better future. As Rorty once said, "You have to be loyal to a dream country rather than to the one to which you wake up every morning".[55] But pragmatists doubt that theory will get us there as fast as change wreaked by the language of the everyday. As Thurman Arnold once caustically noted, in order for a heaven to work it cannot be too close to earth.

Roberto Unger, certainly no friend of conservatives, writes that "even our boldest and most original inventions represent penumbral extensions of [our] legacies".[56] And Unger further notes that the deep-structure social theorist treats the formative institutional and imaginative frameworks of social life as indivisible units, each of which stands or falls as a piece. As a result he, believes that political action always faces a choice between a revolutionary substitution of the entire formative context of social life and a reformist tinkering that merely wards off serious change.[57]

As discussed above, "deep-structure social theorists" on both the Left and the Right disdain Holmes for contradictory reasons. The Left thinks theory should be in service of the oppressed, and that it is necessary to get the right theory of justice in people's heads before we can have a just political structure. Holmes has little patience for this sort of abstract theorizing that purports to answer the big questions of society. The Right thinks that since Holmes distrusts "deep" theory, he puts at jeopardy the foundation of our moral beliefs and paves the road to the worst sorts of excesses found in the French Revolution.

People who see themselves as radical are wedded to the belief that theory is the essential means of discovering injustice and tearing down practices and social structures that are decrepit with corruption and venality. Theory gets to the soul of evil, exposes the distorted practices and beliefs of those in power, and reveals them to be abominations against the people. Without a way to see everything at once, without a means to measure disparate activities against the standard of justice, we are vulnerable to false-consciousness and co-optation by those who are the source of injustice. Theory, totalizing theory, is both a protection against such co-optation and a means of revealing the rotten core of standard practice. Of course, this is a venerable tradition in political and legal intellectual history, that comprises perhaps the most interesting literature to be found in these areas. To tell the average member of a political system that virtually everything she knows and assumes about the law, power, and justice is mistaken, and a carefully contrived product of those who hold power is a good way to bring attention to alternative views. But pragmatists will not make the leap beyond the belief that theory is an interesting point from which to start certain conversations. Theories are the beginnings of discussions, not the ends of them. For pragmatists, politics and philosophy come apart, as Rorty notes:

> Habermas and Bernstein are inclined to think that if a philosopher is any good at all, he is good for political purposes – that if his work has any significance at all, it has political significance, relevance to contemporary political controversies, current social needs ... In contrast, I think that we should see philosophy as, roughly, a branch of literature. Some philosophers (Mill, Dewey, Rawls, Habermas) write books that are relevant to current political practice, as do some novelists (e.g., Hugo, Zola, Dickens, Solzhenitsyn, Orwell). Other philosophers (e.g., Nietzsche, Heidegger, Derrida, Wittgenstein) do not, as other novelists (e.g., Virginia Woolf, Proust, Nabokov) do not. Philosophers whose writings are not relevant to current politics ... are not automatically "irresponsible", nor are they automatically to be assigned to the political right.[58]

Holmes would agree with Rorty's sentiment, and it is this sentiment that causes much of the animosity toward Holmes. Well, what is it then that Holmes is still good for, other than as a source for masterful turns of phrase? Holmes did not see the law as something that needed refinement relative to a particular goal, as something that has a particular path of progress embedded in its history that would be perverted if turned away from. Holmes judged with the belief that the law was one of the greatest public conversations in our culture.

Holmes and the Conversation of Law

Michael Oakeshott famously wrote about the "conversation of mankind", claiming that "[i]n conversation 'facts' appear to be resolved once more into the possibilities from which they were made, 'certainties' are shown to be combustible not by being brought into contact with other 'certainties' or with doubt, but by being kindled with ideas of another order ...".[59] For Oakeshott, conversation writ large was the business of living. These conversations are not fated for any particular goal and are not guided by anything other than the impulses of the conversants. More to the point, Oakeshott asserts the following:

> A morality, is neither a system of general principles nor a code of rules, but a vernacular language. General principles and even rules may be elicited from it, but (like other languages) it is not the creation of grammarians; it is made by speakers. What has to be learned in a moral education is not a theorem such as that good conduct is acting fairly or being charitable, nor is it a rule such as 'always tell the truth', but how to speak the language intelligently ... It is not a device for formulating judgments about conduct or for solving so-called moral problems, but a practice in terms of which to think, to choose, to act, and to utter.[60]

To be human is to be a potential or actual conversant, a participant in the "vernaculars" of the community.[61] And just as in conversations among two people or a small group of people, these communal conversations meander and change and the conversants change with them. We are creatures that have the magnificent power to remake ourselves; a person is "[a] character distinguished on account of limitless powers of self-transformation without self-destruction".[62]

Just because Holmes was not committed to "deep" theory does not mean he was not committed to giving people the chance to remake themselves. We do not remake ourselves through theories, but through conversations that theories and other purported truths start. It is in the give and take, the interaction with people of differing opinions that shapes our vision of how we wish to be and what sort of world we want to be in. Holmes was, and still is, a magnificent conversation starter. But Holmes also acted to make sure the public conversation was not closed off. He may have been largely indifferent to what people did, as is exemplified by his much maligned "bad man" premise.[63] He seems to have claimed in the "Path of the Law", that the law does not say a person may not rob or commit murder, only that if a person's conscience is insufficient to deter her from these activities the state will answer such actions with force. But this indifference to the morality with which people act is part and parcel with his commitment to the civic conversation.

In those cases where state or federal action looked to close off entry into forums for public exchange Holmes frequently voted to stop these efforts. For example, in Nixon v. Herndon, 273 U.S. 536, 47 S. Ct. 446 (1927), Holmes, writing for a unanimous court, found that Texas violated the 15th Amendment by prohibiting African-Americans from voting in primaries. Some have seen Holmes' innovations in the areas involving the First Amendment as out of character, as aberrations of his normal stance of indifference to individual rights. These innovations are not aberrations, but perfectly understandable extensions of his Darwinist and pragmatist roots. Progress, on this score, is making sure that members of the community have access to the conversation of our culture. Holmes' critics, often describing themselves as radical democrats in addition to postmodernists, seem more interested in rigging the conversation to close off paths they see as undesirable. If a person thinks there is a destiny for our culture or that there is a "Great Psalm of the Republic" that is playing out, it begs the question of whether or not such a person is a democrat. Holmes too feared what the "masses" would do and had little respect for the chances the majority could come up with intelligent decisions, but he saw nothing better to carry us forward. Many of his critics who wish to free these same masses from their oppression are not willing to risk the results of a democratic process. The true danger of Holmes and pragmatism to these people is that it seeks to set people free in action, not merely in theory.

Conclusion

Many of those who attack Holmes still want to believe there are "mighty answers to divine questions".[64] They are as much enmeshed in the Enlightenment effort to have society track the motions of something bigger and separate from the wishes of the group as were Locke and Grotius. They are caught in a dilemma: they adhere to an antifoundationalist epistemology, essentially agreeing with Holmes and the pragmatists, but are unwilling to renounce theory as the principle mechanism of progress and finder of truth. Pragmatism and the valorization of theory do not settle very nicely together, and so the main obstacles to such an attempt needed to be removed. This is why the complaints against Holmes often appear identical to those made against Rorty and Posner. Since Holmes' critics share his epistemology, and since these critics see epistemology as entailing a particular political outcome, they must tailor their attacks to appear specific to Holmes and his thinking. They cannot very well attack the epistemology they adhere to. But this is why these criticisms appear strained and unmelodic; the target is not so much Holmes as the pragmatist belief that though theory and efforts to reach beyond the community of humans may promise good conversations, they cannot promise the truth.

Holmes' disagreeable beliefs are seen by the Left as the unfortunate result of forces and causes, but their own beliefs are born beyond the reach of causation, beyond the interplay of politics and psychology; they are a "full presence ... beyond the reach of play".[65] What Holmes had is a perspective, when he should have had the truth. Holmes thought a "democracy of self-devotion" a glorious thing while his critics saw it as a vulgarity. For Holmes, fear and uncertainty provide the forum for greatness. When society is at its worst, in war or depraved government, the citizens may be at their best. A soldier can only be great in war. Holmes would agree with Luther that people need their storks just as much as frogs; the fear of predation and contingency should not be eliminated, even if it were possible. While this feeling is misguided and largely a result of Holmes' experience as a soldier, the impulse does capture something common to most pragmatists: a fundamental romanticism. They place their faith in action and conversation, not in efforts to remove the common and everyday from the formula of life.

Acknowledgement

Thanks to Murray Leaf for his comments on a prior draft.

Notes

1 Oliver Wendell Holmes, Jr., *An address Delivered May 30, 1884, at Keene, N.H., Before John Sedgwick Post No. 4, Grand Army of the Republic*, in *The Essential Holmes*, Richard A. Posner, ed. (Chicago: University of Chicago Press, 1992), 85.

2 Quoted in David J. Seipp, "Holmes' Path", *Boston University Law Review* 77: 515, at 556 (June, 1997). From Westbrook Pegler, "Fair Enough", *Boston American*, Dec. 18, 1950, at 34, 45.

3 See, e.g., Albert W. Alschuler, "Dunwody Distinguished Lecture in Law: The Descending Trail: Holmes' 'Path of the Law' One Hundred Years Later", *Florida Law Review* 49 (July, 1997): 353; Ben Palmer, Holmes, Hobbes, and Hitler, *American Bar Association Journal* 31 (1945): 261; Yosal Rogat, "The Judge as Spectator", *University of Chicago Law Review* 31 (1964): 213; Jan Vetter, "The Evolution of Holmes, Holmes and Evolution", *California Law Review* 72 (May, 1984): 343; Louise Weinberg, "Holmes' Failure", *Michigan Law Review* 96 (December, 1997): 691.

4 Stanley Fish defines foundationalism and antifoundationalism in the following way: "By foundationalism I mean any attempt to ground inquiry and communication into something more firm and stable than mere belief or unexamined practice. The foundationalist strategy is first to identify that ground and then so to order our activities that they become anchored to it and are thereby rendered objective and principled ... [In

contrast] "[a]nti-foundationalism teaches that questions of fact, truth, correctness, validity, and clarity can neither be posed nor answered in reference to some extracontextual, ahistorical, nonsituational reality, or rule, or law, or value". "Anti-foundationalism, Theory Hope, and the Teaching of Composition", in *Doing What Comes Naturally* (Durham: Duke University Press, 1989), 342-44.

5 William James, *Pragmatism* (Amherst, NY: Prometheus Books, 1991), 36.

6 Posner, *supra*, note 1, letter to Alice Stopford Green, August 20, 1909, 116.

7 Thomas Grey, "Hear the Other Side: Wallace Stevens and Pragmatist Legal Theory", *Southern California Law Review* 63 (1990): 1590.

8 Richard Rorty, "The Banality of Pragmatism and the Poetry of Justice", in *Pragmatism in Law and Society*, (Boulder, CO: Westview Press, 1991), 89.

9 The distinction between postmodernism and antifoundationalism seems to be rather confused. Both groups share the same epistemology. But it can be generally said, if one does not push it too far, that postmodernists trace their main influences through Derrida, Foucault, Lyotard, Laclau, Mouffe, Habermas (though strangely), Gadamer, Marcuse, Heidegger, Husserl, and Nietzsche. People who resist the postmodernist label and prefer to be called antifoundationalists generally see their pedigree as running from Richard Rorty and Donald Davidson to Quine to Sellars to Dewey to Wittgenstein to Peirce and James. These two camps roughly divide along continental versus non-continental lines. Even though Wittgenstein was Austrian and perhaps the seminal antifoundationalist it is difficult to think of him as continental. He has little of the characteristics associated with other continental thinkers and is sometimes played off against Heidegger to highlight their difference in style. Richard Rorty once wrote a short piece where he tongue-in-cheek referred to himself as a "postmodern bourgeois liberal". This caused a backlash from postmodernists who missed the playful intent of the phrase. "Postmodern Bourgeois Liberalism", *Journal of Philosophy* 8 (1983): 583.

10 Conversation with Richard Rorty, Charlottesville, Virginia, May, 1998.

11 Vetter, *supra*, note 3, at 344.

12 William E. Nelson, *Americanization of the Common Law*, (Cambridge: Harvard U.P., 1975), 3-4.

13 *Ibid.*, at 4.

14 *Ibid.*, at 89.

15 See William E. Forbath, *Law and the Shaping of the American Labor Movement* (Cambridge: Harvard U.P., 1991), especially chapter 2.

16 Ronald Dworkin, *Law's Empire* (Cambridge: Harvard U.P., 1986), 407.

17 Dworkin would deny this, saying that he does not rely on anything metaphysical. But it is difficult to tell the difference between his notion of justice reified and wrung from the tradition of the community and the belief in an external source for standards of justice.

18 H.L.A. Hart, *The Concept of Law* (Oxford: Oxford U.P., 1961), *passim* 100-110.

19 Daniel Dennett, *Darwin's Dangerous Idea* (New York: Touchstone, 1995), 75.

20 John Locke, *An Essay Concerning Human Understanding*, ed. Roger Woolhouse (New York: Penguin, 1997), 551-552.

21 Richard Rorty, *Philosophy and the Mirror of Nature* (Princeton: Princeton U.P., 1979), 367.

22 John Dewey, *The Influence of Darwin on Philosophy and Other Essays* (Amherst, N.Y.: Prometheus Books, 1997), 1.

23 Richard Rorty, "Untruth and Consequences", *The New Republic,* July 31, 1995, 32.

24 See, for example, *Civilization and Its Discontents*, James Strachey, trans., (New York: Norton, 1961).
25 Dennett, *supra*, note 19, at 206.
26 John Milton, *Paradise Lost*, Scott Elledge, ed., (New York: Norton, 1975), Book XII Ln. 557-571, at 278-279
27 Freud, *supra*, note 24, at 44.
28 Posner, *supra*, note 1, letter to Alice Stopford Green, October 1, 1901, 111.
29 Roberto Mangabeira Unger, "The Critical Legal Studies Movement", *Harvard Law Review* 96 (1983): 675.
30 See e.g. Lon Fuller, *The Law in Quest of Itself* (Boston: Beacon Press, 1940); Grant Gilmore, *The Ages of American Law* (New Haven: Yale U.P., 1979); Henry Hart, "Holmes' Positivism — An Addendum", *Harvard Law Review* 64 (1951): 929.
31 Thomas Nagel, *The View From Nowhere* (Oxford: Oxford U.P., 1986), 109.
32 Weinberg, *supra*, note 3, at 721-722.
33 *Ibid.*, at 722-723.
34 Gilmore, *supra*, note 30, at 48-49.
35 Paul L. Gregg, "The Pragmatism of Mr. Justice Holmes", 31 *Georgetown Law Journal* 31 (1943): 294.
36 Seipp, *supra*, note 2 at 555.
37 Palmer, *supra*, note 3, at 569. Other articles in the series were, "Defense Against Leviathan", 32 (1946): 328, and "The Totalitarianism of Mr. Justice Holmes: Another Chapter in the Controversy", 37 (1951): 809.
38 Jerome Frank, *Law and the Modern Mind* (New York: Coward-McCann, 1949), 253.
39 Often times "radical" is used to disparage thinkers. I mean no such disparagement. I employ the term to distinguish between those thinkers who believe the current legal system can be modified and reformed to achieve tolerably just results and those who think the whole system so rotten as to be unsalvageable.
40 Mary L. Dudziak, "Oliver Wendell Holmes as a Eugenic Reformer: Rhetoric in the Writing of Constitutional Law", 71 *Iowa Law Review* 71 (March, 1986): 863.
41 *Ibid.*
42 P. S. Atiyah, "The Legacy of Holmes Through English Eyes", *Boston University Law Review* 63 (March, 1983): 358-359.
43 Oliver Wendell Holmes, Jr., and Frederick Pollock, *Holmes-Pollock Letters*, Mark De Wolfe Howe, ed., (Cambridge: Belknap, Harvard Press, 1961), letter to Frederick Pollock, March 29, 1922. The "turntable" decisions were the basis for the incarnation of attractive nuisance doctrine. (see, e.g., Sioux City and Pacific RR v. Stout, 84 U.S. (17 Wall.) 657 (1873) and Keffe v. Milwaukee and St. Paul Ry Co., 21 Minn. 207 (1875)). In the late 19th century a number of children were injured by train turntables and other devices when they ventured onto railway property. Historically, in the common law a landowner had differing duties of care depending on whether or not a visitor was an invitee, licensee, or trespasser. Landowners only owed a duty to trespassers not to wilfully or wantonly cause them harm. This doctrine made sense at a time when a person's main wealth was almost always tied up in real property. The law was not about to let a person who illegally enters onto another's property the right to place the landowner's well-being at risk unless the landowner did something affirmatively malicious. But with the advent of large corporations and sophisticated financial institutions, the need for such zealous protection of the landowner disappeared. The lessening of the need for landowner protection eventually led to the

"turntable" doctrine. Some courts held the railways liable for the injuries, arguing that the turntables were an "attractive nuisance" "to children of an age when they follow a bait as mechanically as a fish", *United Zinc*, at 275. Children could not use their faculties to assess the dangerousness of a condition on another's property sufficiently well to say that they should in all or almost all cases bear the burden of the injury.

44 *Buck v. Bell*, at 207.

45 Dudziak, *supra*, note 40, at 863.

46 Alschuler, *supra*, note 3, at 357, note 16.

47 Posner, *supra*, note 1, at ix.

48 *Ibid.*

49 Richard Posner, "Conservative Feminism", in *Feminist Legal Theory*, D. Kelly Weisberg, ed., (Philadelphia: Temple University Press, 1993), 108-09.

50 Ian Shapiro, "Richard Posner's Praxis", *Ohio State Law Journal* 48 (Summer, 1987): 1046.

51 Mark M. Hager, "The Emperor's Clothes are not Efficient: Posner's Jurisprudence of Class", *American University Law Review* 41 (Fall, 1991): 7.

52 David Ray Papke "Problems With an Uninvited Guest: Richard A. Posner and the Law and Literature Movement", *Boston University Law Review* 69 (November, 1989): 1068-1069.

53 Robin West, "Authority, Autonomy, and Choice: The Role of Consent in the Moral and Political Visions of Franz Kafka and Richard Posner", *Harvard Law Review* 99 (December, 1985): 384.

54 The phrase is Cornel West's. See *The American Evasion of Philosophy: A Genealogy of Pragmatism* (Madison, WI: University of Wisconsin Press, 1989).

55 Derek Webster, "Rorty Calls Academics to Activism; Pragmatist Philosopher Brings His Message to Washington U", *St. Louis Post-Dispatch*, April 13, 1999, Section: Everyday Magazine, D1 .

56 Roberto Mangabeira Unger, *Knowledge and Politics* (New York: Free Press, 1975), 246.

57 *Ibid.*, at 249.

58 Richard Rorty, "Thugs and Theorists: A Reply to Bernstein", *Political Theory* (November, 1987), 572-73.

59 Quoted in Glenn Worthington, "Michael Oakeshott on Life: Waiting With Godot", in *History of Political Thought*, XVI (1) (Spring 1995), 105, at 113. From Michael Oakeshott, *Rationalism in Politics* (New York: Basic Books, 1962).

60 Michael Oakeshott, *On Human Conduct* (Oxford: Clarendon Press, 1975), 241.

61 Of course, some people are not potential or actual conversants in community discussions. Anencephalic babies, people in persistent vegetative states, and so forth, are not going to join or rejoin the conversation of our culture. But we have decided these people should be treated with dignity and respect and protected under our regime of law.

62 *Ibid.*, at 78-9.

63 Holmes urged us to look at law as does the bad person in order to see the distinction between law and morals: "if you want to know the law and nothing else ... you must look at it as a bad man, who cares only for the material consequences which such knowledge enables him to predict, not as a good one, who finds his reasons for conduct, whether inside the law or outside of it, in the vaguer sanctions of conscience". As Levinson and Balkin write, "the metaphor of the 'bad man' has haunted Holmes's legacy. Although it seems to mesh well with his unsentimental, positivist approach to law, it has also probably contributed to the recurrent image of Holmes as nothing more

than an insensitive moral skeptic, who regarded law purely instrumentally, and for whom the only real truth was the truth of raw power". Sanford Levinson and J.M. Balkin, "The Path of the Law Today: The 'Bad Man', the Good, and the Self-Reliant", *Boston University Law Review* 78 (June, 1998): 886.

64 Albert J. Beveridge, February 15, 1899, in Lewis Copeland and Lawrence Lamm, eds., *The World's Great Speeches* (New York: Dover Books, 1942), 336-338.

65 Jacques Derrida, *Writing and Difference* (Chicago: University of Chicago Press, 1978), 279.

2 The Dilemma of Democracy: Diversity of Interests and Common Experiences

Charlene Haddock Seigfried

Introduction

Commenting on the fragmented character of experience in modern society, John Dewey (1916: 257) asked, "How shall we secure the diversity of interests, without paying the price of isolation?". Emma Goldman (1969: 214) expressed a similar worry over figuring out "how to be one's self and yet in oneness with others, to feel deeply with all human beings and still retain one's own characteristic qualities". This question, as Dewey further refines it, is one I want to explore further; namely, how the interests of life and the studies stemming from them can enrich our common experiences instead of dividing us from one another. This issue is not only at the forefront of efforts by many marginalized groups to be fairly treated, a position frequently caricatured in conservative media as identity politics, but it is one that anyone interested in democracy as a way of life is led to ponder sooner or later. Diversity of interests is not only a given in democratic societies, but it expresses a value easier to honor in the abstract than in the concrete. This is true even of those who have suffered the most because of their perceived differences from dominant racial and cultural norms. A ten-hour documentary on PBS, which followed the lives of a biracial family, raises the issue in clear terms. As reported in The New York Times (1999), Cicily Wilson, a daughter of a black father and a white mother, found herself rejected by both blacks and whites when she matriculated at Colgate University. The black students wanted her to align herself exclusively with them and the white students were even less accepting of her dual identity. She did not think she should have to choose.

If we are to honor the promise of democracy, then the diverse cultural and social identities that constitute it as a living reality must be protected from enforced uniformity. The problem is that diversity important enough to be worth protecting involves expressions of beliefs and patterns of behavior unsettling enough to invite suspicion, intolerance, even suppression, if steps are not actively taken to avoid such outcomes. What steps are relevant and effective today? How can diverse interests and such varied academic approaches as multi-cultural, women, lesbian, gay, and black studies both celebrate and enhance a person's sense of belonging to a particular group otherwise devalued by the general population and still enrich common experience instead of further dividing us?

Jane Addams (1981: 40) who, together with John Dewey and George Herbert Mead, gave pragmatism a distinctly social emphasis, characterized her turn-of-the-century generation as one which could no longer take for granted that as Americans they shared a fund of common experience.[1] She was acutely aware of the loss of a common civic identity as a result of the civil war, which demonstrated the deep divisions between north and south; the industrial revolution, which opened a yawning gulf between those who benefitted from capitalism and those whose exploitation provided the means for those benefits; the waspish disdain for the waves of foreigners whose labor was needed as a result of rampant industrialization; and generational conflicts between working class and college educated young women and the paternalistic institutions, family structures, and customs that constrained them. As we begin another century, the divisions which prevent appeals to a common experience, whether as members of a nation or of the human race, have only multiplied and worsened. Appeals to normalcy, to a fund of common experience, have become the battle cry of right wing, reactionary forces who seek to impose a mythical sameness of whiteness, patriarchy, English language hegemony, evangelical religious dogma, and heterosexism on targeted groups who ever more vocally defend their right to be different. If Dewey is right that reciprocity of interest is required for uncoerced social life, then such one-sided demands are evidence of an increasingly hostile environment. We seem to be facing ever more draconian attempts to enforce common experiences and common outlooks, but not the ones he and Addams intended. At the same time, the right to be different at all costs, not reciprocity, seems the order of the day, whether from the right or the left. But there are costs and they have to be weighed against alternative ways of conceiving the relationship between what individuals and groups have to uniquely contribute to the enrichment of society and what role the search for common experiences play in furthering democratic goals.

In explaining the importance of forging common experiences in a diverse democratic society, I will also explain the nature of the shared experiences desired and begin developing the means required for bringing them about. The basic reason common experiences are a necessary condition for the survival of democracy and its thriving as a morally responsible way of life is that without them other important constituents of democracy, namely, the ultimate dignity and value of each person and their free association into units protective of such expressions of individuality will generate conflicting forces strong enough to split such identity groups into opposing forces destructive of democratic values. Reciprocity of interest is one such core democratic value. It is based on the biological and social fact of human interdependency.[2] Such interdependency is both a fact of life and a goal to be consciously achieved. The referent of pragmatist interpretations of democracy should thus be called 'social democracy' to distinguish it from the liberal model of isolated individuals with innate human rights.

Interdependency and Reciprocity

The mutuality of the biological and the social in human growth and development can be seen in Dewey's (1980: 48-49) characterization of children as being "marvelously endowed with *power* to enlist the cooperative attention of others ... From a social standpoint, dependence denotes a power rather than a weakness; it involves interdependence". The dependency and adaptability of immature children are in fact what makes possible such human abilities as the power to develop dispositions and to acquire habits; it is a prerequisite for understanding. "It is essentially the ability to learn from experience; the power to retain from one experience something which is of avail in coping with the difficulties of a later situation". It is this power to learn from experience that characterizes the pragmatist understanding of reasoning that Murray J. Leaf explains in this volume. So much is at stake in recognizing and valuing human interdependency and its corollary of reciprocity, which inform the normative dimension of practical rationality, that Dewey (1980: 49) calls the illusion that one can think and act alone a form of insanity that is responsible for much of the avoidable suffering in the world.

Non-reciprocal behavior is anti-social, as when the more powerful use others without regard to their emotional or intellectual dispositions and without their consent. In the communication that establishes social life, an imaginative grasp of one another's experience takes place. It is necessary to get outside of one's own experience and see it as others would see it and to establish some point of contact with their life, if the other is to appreciate its meaning. An indispensable disposition and core value that must be developed in socially democratic societies, therefore, is the ability and intention to view the consequences of one's "own acts as having a bearing upon what others are doing and" to take "into account the consequences of their behavior upon himself" or herself (Dewey, 1980: 35).[3] This is an intentional attitude that must be learned, and it expresses the moral requirements of a sound democracy.

Addams (1964: 7-10) also argues that we need diverse experiences for the opportunities they provide for sympathetically appreciating ways of life unlike our own. Such experiences are the foundation and guarantee of democracy because they give us social perspective and sanity of judgment; they provide "the surest corrective of opinions concerning the social order". She attributes the misconceptions and prejudices that lead to injustices "to the lack of imagination which prevents a realization of the experiences of other people".[4] Because of the indispensable role that diversity plays in democratic societies, she concludes "that we are under a moral obligation in choosing our experiences, since the result of those experiences must ultimately determine our understanding of life".

We need standards by which to measure the worth of actual interactions and outcomes. The standard Dewey (1980: 90) proposes is reciprocity of interest since all associations lacking it enslave rather than liberate their members. He says that without "a large variety of shared undertakings and experiences ... the influences which educate some into masters educate others into slaves". Rigid class lines, for example, prevent the adequate interplay of experiences, the less advantaged class being more subject to routine and those more materially fortunate tend to self-indulgence, capriciousness, and explosive behavior. Slavery goes beyond the legal slavery Plato had in mind when he defined it as accepting the purpose of one's conduct from another. Whenever someone is engaged in activities they do not understand and have no interest in, they are enslaved. The efficiency sought in scientific management of labor, for example, reduces workers to alienating mechanical routine which prevents them from seeing "the technical, intellectual, and social relationships involved in what they do" (Dewey, 1980: 91).

Criticisms of the harms caused by the public/private split are an integral part of Dewey's socially democratic philosophy. He says that groups cut off from productive relations with the larger society tend to protect what they have rather than reorganize themselves in light of changed conditions. He shows that the negative effects of rigid distinctions between the public and the private in the case of the family are not an isolated phenomenon, but are part of a continuum of isolation and special pleading. Included in his (1980: 91) indictment are "nations in their isolation from one another; families which seclude their domestic concerns as if they had no connection with a larger life; schools when separated from the interest of home and community; the divisions of rich and poor; learned and unlearned". In another context, he (1980: 343) adds the dualistic perspectives of men and women. By uncovering an underlying similarity of oppression in disparate social organizations and beliefs, he could not have better illustrated the folly of competition among subjugated groups and the need for cooperative alliances. He also points out that isolation makes for rigidity, especially in reproducing past customs rather than questioning them. Eliminating the distance between peoples and classes historically cut off from one another encourages the dissolution of customs meant to keep them apart and hostile to one another and encourages reconstruction of institutions and society.

What Dewey deplores in the radical feminist identification of men as the cause of women's oppression is not the recognition and rejection of dominating uses of power, but the polarization such an analysis implies. Since he argued for a pragmatist version of standpoint theory, he is not denying that significant differences and unequal relationships often or even most of the time separate women from men. He himself (1982: 45) provides reasons why women's different socialization, interests, and experiences will lead to different viewpoints and values than men's.[5] He also thinks that until women's views have been heard, and their criticisms followed out, many social and political issues will not be satisfactorily resolved. As we will see, Addams brings this pragmatist version even more into line with contemporary feminist standpoint versions by her suggestion that since abused women directly suffer the effects of injustice, they are in a better position to recognize what is wrong with society than those who are more integrated into the mainstream and who benefit from it. But Dewey (1985: 20-21) also thinks that however widely a person's direct experience reaches out into the world of things and persons, it remains "personal, curtailed, one-sided, distorted". The limitations of each woman's point of view need to be supplemented and her biases corrected through the experiences of others, both living and as recorded in history and dramatized in literature and the arts. Without falling back on a non-relational self and non-contextual causal explanations, what grounds could there be for an *a priori* rejection of men's perspectives as irretrievably tainted? "Dogmatism, adherence to a school, partisanship, class-exclusiveness, desire to show off and to impress, are all of them manifestations of disrespect for experience: for that experience which one makes one's own through sympathetic intercommunication" (Dewey, 1985: 21).

A democratic society is one that not only cherishes numerous and various points of view, but one that seeks the recognition of mutual interests.[6] Through free interaction among groups it engages in continuous readjustment to new conditions as they develop through such interaction. The normative status of democracy in pragmatist theory and practice cannot be understood without recognizing, as Dewey (1980: 93) so elegantly puts it, that it represents "more than a form of government; it is primarily a mode of associated living, of conjoint communicated experience".

Ends-in-View and Power Disparities

Education in a democracy so conceived substitutes ends-in-view for external ends imposed by authority, whether that authority resides in efforts to consolidate already existing power arrangements in contemporary society or to impose traditional ends developed in rigidly hierarchical societies of the past.[7] In order to liberate and organize the capacities of each person to direct the outcomes of the concrete situations in which they find themselves, they need to learn procedures to test, correct, and amplify their aims (Dewey, 1980: 114-115). Since, according to Dewey (1980: 118), ends-in-view "are but prospective points of view from which to survey the existing conditions and estimate their possibilities, we might have any number of them, all consistent with one another". But what if they are not consistent with one another, as seems all too common today?

One thing that is apparent from the analysis so far is that rigid and unbending protection of what are perceived to be one's interests is counter-productive. It sets up the very barriers to communication and mutual understanding that allow better-advantaged groups to extend and consolidate their power. But how is it possible to secure one's legitimate interests when one is in a minority or relatively powerless without holding fast to them despite attempts by the larger society or more powerful groups to ridicule, undermine, and ultimately defeat them? It seems obvious that in the conflicts Dewey gives as illustrations of a public/private split illustrative of isolation and special pleading the two sides are unequally situated. Some nations can dominate over others because of their more advanced technology, stronger economies, and more powerful weapons; the perpetrators of domestic violence unilaterally benefit by shielding their activities from outside scrutiny; and the power imbalance between rich and poor, learned and unlearned, men and women, needs no further comment. It can be granted that one way of eliminating the distance between groups historically cut off from one another through unjust social, economic, religious, and political barriers may well be through exposing the special pleading and the unfairness of appealing to past customs to justify oppressive situations since these are strategies by which those in power maintain and extend their power. But does the same remedy apply to the disadvantaged side of the conflicts?

Can they really recognize mutual interests without being submerged in a majoritarian consensus or being further suppressed by those who have the power to impose their perspectives and enforce their interests? How do ends-in-view substitute for the external ends imposed by authority when that authority has the power to enforce already existing power arrangements? How can those who are less powerful direct their concrete situation to bring about the better ends they desire through learning how to test, correct, and amplify their aims? Is not what is needed simply the power to carry out their aims?

To begin answering these questions, it is first necessary to recognize that aims do not transparently spring, complete and pure, from the interests of any group, but are influenced by past traditions, take account to a greater or lesser extent of present conditions, and are limited by imagined possibilities. According to Dewey, social groups are democratic if their members are free and they seek to secure in individuals a consciously socialized interest instead of following customary norms favoring a superior class. Therefore, one should be suspicious of the refusal to question customary norms and seek to determine who benefits and who suffers from the cultural arrangements already in place. Yael Tamir (1999) makes a similar argument that in liberal efforts to secure group rights, the interests of the more powerful and conservative leaders of non-Western societies are often upheld at the expense of dissenting members of those societies. The assumption that 'a' group has 'a' tradition and one set of interests that outsiders ought not to question lest they exhibit Western ethnocentric hegemony is a failure to recognize and grant to other cultural groups what is granted to one's own; namely, that "cultures are permanently changing and developing, at that there is no reason to 'freeze a culture in order to preserve it'". Dewey recognizes hierarchies of authority and power and argues that they can be overcome to the extent that interdependency is recognized as a fact and its value expressed through a genuine reciprocity of interest. This democratic criterion implies the ideal of a continuous reconstruction of experience by members of society who as a matter of course have been empowered to do so. Such empowerment is an ongoing process and expresses "the ideal of a continuous reconstruction or reorganizing of experience, of such a nature as to increase the capacity of individuals to act as directive guardians of this reorganization" (Dewey, 1980: 332). Such an ideal of continuous reconstruction and personal empowerment are as valuable, if not more valuable, for those who are marginalized as for those in power.

Utilizing Diversity to Craft Common Experiences

Addams consciously and continuously seeks to empower the more marginalized members of society to actively engage in such social reconstruction. She (1916: 112) particularly speaks to, for, and with "that vast multitude of women whose oppression through the centuries has typified a sense of helpless and intolerable wrongs". Women are not treated as an undifferentiated, homogeneous class. Addams perceptively and sensitively enters into the multiplicity of women's experiences arising from the different situations of newly industrialized workers and homebound women from the different backgrounds of elderly immigrant women and a younger generation eager to Americanize, all with various ethnic traditions and class differences. In *The Long Road of Woman's Memory* she develops an interpretive model of utilizing the specificity of each person's experiences by putting them to social uses in order to show that in doing so, they benefit themselves as well as others.

Memories selectively retain the accumulated values of past experiences. Sometimes they reconcile one to life, but at other times they can function to challenge existing conventions. According to Addams (1916: 53), "when these reminiscences, based upon the diverse experiences of many people unknown to each other, point to one inevitable conclusion, they accumulate into social protest". One social protest she had in mind was the campaign the women's movement waged against the stigma of illegitimacy. Although women of different nationalities, classes, and religions experienced society's harsh attitudes and laws against both unwed mothers and their illegitimate offspring differently, they all either suffered or could empathize with the suffering of others like themselves in a way that had the power to sensitize them to the injustice of society's judgment (Addams, 1916: 64). But because women of the time were particularly restricted by tradition and convention and hampered by their limited access to higher education and wider social and political activities, the path from condemning fallen women and bastard children to condemning the injustice of such cruel judgments and punitive laws was neither inevitable nor easy.

What needs to be recognized by the righteous upholders of traditional morality is that "no conventionalized tradition is perfect, however good its intent" (Addams, 1916: 53-54). When a particular tradition is challenged, an opportunity arises for reflecting on the actual sufferings experienced because of that tradition with a view to mitigating them. Association and communication are necessary both to utilize the insights gained from diverse experiences and to recognize common injustices. Addams believes that commonalities arise from such accidental associations as that of young women thrown together in the backbreaking work of early industrialized factories and sweatshops and that such association can be the basis for more conscious organizations formed to combat the unjust social conditions they experience.

Several conclusions can be drawn from Addams' analysis of the diversity of women's interests in any form of discrimination, such as that surrounding illegitimacy. She undercuts the belief that there is a uniform feminine response to sexual discrimination, arguing instead that diverse interests should be expected since they reflect different experiences as filtered through various traditions, beliefs, and levels of participation in extra-marital sex. As a matter of fact, they can run the moral gamut from condemnation, to pity, to eventual outrage. Still, she concludes that they can, nonetheless, lead – through reflection and communication – to challenging the injustice of existing conventions. Furthermore, when deeply enough felt, such challenges can amount to social protest. Another conclusion is that for such protests to be effective, the basis of the grievance must be effectively articulated and appropriate actions initiated. And, lastly, for this stage of social reform to take place, Addams (1916: 113) says, "people must come together in order to exercise justice".

In the sharing of deeply personal but troubling experiences which association encourages, links can be made to a more pervasive prejudice as motivating seemingly disparate injustices. Addams pointed out, for example, the link between prohibitions against illegitimate children seeking to identify their fathers and on the one hand denying custody of children to married women on the other, and between states in which laws considered a ten year old girl the seducer rather than the adult male partner on the one hand, and the denial of property rights to married women on the other. In doing so, she began with some of the most ingrained special interests that defined the differences in women's status in order to demonstrate that they masked a more fundamental, shared, discriminatory situation. The societally sanctioned distinction between married and unmarried women, a distinction many women learned to cherish as the basis for their social position and dignity, led them to be particularly censorious towards so-called fallen women. A woman felt stigmatized once she stepped outside the accepted sexual boundaries which covered over their shared origins in a male dominated social and legal system that encoded and enforced masculine power. Grievances originally experienced in isolation can thus come to be seen as having common social, political, religious, and economic causes. Out of the initial passions of different interests which originally separate us, common experiences can be forged in seeking justice through identifying shared issues and developing and implementing plans of action.

Concern for Others

For Dewey, democracy as a way of life requires faith in a personal day-by-day working together with others. He (1988: 228) says, "democracy is the belief that even when needs and ends or consequences are different for each individual, the habit of amicable cooperation – which may include, as in sport, rivalry and competition – is itself a priceless addition to life". Like Addams, he wants to develop dispositions of interdependency and concern for others to the point where the inevitable conflicts of life are taken out "of the atmosphere and medium of force, of violence as a means of settlement into that of discussion". In direct contrast to the increasing tendency in our times towards escalating conflicts into violent confrontations, a democratically social intelligence would treat "those who disagree – even profoundly – with us as those from whom we may learn, and in so far, as friends".

However, this expectation that conflicts can be settled by considerations of friendship seems beyond the limits of possibility or even of desirability for those who have suffered or whose friends or relations have suffered at the hands of twentieth century dictators, in massive campaigns of extermination, or through traditional misogynistic practices such as rape as a weapon of terror in times of war. In a situation of oppression, the oppressor often thinks of himself as a friend to the other – think of the Southern defense of slavery as a benign institution – but the reverse is neither true nor emancipatory. As long as an abused woman identifies with the one who batters her or the slave with her master, they will continue to be exploited. On the other hand, were it possible for this concern for the other to become the explicit goal of socialization in democratic societies, then such oppressive situations would be less likely to arise in the first place. If we take Dewey literally when he says that the characteristic of friendship which he is appealing to is the willingness to learn even from those with whom we profoundly disagree, then perhaps such a goal is not as unrealistic as it at first seems to be. When Studs Terkle refused to take the loyalty oath during the McCarthy era, for example, a government official asked him incredulously, "Surely you do not accept the goals of the Communist Party?". Without a pause Terkle responded, "And if they are against pneumonia, are we for it?".[8]

It is not necessary to think of the other in the intimate terms of friendship in order to achieve the benefits sought for in a genuinely democratic faith which believes, according to Dewey (1988: 228), "in the possibility of conducting disputes, controversies and conflicts as cooperative undertakings in which both parties learn by giving the other a chance to express itself, instead of having one party conquer by forceful suppression of the other – a suppression which is none the less one of violence when it takes place by psychological means of ridicule, abuse, intimidation, instead of by overt imprisonment or in concentration camps". What is required, however difficult this is to achieve in practice, is a profound change in attitude away from the self-centered regard encouraged in liberal societies towards one of mutual and reciprocal empowerment. "To cooperate by giving differences a chance to show themselves because of the belief that the expression of difference is not only a right of the other persons but is a means of enriching one's own life-experience, is inherent in the democratic personal way of life". This way of putting the issue was most strongly expressed in Jane Addams' work; for example, a unifying theme in *Twenty Years at Hull House* is her contention that in their work with the disadvantaged members of society the settlement workers were not so much doing them a favor as enriching their own lives.

Consensual Decision Making

In her early essay, "A Modern Lear", Addams (1982) gives a concrete example of how reciprocity of interest works to resolve conflicts in which the participants are unequally positioned. She explicitly draws on her account of fathers and daughters to provide an ethical approach to the massive social problems caused by the industrial revolution. The shocking experiences of the violent Pullman railway strike that exploded in Chicago in 1894 are approached through an extended comparison with the familial despotism of King Lear over his daughters. "A Modern Lear" was written in 1894 and presented in lectures, but not published until 1912 because Addams was told that its attack on George M. Pullman, the powerful president of the Pullman railway company, was too inflammatory to be published. Although she did publish an account of the strike in 1902 in *Democracy and Social Ethics*, one which was just as critical of Pullman, which incorporated the gist of her earlier analysis of his role in the labor dispute, the extended comparison with King Lear was dropped. Readers had no way of knowing the context which shaped Addams' own analysis. By calling attention to this hidden subtext, I would like to emphasize the audacity of Addams' using a domestic context as mediated through drama, albeit a political drama about a royal family, to illuminate the public sphere. Moreover, she does not just bring the values of the private sphere to the public sphere, but does so on the basis that both are deeply flawed in such a way that the failings of the paternal family are reproduced in the public world of industrial relations. She argues that benevolent paternalism is obsolete in the new industrial order and should be replaced with consensual decision-making.

Addams (1982: 116) still expresses gratitude to "the father", her own father, and does not want to lose any of the virtues learned from him. Despite such piety, she demolishes the individualist ethics the paternal order represented and argues that it should be replaced with social ethics. But because she begins her reflections from the perspective of a benevolent paternalism instead of an oppressive patriarchy, she (1982: 120) argues, "the emancipation of the working people will have to be inclusive of the employer from the first or it will encounter many failures, cruelties and reactions". What evidence does she give for this claim? She draws this conclusion in the first place from analyzing the ethical dimensions of Shakespeare's *King Lear*, according to which she praises the position of the repentant Cordelia over that of the two older daughters. She does so by evaluating the welfare each of the daughters achieves as a result of their varying approaches to a distressing situation. By analogy, she also evaluates what brings about the greater well being of the worker: violent confrontation or binding arbitration. She contrasts the brutal suppression of workers in the union strikes in 1890s Chicago made possible by the overwhelming strength of the colluding forces of industrial tycoons and the government with the gains achievable by arbitration. The first approach follows from each side assuming a non-negotiable position based on the righteousness of their cause; the second method requires that each side is willing to take the perspective of the other into account. But such perspectivism is not value-free. It requires that the criterion used is the well being of those on the less powerful side of the conflict where well-being has a strong moral as well as material dimension.

In *Newer Ideals of Peace*, Addams (1957: 150) points out the problems that follow from what Schneider and Ingram call in this volume, "a particularly degenerative version of pluralism". According to Addams, "Class and group divisions with their divergent moralities become most dangerous when their members believe that the inferior group of class cannot be appealed to by reason and fair dealing". The result is predictable:

"Terrorism is considered necessary and legitimate that they may be inhibited by fear from committing certain acts". This justification was frequently invoked during the late nineteenth and early twentieth century industrial revolution, the turbulent decades of predatory capitalism and government suppression of labor strikes by force. In recent times, similar sentiments have led to dramatic and racially biased increases in prison populations. Given such negative social constructions of what are perceived as being an "underclass", Addams' example of employers exhibiting this attitude toward workers is not surprising. What is surprising is that she includes trade unionists adopting this point of view in regard to non-unionists as equally contributing to the use of brute force. She derives from her experiences of what she calls the modern exploitation of an enlarged industrialism the danger of hardening legitimate differences and grievances between groups into an intransigence that makes recourse to the methods of warfare the only plausible recourse. The fact that she sided with the moral righteousness of the oppressed workers did not blind her to the downward spiral to violence that group polarization portended. What she was searching for was a way to recognize the legitimate grievances of the oppressed that could avoid such violence. Like Dewey, she was convinced that a contributing factor to the violent actions that seem inevitable was the hardening of group identity to the point where communication with others was scorned as collaboration with the enemy.

Addams was appalled by the rioting in the Blue Island community in connection with the Pullman strike and the violence unleashed against the workers, most of whom were black, by local police and federal troops which ended in the complete defeat of both the Pullman workers and the American Railway union. She reflected on what could be learned from the experiences of the industrial clashes of the summer of 1894 in which rage and violence dominated, class lines hardened, and ultimately a legacy of distrust and bitterness was left behind. Her surprising approach was to begin with her own complicity, however remote, rather than begin by demonizing the perpetrators. The perplexities raised by the ease with which violence rather than peaceful mediation was chosen should be an occasion for asking oneself the question: "How far am I responsible for this social disorder?". Such responsibility is always connected for pragmatists with a call to action, so her second question is: "What can be done to prevent such outrageous manifestations of ill will?" (1982: 120). What can be practically done, that is, to replace the incitements to riot and to murder with methods of conciliation and control?

Nothing short of "the complete participation of the working classes in the spiritual, intellectual and material inheritance of the human race" would suffice. This is the fund of common experiences in which all members of society should be able to take part. But drawing on the lessons Cordelia learned when she first abandoned and later included her father, King Lear, in her redemptive reconciliation, Addams argues that employers have to be emancipated along with their workers or failures and cruelty will result. Insofar as both the captains of industry and the workers struggled for power over the other, as long as emancipation was conceived of as the expropriation of power or its unilateral use, then they were simply continuing ancient patterns of valorizing and justifying the dominating sense of possession and exclusion of others seen in the claims of Lear's older daughters as well as in Lear himself. They would also reap its attendant cruelties and contempt for perceived rivals. The alternative is to seek for social justice. Addams (1982: 120-121) explains that such a "doctrine must be strong enough in its fusing power to touch those who think they lose, as well as those who think they gain. Only thus can it become the doctrine of a universal movement".

Universalizing Particular Experiences

This sense of how moral universals are achieved is deeply pragmatic. Dewey says he suspects any universals that are not rooted in neighborly friendliness. Universals which are found only in academic discourse or arrived at by imagining such a patently artificial state of affairs as John Rawls does in his admonition to put oneself behind a veil of ignorance, may well be ideal types, but are insufficiently rooted in the perplexities of the human situation to be of much help.[9] Like Addams, Dewey (1985: 21) distrusts "universals that are not reached by way of profound respect for the significant features and outcomes of human experience, as found in human institutions, traditions, impelling interests, and occupations".

But Addams is the only one of the original pragmatists who actively explores how people outside academia transform their experiences into moral values, how these experiences can be strong enough to overturn tradition instead of reflecting it, and how such new values can spread and gain momentum toward universalization. In *The Long Road of Woman's Memories*, she recounts many instances of ordinary women who challenged moralistically righteous conventions and developed new, more inclusive values. She tells their stories as much as possible in their own words and in enough detail to disclose the means by which their reflections led them in new directions. In her pragmatist version of standpoint theory, she (1916: 112) says that many women who have been oppressed for centuries have developed social values out of their sense of helplessness and undergoing of intolerable wrongs, and they are becoming conscious that these experiences are related to larger issues. She (1916: 64) also suggests, "individual women, driven to modify a harsh convention which has become unendurable to them, are perhaps those most sensitive to injustice". The struggle for social justice, which is a struggle among competing ideas long before it is expressed in contending social groups, may sometimes have its origins in individual women who assert an unconventional value as a resolution to their own warring emotions and conflicting values.

She recalls one such story told by a widow who stopped by Hull House with her grandson and then proceeded to explain not only that he was illegitimate, but that he was not even really her grandson. He was, in fact, the child of a woman who fooled her son into thinking he was. Then follows a heart-rending explanation of how her bitterness and righteous indignation were gradually transformed into an understanding of how conventional morality can cause the very social transgressions which it then condemns. This is further linked to the campaign against the stigma of illegitimacy being waged by the Woman's Movement, thus relating individual revaluations of values to more broad-based movements aiming at universal acceptance of a new social order based on such revaluations as the ultimate goal. In this case, it is a matter of women in a position of power because of their conventional respectability and class privilege undergoing a conversion of their beliefs as a consequence reaching out to those ostracized by society. But in conversing with women in war-torn Europe, who had struggled through their patriotic acceptance of their country's wartime goals and decided to reject them and adopt pacifist goals, Addams directly addresses the issue of individual powerlessness in the face of overwhelming governmental, military, and cultural power.

Addams (1916: 115-140) lets two women from different social classes tell their own stories. But she also frames them as conversations in which she has herself participated and thus affected. Again, her goal in doing so is to show how reflections on one's own experiences can lead to challenging conventions – in this case war as a means of solving problems – and towards actively working for a more just society. This entails linking the personal with the wider society and the state and recognizing that the welfare of one's own country is indissolubly bound up with that of other countries in the family of nations. The more educated of the two women confesses that she has never been a feminist and did not think women had any particular contribution to make to the state beyond supporting it. But after a long reflection on the death of her son in the (First World) war, she comes to the conclusion that feminism and militarism are irreconcilable.

Despite their high-sounding patriotic rhetoric, the militarists rest the power of the government on physical force which, in war, is expressed in the crudest forms of violence. Since it would be absurd to think that women could win equal rights in a world ruled by physical force, they must resist militarism and assert moral agencies as the ultimate guiding force.

At this point, the woman admits that she has always agreed with feminists in their contention that societies are being more and more organized by other means than merely physical force and that women's lesser strength should be no barrier to their full participation in society. Arresting this development has been one of the wretched consequences of war and women should do all in their power to strengthen non-militaristic social development. One can only conclude that for Addams, the disadvantaged members of unequally positioned subjects in conflict cannot win the conflict and claim the moral high ground through forcefully wresting power from the stronger. Not only will the weaker members be more likely to suffer defeat in such an uneven struggle, but society will not ultimately benefit. Differences will not be resolved by treating the other simply as the enemy or as a homogeneous unit best ignored or opposed. Addams shows how large and eventually successful social movements can begin with apparently powerless individuals who first challenge their own beliefs, begin recognizing wider connections, and take action through cooperative endeavors (see Seigfried, 2001b).

Conclusion

Many decades after Addams and Dewey wrote, more and more people active in social reform have come to share their pragmatist goal of inclusiveness. It is no longer heretical for reformers to admit the need to appeal to those in power as well as to the less powerful members of society as a condition of ultimate success (see Faludi, 1999). But well-publicized partisan political activities demonstrate that the principle of working with, instead of against perceived enemies, is still not widely held. Pragmatist theory and its feminist practices showing how diversity of interests can foster common experiences rather than subvert them can be helpful resources for overcoming such tendencies to isolation and self-righteousness. The pragmatist understanding of interdependency and its corollary of reciprocity of interests grounds its social democratic theory and practice. Solutions, to be just, must reach up and out from below and not be imposed from above or unilaterally by force. It is this democratic commitment to keeping faith with others that led Addams (1981: 97) to seek "to accentuate the likenesses and to ignore the differences which are found among the people whom the [Hull House] Settlement constantly brings into juxtaposition". The need for such efforts is more apparent than ever.

Acknowledgements

Thanks to Alfonso Morales for encouraging the contributors to this volume to make it a pragmatist collaborative project as well as a book on pragmatist theory.

Thanks to Murray J. Leaf for pointing out that the recovery of Addams' pragmatism is too recent to be widely recognized.

Notes

1 For Addams' role as a founding member of the Chicago school of pragmatism, see Seigfried (1996: 58-59, 73-79), and Seigfried (1999: 207-230).

2 In pragmatic theory the biological and the social mutually inform each other without either being reducible to the other.

3 Richard Rorty (1998: 176) seems to be urging a similar claim when he says that in order to overcome the foundationalist idea "of a sui generis sense of moral obligation, it would help stop answering the question 'What makes us different from other animals?' by saying, 'We can know and they can merely feel'. We should substitute 'We can feel for each other to a much greater extent than they can'".

4 See Rorty (1996: 123), where he gives the example of feminist lawyers in Canada who in 1927 lost a case in which they argued that women could be elected to the senate because the relevant phrase in the Canadian constitution was "any person may be elected to the Senate who", without mentioning sex. They lost, not because they did not have an absolutely airtight argument, but because of the lack of imagination of the Supreme Court judges, who thought that it was so ridiculous that women should be members of the senate that they held that the word 'person' in the constitution must mean 'men' in this case, even though this contradicted the way 'person' was applied in every other statute and constitutional provision.

5 For feminist standpoint theory, see Harding (1993).

6 See Anne Larason Schneider and Helen Ingram for the importance of this pragmatist principle in shaping policy analysis.

7 See Murray J. Leaf on how legal decisions that take factual considerations as being crucial still lie within the law for Holmes because they consider the adjustments needed in light of the consequences of the particular purposes at work in a particular case.

8 The quotes are not verbatim, but express the sense of the anecdote Studs Terkel told at a book signing session at Great Expectations Book Store, Evanston, Illinois, October 24, 1999.

9 For the important role perplexities play in both Dewey's and Addams' methods of social inquiry, see Seigfried, 2001a.

References

Addams, J. (1907), *Newer Ideals of Peace*. Chautauqua, New York: Chautauqua Press.

Addams, J. (1916), The *Long Road of Woman's Memory*. New York: Macmillan. Rpt. Seigfried, 2001b.

Addams, J. (1964), *Democracy and Social Ethics*. Cambridge, MA: Belknap Press of Harvard University. Rpt. Seigfried (2001a).

Addams, J. (1981), *Twenty Years at Hull House*. New York: Signet Classic.

Addams, J. (1982), "A Modern Lear", in Christopher Lasch (ed), *The Social Thought of Jane Addams*. New York: Irvington, pp. 105-123.

Dewey, J. (1980), "Democracy and Education", in Jo Ann Boydston (ed), *John Dewey The Middle Works*, vol. 9:1916. Carbondale and Edwardsville: Southern Illinois University Press.

Dewey, J.. (1982), "Philosophy and Democracy", in Jo Ann Boydston (ed), *John Dewey The Middle Works*, vol. 11:1918-1919, Carbondale and Edwardsville: Southern Illinois University Press.

Dewey, J. (1985), "Context and Thought", in Jo Ann Boydston (ed), *John Dewey The Later* Works, vol. 6:1931-1932. Carbondale and Edwardsville: Southern Illinois University Press.

Dewey, J. (1988), "Creative Democracy the Task Before Us" in Jo Ann Boydston (ed), *John Dewey The Later Works*, vol. 14:1939-1941. Carbondale and Edwardsville: Southern Illinois University Press.

Faludi, S. (1999), *Stiffed: The Betrayal of the American Man*. William Morrow.

Goldman, E. (1969), *Anarchism and Other Essays*. New York: Dover.

Harding, S. (1993), "Rethinking Standpoint Epistemology: What is Strong Objectivity?" in Linda Alcoff and Elizabeth Potter (eds), *Feminist Epistemologies*. New York: Routledge.

James, C. (1999), "In a Family Portrait, the Future". *New York Times*, Sec. 2 (Sept. 5), pp.1-27.

Seigfried, C. H. (2001a), Intro. *Democracy and Social Ethics*. Champaign: University of Illinois Press.

Seigfried, C. H. (2001b), Intro. *The Long Road of Woman's Memory*. Champaign: University of Illinois Press.

Seigfried, C. H. (1999), "Socializing Democracy: Jane Addams and John Dewey", *Philosophy of the Social Sciences*, vol. 29 (June), pp. 207-230.

Seigfried, C. H. (1996), *Pragmatism and Feminism*. Chicago: University of Chicago Press.

Tamir, Yael. (1999), "Siding With the Underdogs", in J. Cohen, M. Howard, and M.C. Nussbaum (ed). *Is Multiculturalism Bad for Women? Susan Moller Okin with Respondents*. Princeton: Princeton University Press.

3 A Pragmatic Response to the Embarrassing Problems of Ideology Critique in Socio-Legal Studies

Brian Z. Tamanaha

Ideology critique has been a major theme of socio-legal studies for the past twenty years (Special Issue 1988). It has also been one of the central themes of critical legal studies throughout its existence. Yet it is plagued by serious conceptual difficulties. The concept of ideology and its relationship with truth has been formulated in ways that are at best fuzzy, at worst inconsistent or vacuous. Despite its manifold problems, most of which are widely recognized, ideology critique continues to thrive in socio-legal studies. There is something essential about the argument that a certain point of view and set of beliefs is ideologically induced and wrong in ways that resist recognition. The dilemma is to figure out how the critique of legal ideology can be conducted with a satisfactory response to its theoretical difficulties. This chapter will explore the problem and will draw upon pragmatism for a possible solution.

General Problems with the Concept of Legal Ideology

A formidable threshold problem for ideology critique is that there is scant agreement upon the concept itself, on what "legal ideology" means, or on how it can or should be formulated for the purposes of social scientific application. In the absence of agreement upon what the notion of ideology represents, it is impossible to engage systematically in ideology critique (or even to know what that entails).

The multitude of definitions of ideology in general, and legal ideology in particular, can be divided roughly into two basic versions: the pejorative version and the neutral version. The pejorative (or critical) version, grounded in Marxism, has been the dominant understanding of ideology. "Unlike neutral conceptions, critical conceptions imply that the phenomena characterized as ideology or ideological are misleading, illusory or one-sided; and the very characterization of phenomena as ideology carries with it an implicit criticism or condemnation of them" (Thompson 1990: 52). "Particular ideologies, then, are held to be not only distortions of reality, but socially induced distortions, arising from the class interest of the proponents and victims of ideological beliefs" (Hesse 1980: 30). An ideology, under this view, is a set of beliefs or understandings or ideals that travel under the banner of universality or neutrality, but serve the interests of the dominant class. "There are a number of 'legal ideologies'. These include the elite production called legal doctrine and everyday understandings about law" (Trubek and Esser 1990: 175-76). These understandings are strongly influenced by and support the interests of the elite who produce it (Pashukanis 1989). Deluded by this legal ideology, the subordinate classes in society suffer from false consciousness in their willing support of the institutional and legal structures of society that operate to their disadvantage. Unaware of the effect of the dominant ideology, the oppressed voluntarily participate in bringing about their own oppression. In the pejorative version, an ideology is false or deceptive. Appending the label ideology to a set of beliefs is tantamount to an accusation.

The neutral version avoids the negative connotations attached to the pejorative version. "Neutral conceptions are those which purport to characterize phenomena as ideology or ideological without implying that these phenomena are necessarily misleading, illusory, or aligned with the interests of any particular group" (Thompson 1990: 53). Ideology in this sense constitutes a complex of ideas that inform the understanding of groups about the nature of their society. To distinguish it from the general notion of culture, some proponents of this version of ideology restrict its application to political ideas. "Legal ideology" is limited to legal ideas. "Legal ideology consists of currents of 'common sense', taken-for-granted understanding, and belief that are informed and sustained by legal doctrine and which, in turn, reinforce it and are to some extent expressed in it" (Cotterrell 1995: 10). The neutral version of ideology differs from the pejorative version in that it does not necessarily entail the assertion that the ideas and beliefs labeled ideological are false.

Although most approaches to the notion of legal ideology can be fit into one of these two versions, it should be emphasized that there are a variety of individual formulations with different crosscutting axes. For example, some analysts—of both versions—insist that ideologies are unified and internally coherent, while others insist that ideologies consist of various separate streams of thought some of which can be internally conflicting (see Cotterrell 1995: 13). Some analysts hold that ideologies are hegemonic, while others say ideologies are in a battle to become hegemonic (see Ewick and Silbey 1995: 212). Some analysts assert that ideologies constitute lived social relations, while others assert that they exist only on the plane of ideas (see Pashukanis 1989). Some analysts insist that all knowledge systems are ideological while others assert that only certain knowledge systems are ideological (see McLellan 1986). This inconsistency and lack of agreement among views about the nature of legal ideology is one of the fundamental problems with the concept.

Another problem, one specifically attached to the notion of legal ideology, especially the neutral version, is that it is exceedingly difficult if not impossible to draw lines separating legal from political, economic, moral, and religious ideas. A great deal of the culture can be considered a part of legal ideology when viewed expansively as ideas about law. Moreover, the neutral version of legal ideology is virtually identical to the decades old concept of legal culture (Friedman 1969, 1975). Despite the passage of a lengthy period of time and efforts by various theorists, the concept of legal culture has never been developed into a serviceable analytical concept or research tool for many of the same reasons that the concept of culture has not functioned well in the social sciences generally. No good reasons have been offered for supplanting the notion of legal culture with the equally elusive and more baggage-laden notion of legal ideology.

Problems with Ideology Critique and the Notion of Truth

The above difficulties render the notions of ideology and legal ideology highly problematic. The fundamental difficulty with ideology critique I wish to address, however, is different and runs deeper. The pejorative version of ideology has a distinct meaning and powerful use. It asserts that a set of ideas and beliefs are false in a way that resists recognition by those holding them—that owing to false consciousness the oppressed are blind to the fact that their own ideas hold them in chains. The assertion that there are entire bodies of false ideas and beliefs about society, politics, morality, and law necessarily entails the assertion that there are in fact true ideas and beliefs about these matters. Furthermore, the assertion that a person suffers from false consciousness suggests that the analyst or observer making the claim possesses a "true consciousness". A charge of falsity makes sense only if truth is a possibility, and if the person making the charge knows that truth.

Many practitioners and advocates of ideology critique identify themselves with interpretivism, holism, and social constructionism which are perhaps the leading (or at least most popular) complex of views in social science epistemology and ontology today. However, these theories struggle mightily with the notion of truth (Norris 1997). The core ideas behind these schools of thought can be summarized as follows: 1) we interpret and act in the world through our ideas and beliefs; 2) these ideas and beliefs, shaped by and grounded in language and culture, are socially generated and shared (and thus are intersubjective); 3) there is no strict separation between theory and fact (all facts are theory laden); 4) there is no way to get outside of or beyond a perspective-based view; and 5) reality, or at least social reality, is constructed through our ideas and beliefs. The question is whether and how truth and falsity can be asserted and understood once one accepts these basic postulates which seem to carry necessarily relativistic implications. One person's ideology is another person's truth. The problem is heightened because the charge of false consciousness reaches behind the allegedly false ideas and beliefs to challenge the entire worldview upon which they are based, which directs the accusation of falsity back to the level of perspectives. Interpretivism suggests that shared language and perspectives are what generate our ideas and beliefs, but the perspectives themselves, the world views, are not themselves subject to the charge of truth or falsity, at least not in their entirety. This point can be understood in terms of Peter Winch's (1958) claim that forms of life contain their own internal criteria of intelligibility that cannot be evaluated by criteria of intelligibility derived from other forms of life.

A concrete example of ideology critique will help illustrate some of the complex issues involved. Joel Handler has argued that the consciousness of disadvantaged people has been manipulated through ideology (1992: 342-3). This can be seen, according to Handler, in the attitudes of recipients of public assistance who believe that they bear certain obligations in return for the benefits they receive. Handler asserts, "To the extent that the applicant for assistance has internalized these values ... then the dominant group has prevented even the conception of the grievance" (343).

The first issue raised by this series of assertions is whether truth or falsity is even applicable to the kinds of beliefs identified by Handler. They involve questions of values. Consistent with the fact/value distinction, it is generally recognized that questions of truth and falsity apply to questions of fact, but not to questions of value. Moral realists and natural law theorists insist that moral statements, or at least a certain class of moral statements, can also be true or false. Outside these schools of thought, however, the general view is that moral assertions are questions of personal choice or belief to which truth and falsity are inapplicable. Even within these narrow schools of thought there is disagreement about the kinds of moral questions that can be considered true or false, and, furthermore, disagreement about which ones are true or false.

The second issue relates to the self-defeating nature of the charge. Many socio-legal scholars who engage in ideology critique deny the fact/value distinction. Even our perception of the facts, according to this view, is influenced by our value commitments contained in our language and grounded in our form of life. Thus, questions of fact cannot be clearly labeled true and false. Holism, mentioned earlier, is the name for a philosophical position that presses the point at a higher level of generality. It holds that factual assertions exist relative to a broader network of theoretical statements. Accordingly, "there is no theoretical fact or law like relation whose truth or falsity can be determined in isolation from the rest of the network" (Hesse 1980: 86). "Any statement can be held true come what may, if we make drastic enough adjustments elsewhere in the system ..." (Quine 1953: 46). The truths of facts are thus relative to the particular complex of theoretical (factual) statements within which the facts exist. According to the tenets of holism, critics of ideology are in effect asserting—without stating it—that their theory and value laden perspective-based view of the facts leads them to conclude that the Subjects suffer from false consciousness. Subjects, of course, can return exactly the same charge against the critic. The result is a stalemate.

The third issue raised by Handler's assertions is elitism. Handler is a committed advocate for the disadvantaged and makes the argument on their behalf, but there is a condescending quality to the argument that condemns an entire population to delusion while the analyst sees the light. Any response they might give to explain and support their belief—that they find it important for their own sense of dignity that there be some responsibility attached to their receipt of assistance—is invalidated at the outset because the reasons given are likewise the product of the ideological beliefs. Handler must be prepared to answer the obvious retort that it is his views, which he assumes to be superior, that are false, the product of leftist delusions; the disadvantaged, however, rarely engage on equal terms in the arena of academic discourse and, thus, will have no opportunity to make this response. Handler recognizes the questions raised by his assertions: "[H]ow do we know whether the consent is genuine or manipulated? How does the researcher…avoid imputing her values, the social construction of meaning, to the quiescent?" (344). But he offers no answer. Interpretivism and holism suggest that indeed the researcher is imputing her values.

Karl Mannheim was caught in a similar box when he extended Marx's partial theory of ideology to a total theory of ideology, asserting that all beliefs about society are the product of social context. The resultant dilemma:

> For if all beliefs distort, how can there be true beliefs about the real, and in particular how do we know there is a 'real' to be distinguished from the distortion? This reflexive argument certainly hits Mannenheim's own theory, for this is quite clearly a social theory of the same kind as it refers to, and must therefore itself be socially induced according to its own principles (Hesse 1980: 31).

Mannheim avoided this self-refutation by asserting that "intelligensia is a disinterested class whose beliefs are minimally distorted" (Hesse 1980: 31). Handler does not take this path, perhaps to avoid the charges of self-privileging and elitism, but he is left unable to explain how or why others suffer from delusion while he does not, at least with respect to this set of views. Handler might respond that this reflexive argument misses a key characteristic of ideology that it operates to the benefit of the dominant class. This response, however, ignores the possibility that the intelligensia is one of the dominant classes in society.

Mannheim suggested another possible solution to the question of truth. Through a consideration of many different points of view, we could develop an ever expanding, more encompassing framework which, consequently (over time) solves the problem of different world views, reducing their number through a process of absorption into an overarching world view (Mannheim 1985: 300-302). Given the extraordinary profusion of extant perspectives in the world today, this scenario is unduly optimistic—while ignoring questions about what we would lose in this homogenizing process—and in any case would not solve the problem well into the future.

In recognition of the problems with truth and falsity identified above, practitioners of the critique of legal ideology have made a subtle, yet significant shift in the way in which ideology and the critique of ideology is understood, as reflected in the following excerpt from the Introduction to a special issue of the *Law and Society Review* dedicated to the subject:

> In studies of law and ideology, the power of law resides in part in its capacity to inscribe the arbitrary and cultural features of social life with the aura of the natural and inevitable. All of the articles in this issue illustrate the power of law associated with the capacity to forge authoritative understandings of social relationships. In addition to the ability to 'naturalize' what is conditional and arbitrary legal ideologies can also be powerful as they conceal, falsify, or distort. It is not the immutable natural reality assumed by positive science that is concealed, however, but alternative social constructions forged from diverse experiences and competing visions. By rejecting alternative interpretations, legal ideologies are powerful to the extent that they deny that they are themselves constructions (Special Issue 1988: 633).

This account of ideology continues to makes claims about falsity and distortion, but with a substantial modification. The falsity is less in the traditional sense of a failure to correspond with reality (though those connotations have not been discarded completely); rather, the falsity lies in the claim to naturalness or inevitability, in the failure to acknowledge the possibility of alternative constructions.

David Trubek, a leading socio-legal scholar and practitioner of ideology critique asserts a similar position:

> Critical scholars see social order as maintained by a system of beliefs. The belief systems that structure action and maintain order in capitalist societies present as eternal and necessary what

> is only the transitory and arbitrary interests of a dominant elite. This commonly accepted body of ideas justifies the unequal and unjust power of the dominant group. These systems of ideas are reifications, presenting as essential, necessary, and objective what is contingent, arbitrary and subjective. Furthermore, they are hegemonic, that is, they serve to legitimate interests of the dominant class alone (Trubek 1984: 606).

This approach to ideology sidesteps the problem of truth by specifically identifying that what is false is the contingent complex of legal ideas posing as if they were necessary. However, this argument fails to appreciate the thoroughgoing nature of the social construction thesis. If meaning is socially constructed, as the thesis asserts, then every system of ideas is as "contingent, arbitrary and subjective" (or intersubjective) as any other. Each and every entrenched construction takes on the aura of the 'natural and inevitable'; each and every prevailing social construction forges authoritative understandings of social relationships. No body of ideas and beliefs—including those espoused by the practitioners of ideology critique—announce that they are merely social constructions; the social construction thesis itself does not announce that it is a social construction (which it is by its own tenets). The social construction thesis has this quality because it applies to all bodies of meaning, to all ideas and beliefs. If these characteristics are what make ideas and beliefs false and ideological, then virtually everything in social life is subject to the same charge. Everything is false in this sense. But if everything is a false ideology, then ideology has no sting, no power, no meaning. Under this interpretation of falsity the pejorative version is in effect transformed into the neutral version.

There is another sense in which the social construction thesis cannot easily coexist with the pejorative notion of ideology. The central idea behind social constructionism is that social reality is constructed through socially shared bodies of ideas and beliefs. Ideas and beliefs that people hold and act upon cannot be consistent with the social construction thesis and are false in their totality because it is these very ideas and beliefs, and the actions based upon them, which give rise to and create social reality. Pashukanis (1989) made an analogous point when he insisted that ideology gives rise to actual lived social relations and, thus, is not properly understood exclusively in terms of false ideas. Although there may also be unintended consequences to action, the social construction thesis suggests that they can only be partial or deviations, not systematic or comprehensive. To provide a specific example, it is the belief in the liberal rule of law system and actions pursuant to these beliefs, which give rise to the creation of the rule of law and allows us to distinguish this orientation from other kinds of systems, like those oriented toward substantive justice.

Drawing from the preceding discussion, here is a summary of the complex of problems raised above by the notion of ideology, or, more specifically, legal ideology, when combined with interpretivism, holism and social constructionism. The neutral view of legal ideology has questionable value because it faces a threshold difficulty of delimiting the distinctively legal complex of ideas and beliefs in society from among other ideas and beliefs and is indistinguishable from the longstanding (unsuccessful) notion of legal culture. The pejorative version of legal ideology has difficulty identifying what are true beliefs about law; it cannot avoid the reflexive sting—that its own position is merely ideology; it has elitist overtones; and it appears to be inconsistent with the social constructions thesis—that widely held ideas and beliefs are acted upon to construct social reality (and therefore cannot be systematically false). The modified pejorative version, which abstains from making claims about reality, instead asserting that the falsity lies in a false claim to naturalness, has absolutely no bite because the same charge applies to all ideas and beliefs. This modified pejorative version, furthermore, when giving up the claim about falsity in relation to reality, emasculates the very point, which has made the notion of ideology so powerful.

A Pragmatic Approach to Knowledge and Truth

Considering the complexity and lack of apparent solutions, it makes sense to conclude that ideology critique should be suspended, and indeed that is what I argued in an earlier exploration of this problem (1997: 84-89). The issues involved, it should be noted, are not limited to the problem of ideology. A raging debate is taking place within the philosophy of science generally with regard to the implications of interpretivism, holism, and social constructionism for our ability to make claims about truth and reality (Norris 1997). That is the post-modern condition. The highly influential work of Richard Rorty (1979) and Thomas Kuhn (1962), among many others, suggests that science itself is just another worldview, practice, or language game. These arguments, it should be noted, are aimed directly at the natural sciences, which at least have concrete objects and achievements to point to for vindication even as their epistemological underpinnings have been thrown into doubt. The weaker and less secure social sciences have no obvious object of study and few obvious achievements to claim in validation.

When viewed in this broader framework, the fate and self-understanding of the social sciences generally are at stake. The dilemmas faced by ideology critique appear minor by comparison. Yet there are two important reasons to continue ideology critique: it raises an argument that is crucial for social justice, and it is a highly effective form of argument. Its value for these purposes provides compelling incentives to strive to locate a resolution to the problems identified above. Working out this understanding will also have broader implications for social science as an enterprise.

I will draw upon pragmatism to provide a basis for this understanding. There are many strains of pragmatism, including Rorty's version. The approach I take, building upon the work of Dewey and James, will emphasize the realistic side of pragmatism, an aspect of pragmatism that Rorty sublimates. Pragmatism is especially useful because it adheres to the core ideas underlying interpretivism and holism while holding to a notion of truth.

The basic argument I will press is that the emphasis in interpretivism and holism on shared bodies or networks of meaning is only one side of a necessarily two-sided relationship. The other side is the reality within which meaning, language, concepts, and theories arise. This emphasis on the reality side of the relationship, it should be noted, while necessary as a corrective matter, is also misleading because the key is not to be found in either or both poles, but in the inseverable relationship that connects them. Pragmatism builds truth and knowledge upon this relationship. Meaning, language, truth, and knowledge are always grounded in and derived from our meaningfully informed activities in the world. The following discussion will lay out the pragmatist theory of truth and how it relates to reality and our access to this reality. With the pragmatist approach to truth and knowledge in hand, the next Section will revisit the problems raised by the critique of legal ideology.

The first crucial step taken by the pragmatists was to replace the contemplative, spectator view of knowledge with an active, constructive account of knowledge. Knowledge is obtained through experience gained in the course of working in the world to achieve our projects. According to Dewey, "Knowing means a certain kind of intelligently conducted doing; it ceases to be contemplative and becomes in a true sense practical" (Dewey

1948: 21). This intelligently conducted doing takes place within a material environment and a context that involves both preexisting ways of doing (knowing) and a community of doers; it takes place within practices. "For Peirce and Dewey, inquiry is cooperative human interaction within an environment; and both aspects, the active intervention, the active manipulation of the environment, and the cooperation with other human beings, are vital ... For the pragmatists, the model is a group of inquirers trying to produce good ideas and trying to test them to see which ones have value" (Putnam 1995: 70-71).

This view of knowledge leads to the pragmatist theory of truth, as expressed by Dewey:

> If ideas, meaning, conceptions, notions, theories, systems are instrumental to an active reorganization of the given environment, to a removal of some specific trouble and perplexity, then the test of their validity and value lies in accomplishing this work. If they succeed in their office, they are reliable, sound, valid, good, and true. If they fail to clear up confusion, to eliminate defects, if they increase confusion, uncertainty and evil when they are acted upon, then are they truly false? Confirmation, corroboration, verification lie in works, consequences ... That which guides us truly is true—demonstrated capacity for such guidance is precisely what is meant by truth (Dewey 1948: 156).

The pragmatist slogan that truth is "what works" has a technical meaning that entails several different aspects which I will roughly (and artificially) separate into three elements. Something is true if we can 1) successfully rely upon it in the pursuit of our projects, which are 2) conducted by a community of investigators, and 3) take place within a material context or environment (including other persons). An additional point must be made about each of these three aspects.

As to the first aspect, the notion that truth is what works, what satisfies, does not imply 'a meeting of purely personal need...It includes public and objective conditions" (Dewey 1948: 157). In a sense, it involves successful prediction, that is, things work out based upon a certain understanding of the facts of the situation. When that understanding is correct—or true—the project at hand plays out consistent with what was anticipated. It is true that water freezes at 32 degrees (as determined relative to a constructed measuring system), and this fact can be relied upon every time it is necessary for us to make (or melt) ice.

The second aspect, involving the community of investigators, is tied to the fact that the theory of truth has nothing to do with what the individual desires, but rather is the product of a community of inquirers operating within shared practices. "Truth [James insists], is a notion which presupposes a community, and, like Peirce, he held that the widest possible community, the community of all persons (and possibly all sentient beings) in the long run, is the relevant one" (Putnam 1995: 24 n.7). William James emphasized that truth in the long run is what matters: "for it is notorious that the temporarily satisfactory is often false" (James 1975: 220).

The third aspect, the material environment, is also crucial. This is where the strong strain of realism in pragmatist thought emerges. James repeatedly pointed out that pragmatists "carefully posited 'reality' ab initio"; (272) that is, each individual is up against the world, a world that consists of material objects (including other people) that are not malleable to thought or desires. The "notion of reality independent of either of us, taken from ordinary social experience, lies at the base of the pragmatist definition of truth. With some such reality any statement, in order to be counted true, must agree" (283). Thus, while the pragmatists recognize that there is no unmediated access to the world, and they accept that in a certain sense the world is constituted through our ideas and beliefs, that it is carved up and available to us only through the prism of our perspective-based interests and concerns, they continue to insist that there is a world out there which has its own facticity, albeit one we can never have access to in any raw form (whatever that might mean). Although pragmatists posit the existence of reality, their position is not the metaphysical realist one that there are transcendent truths about the nature of this reality regardless of the presence of sentient beings. Knowledge and truths are social achievements that cannot exist—that make no sense—in the terms understood by metaphysical realism.

The above approach to truth and knowledge allows pragmatism to straddle what are ordinarily considered to be two alternative theories of truth: correspondence and coherence. It must be emphasized that the pragmatists reject the correspondence theory of truth in its standard epistemological dress which holds that truths, especially scientific truths, connect up with reality, that truths in science have discovered the essential language or structure of the nature. There is no one language in which nature is written, according to pragmatism, no one theory that connects up with the essential structure of reality, only alternative webs of meaning within which reality can be experienced and understood. But it would be a mistake to conclude from this that correspondence is irrelevant. A strong sense of correspondence is contained in the first and third elements set out above. A project works, is successful, precisely because the knowledge and understanding which guides it fits within, and corresponds to the enveloping material conditions—the reality—within which the project takes place. Projects may conceivably also succeed under circumstances in which the knowledge does not correspond to reality when conforming conditions, nevertheless, hold as a matter of coincidence (like a rain dance that happens to be followed by a storm). However, it is less likely that a project will fail when the knowledge does in fact correspond to the reality; and such failures will usually be based upon features that cannot be predicted or controlled (knowledge is never complete, and contingencies are always present). As a general matter, confirmation, corroboration, and verification, that is, success will not come about in a sustained way in the absence of some degree of correspondence.

The pragmatist incorporation of the coherence approach can be seen in the second element. According to coherence theory, beliefs are true based upon their relationship with other beliefs, or, more broadly stated, based upon consistency with the entire complex of beliefs. The second element indicates that a key aspect of the inquiry is that it takes place within a community of investigators (identified in the broadest possible terms, over the long run) which indicates that for the knowledge to be accepted it must fit within the prevailing complex of intersubjective meaning, within the world view or the network of theories and facts which informs the community of investigators.

If the purported knowledge either does not correspond to the material conditions of the project, or does not cohere with the overarching network of meaning within which the investigation takes place, it will not be knowledge; it will not be true. This discussion should reveal that, owing to the pragmatist account of knowledge as always intersubjective and always context grounded, coherence and correspondence are actually connected at a fundamental level. Neither makes sense without the other. Our language, ideas and concepts, with which and within which we perceive and organize the world arise and are formulated naturalistically: that is, within existing webs of meaning, and within a material context that is always already present. Thus, these ideas, beliefs and concepts are a product of both other ideas, beliefs and concepts (which they cohere within), as well as the situated context within which they arise (and which they correspond to).

Combining correspondence and coherence is not unique to pragmatism. Mannheim, despite developing a total theory of ideology and the sociology of knowledge in a manner that potentially eviscerates claims to truth, in fact held a rather strong realist view. In the following observations, the coherence and correspondence aspects, respectively, of his thought are apparent (albeit without using the terms): "Relationism signifies merely that all of the elements of meaning in a given situation have reference to one another and derive their significance from this reciprocal interrelationship in a given frame of thought … All knowledge is oriented toward some object and is influenced in its approach by the nature of the object with which it is preoccupied" (1985: 86). Hans Georg Gadamer (1991), the foremost hermeneutic philosopher of this generation, likewise has a consistent realist strain in his work which combines correspondence and coherence. As Brice Wachterhauser (1994: 153) observed, Gadamer "feels confident in repeatedly claiming that though knowledge is mediated by language and history the truth of our knowledge-claims must still be conceived in terms of their adequacy or correspondence to the things in themselves". Although Mannheim and Gadamer do not describe the relationship between the two ways of approaching knowledge in the pragmatist terms set out above, there are parallels (especially with Mannheim); more importantly, their positions demonstrate the viability (and perhaps necessity) of the combination from the standpoint of strong interpretivist positions.

This straddling of correspondence and coherence helps provide a partial solution to a puzzle generated by the holism. With a sharp separation between theory and fact, any recalcitrant purported fact can be viewed in one of two ways: the purported fact can be false (because inconsistent with a true theory), or the theory can be false (because refuted by a true fact). The holistic blurring of theory and fact, however, gives rise to the possibility of a third option: adjusting the theory (which may include recharacterizing the fact) until the fact fits. If a fact apparently inconsistent with a prevailing theory can, nevertheless, be made consistent through adjustments elsewhere in the web of theoretical postulates, thereby continuing to maintain coherence, then it is not clear on what basis a theory (or indeed a fact) will be determined false. This, in turn, suggests that existing theories are overthrown, or new theories adopted, for political (or ideological) reasons, rather than because the newer theory is more adequate to the facts. Truth and falsity have little apparent role to play in this scenario.

While it would appear that, pursuant to this understanding, the coherence of a set of facts and theoretical postulates can be preserved no matter what the contrary evidence, the constraining presence of reality (element 3), the demands of a project (element 1), the requirement of correspondence (combining elements 1 and 3), as well as the understandings of the community (element 2), set limits on the freedom to revise. The community of investigators will not easily give in to revisions in the theory, especially for those postulates that have long been accepted. Although an adjustment of theoretical postulates might be preferable to a complete overthrow of the theory, the requirement of coherence, whereby the existing body of theories and facts fit together, would indicate that any disconfirming fact of sufficient import would require extensive theoretical revisions or factual recharacterizations if the overall coherence of the theory is to be preserved. The correspondence aspect matters because it will not allow a superficial papering over of the recalcitrant fact or theoretical adjustment. Any adjustments must fit with, or correspond to the constraining conditions presented by the surrounding reality. The project-grounded aspect of knowledge matters in both a general and a specific sense. In the general sense, all scientific projects carry with them certain norms common to the practice of science—i.e. attention to evidence, experimental confirmation, repeatability, resistance to falsification, acceptable modes of discovery and justification, and so forth—which set limits on the amount and kinds of revisions that can be done. The more specific sense has to do with the fact that a great deal of knowledge has instrumental benefits with respect to particular projects; the recalcitrant fact is a potential warning that the existing theory contains limitations which means that there may be limitations in its instrumental exploitation when relied upon or implemented in the form of technical or other knowledge. In a competitive environment (i.e. the presence of other projects, as well as other theories), it is quite possible that another theoretical framework, one which is able to account for the recalcitrant fact, will be more successful in key instrumental respects. This relatively greater success will render irrelevant, or less attractive, efforts to revise the original theory to the point that the theory may be considered falsified, or at least inadequate by comparison.

This description of the constraints involved is consistent with James' comments on the subject. New knowledge comes about when experience throws up a problem—something unusual or unanticipated that does not easily fit, or an apparent contradiction—that strains existing beliefs. New truths are adopted in a conservative and patchwork fashion, preserving "the older stock of truths with a minimum of modification, stretching them just enough to make them admit the novelty, but conceiving that in ways as familiar as the case leaves possible" (James 1975: 35). His observation suggests both that the theoretical adjustments to the existing stock of knowledge can only be stretched so far, and, on the other hand, that the recalcitrant reality cannot be entirely ignored.

An avowed post-modernist will contest the above account by asserting that the constraints identified are either weak or non-existent. The primary flaw of this account, she would assert, is that it fails to appreciate the extent to which our worldview constructs the very reality we see; reality can hardly serve as a constraint on knowledge and truth for the purposes of coherence and correspondence if reality is constituted by those very ideas and beliefs. Furthermore, world views are incommensurable, and contain their own standards of truth and rationality; thus, not only is there no shared view of reality, but it is impossible to come to an agreement across world views; it is impossible to find truths across or outside of particular world views. Accordingly, the term truth is nothing more than a redundant affirmation of one's belief, a meaningless carryover from dated objectivist rhetoric, which should be discarded.

The pragmatist response is that while we can perceive reality only from within a perspective which shapes what that reality is for us, this does not mean that reality is whatever we wish to make of it. Reality has an independent existence which serves as more than a test for knowledge; prior to this moment, it has a substantial formative influence on the worldview itself, which, as indicated, naturalistically arises always a part of and always already shaped by this material context. The pragmatist will also respond that the revisability of theory is constrained by the practices of the community of investigators, practices which, at least in the case of science, have been influenced by the instrumental success of the knowledge generated pursuant thereto; it is undeniable that certain ideas and beliefs are more successful (or reliable) than others. Finally, the argument of incommensurability is belied by the fact that science has been able to generate a body of knowledge that holds across many different culture and language groups. Whether this is because reality is a universal constraining condition, or because aspects of the scientific worldview have colonized other worldviews (along the lines Mannheim suggested) need not be determined. The point is that incommensurability is not inevitable. Admittedly, the range of accepted scientific knowledge is narrow by comparison to the total body of knowledge. Even outside of this range, however, the incommensurability point is exaggerated, as demonstrated by the fact and practice of the translatability of language. Acknowledging all of the limitations and imperfections of translation, the fact remains that we are able to overcome differences in world view for the purposes of understanding one another, as demonstrated and confirmed every day in the practice of inter-language and inter-cultural communication. From the possibility of understanding immediately follows the possibility of locating shared knowledge and truths about (core aspects of) the reality within which we mutually exist. Donald Davidson's (1984: 183-98) often cited "Charity Principle", which holds, "if we want to understand others, we must count them right in most matters" (197), comes to basically the same point, suggesting that there is always some common ground to be found between forms of life upon which understanding, and often evaluation, can be based.

An objectivist or absolutist will also remain unconvinced by the above account of knowledge and truth. The constraints it provides are soft or pliable, not the kind of certainty and universality that knowledge and truth require. Moreover, it leaves untouched the fundamental point that knowledge and truths are relative to a perspective or world-view. The pragmatist response: this is the human condition; absolute certainty and objectivity are simply beyond our reach; there is no Archimedean standpoint, at least not one we have access to, and we have been getting along quite well in generating useful knowledge and discovering reliable truths regardless of these constraining conditions. The dreaded objectivist charge of relativism, which serves in the debate more as a smear than as a refutation of the pragmatist account of truth, is descriptively accurate, but epistemologically irrelevant. If pragmatism is correct, this relative aspect is an enabling condition (as well as limitation) of all knowledge. To say that the pragmatist account of knowledge is relativist is not a critique of the account, but a restatement of it (see Tamanaha 1997: 26-35). A valid critique would be to establish the possibility or existence of a non-relative account of knowledge and truth which no objectivist has satisfactorily accomplished. In effect the objectivist asserts the inadequacy of the pragmatist position by comparison to a non-existent alternative.

There is a telling underlying identity in the criticisms directed by the avowed objectivist and the avowed post-modernist—two schools thought to be diametrically opposed—against the (realistic) pragmatist approach to truth and knowledge asserted herein: both are arguing from the standpoint of an absolutist theory of truth. According to this shared view, truth must be absolute (i.e. non-relative), or it is not truth (objectivist), or there is no such thing as truth (post-modernist). The pragmatist response to both is that the fact that truths about the reality within which we exist are generated in the context of our social practices relative to communities of inquirers does not render them any less reliable or useful. They are still truths in the most important senses of the term.

A Pragmatic Approach to Ideology Critique

The pragmatist account of knowledge and truth established above can be applied in the context of social science to provide an understanding of the pejorative version of legal ideology and to license ideology critique, consistent with interpretivism, holism, and social constructionism. A cost is attached to accepting this pragmatist basis for ideology critique—it restricts the range of application of the pejorative version of legal ideology. The account of truth offered above was based upon the positing of a reality that serves as a constraint upon, or check for, knowledge and truth in terms of both coherence and correspondence. Reality in this sense is limited to matters of fact (understood in holistic terms) to empirical claims.

While the application of this conception of knowledge is apparent with regard to the natural sciences with their usually concrete, physical referents or objects of study, talk about reality in the context of the social sciences is less certain. An example of the magnitude of the problem of what constitutes "reality" for the social sciences can be seen in a threshold dispute of how to understand the subject matter of sociology. Strict methodological individualists deny that social phenomena exist in any real sense (see Maniacs 1987: 266-93) while others, those who believe in social phenomena, argue, for example, that structures or mass behavior are *sui generis* real, according to certain radical views more real even than the individuals who make them up (Black 1995).

Rather than attempt to resolve this debate, I will instead approach from a different direction. The point of mentioning it is to highlight that "reality" in the context of the social sciences which is a contestable notion that cannot be determined for all instances and possibilities in advance. Hence, in this exploration I can do no more than indicate one significant context in which there is a kind of concrete reality parallel to that which exists with regard to the reality for the natural sciences, which would therefore be an appropriate subject matter for ideology critique. Before describing this context, however, it is necessary to repeat a reminder by Dewey on the limited scope of truth in the realm of meaning:

> But the realm of meanings is wider than that of true-and-false meanings; it is more urgent and more fertile. When the claim of meanings to truth enters in, then truth is indeed preeminent. But this fact is often confused with the idea that truth has a claim to enter everywhere; that it has monopolistic jurisdiction. Poetic meanings, moral meanings, a large part of the goods of life are matters of richness and freedom of meanings, rather than of truth; a large part of our life is carried on in a realm of meanings to which truth and falsity as such are irrelevant (Dewey 1925: 332).

As difficult as it might be to draw precise lines, the general distinction Dewey makes is understandable. His basic point is that there are many aspects of meaning to which the question of truth or falsity is inappropriate. In these contexts ideology critique is inappropriate (though other forms of criticism will be available). Unfortunately, a great deal of extent ideology critique, which inevitably touches on matters of meaning, traverses this line.

In the social sciences, the realm of activities provides a reality parallel to the physical reality that is the object of the natural sciences. Activities consist of the actions of people engaged in meaningfully oriented conduct. So defined, behavioral, as well as meaningful components, are present in all activities. The meaningful aspect in the first instance refers to the purposeful (subjective) orientation of each individual actor; consequently, an orientation which always and inevitably draws upon socially shared and generated (intersubjective) meaning strains. The behavioral aspect refers to what the people do in a concrete physical sense to physical action taking place within a material context. A useful heuristic notion in the social sciences that has captured these qualities of activities is the concept of a practice (see Tamanaha 1997: 167-72), though the realm of activities to which ideology critique can be applied is broader than just practices. Activities provide a kind of reality because they too consist of physical manifestations, both in terms of the movements of bodies in space and in terms of the concrete physical manifestations of, or consequences of, the activities. Wars, skyscrapers, automobiles, ice cream, intercourse, and legal systems are all the products of meaningfully oriented behavior and are all manifested in physically observable conduct, as well as in concrete physically manifest consequences or traces.

One irony of centering on activities is that it turns upside down the traditional focus of ideology which originated in and has heretofore emphasized the realm of ideas. Although ideas are still key under this approach, the point of access and reference is activities related to the ideas. Absent activities, there is no tangible reality that can provide the grounding necessary for correspondence and coherence to operate. When identifying truth and falsity for the purposes of establishing the pejorative usage of ideology, in answer to the question—"correspondence (or lack thereof) to what?"—we are able to point to the products and consequences of intentional activities. Since the social sciences themselves also consist of activities, in answer to the question—"cohere to what?"—the answer is the intersubjective communities of the social sciences as meaningfully informed practices oriented toward generating knowledge about reality. As indicated earlier, the pragmatist account of truth is itself directly based upon activities. Thus, this approach is not only consistent with the pragmatist approach to truth, but it is reflexive in the sense that the very same standard applies to test whether those engaging in ideology critique from a social science standpoint are themselves suffering from false consciousness.

When the relevant meaningful activities have been identified, they should be examined with three connected foci in mind. One focus is on what the people engaged in those activities understand to be the nature, point, purposes, effect, consequences, and so forth, of their activities. We must uncover the meaning those activities have for them, as interpretivism suggests. Another focus is on observing what they are in fact doing—on whether their actual conduct is consistent with what they claim to be doing. This second focus will be more behaviorist in orientation (though not ignoring meaning), striving to uncover actual patterns of conduct that can be checked against espoused intentions. The third focus involves attention to the direct as well as secondary or collateral effects or consequences of the activities, and to examine and test whether they are consistent with the expressed intentions of the actors. The distinction between the final two foci is that for the second, the question is whether people are in fact doing what they claim to be doing, whereas for the third, it is whether the consequences of their actions are consistent with their stated purposes or goals.

The final matters to be indicated are the circumstances under which the label ideology can be appropriately attached. In any situation in which the actions (2nd) or the consequences of the activities (3rd) are contrary to the expressed meaning and intentions of the actors, unbeknownst to the actors, ideologically induced false consciousness is a possible explanation for the inconsistency. Insincerity must be ruled out, which is why the contradiction must be unbeknownst to the actors. Plain mistake or misunderstanding, or simply inadequate information, with regard to what the appropriate kinds of activities consist of, or with regard to how to effectively achieve the stated objectives, must also be ruled out. Thus, unrecognized inconsistency between expressed intentions and actions, or consequences alone is not sufficient to narrow the explanation to ideology. Two additional pieces are necessary. The first piece is that core aspects of the knowledge and beliefs which shape the understanding of the actors with regard to the nature and consequences of their actions must be shown to be wrong or false (as determined in pragmatist terms); the second piece is a demonstration that the real consequences of the actions operate in a systematic fashion either against the interests of the actors or for the interests of a different group (what qualifies as "interests" are to be determined by reference to the respective world views involved). As an aspect of the latter demonstration, it should be shown how—i.e. the actual or likely manner or mechanism by which—the (false) core ideas and the activities they inform operate against the interests of the actors, or for the interests of others.

When the above circumstances are present, there is a strong basis for asserting that the actors suffer from ideologically induced false consciousness. This approach, it should be noted, does not run afoul of the social construction thesis because it operates within a limited scope to show the ways in which intentional actions can, in selected circumstances, lead to unintentional consequences (often owing to the intentional actions of others). It is also reflexive, as noted, because the social scientist must be prepared, when challenged, to demonstrate that her activities that generated the charge of ideology against another group's activities and beliefs can withstand the same scrutiny. There is, however, one significant modification. One of the key assertions of the social sciences (and common to many professions) is that its activities are not oriented toward the advancement of its own interests as a group; if along with the other indicia set out above it is systematically demonstrated that the interests served are in fact those of the (purportedly not self-interested) group itself, the final piece identified above will be satisfied.

The above guidelines have immediate application in socio-legal studies. If the above suggestions are complied with, a greater degree of confidence can be accorded to claims; for example, that the rule of law is an ideology or that rights talk is ideological. A grounding in this (realistic) pragmatic approach to truth can help socio-legal scholars avoid most of the puzzles and dilemmas that have plagued assertions of ideologically induced false consciousness.

It should be evident from the above description that much of the recent work that identifies itself as ideology critique can still be conducted under the approach proposed herein. The best and most persuasive studies already comply with the above guidelines. This overlap is not coincidental. These guidelines are consistent with what should be demonstrated if the charge of ideology is to be pressed in a manner consistent with the historical identity of the social sciences as an enterprise concerned with gathering and conveying reliable knowledge about the reality of social life.

References

Black, D.J. (1995), "The Epistemology of Pure Sociology", *Law and Social Inquiry*, vol. 20, pp. 829-70.

Cotterrell, R. (1995), *Law's Community: Legal Theory in Sociological Perspective*. Oxford: Clarendon Press.

Davidson, D. (1984), *Inquiries Into Truth and Interpretation*. New York: Oxford University Press.

Dewey, J. (1925), *Existence and Nature*. New York: Norton.

Dewey, J. (1948), *Reconstruction in Philosophy*. Boston: Beacon Press.

Ewick, P., and Silbey, S. (1995), "Subversion Stories and Hegemonic Tales: Toward a Sociology of Narrative", *Law and Society Review*, vol. 29, pp. 197-226.

Friedman, L.M. (1975), *The Legal System: A Social Science Perspective*. New York: Russell Sage Foundation.

Gadamer, H.G. (1991), *Pragmatism and the Meaning of Truth* (2nd ed.), trans. J Weinsheimer and D.G. Marshall. New York: Crossroad.

Handler, J. (1992), "Discretion, Power, Quiescence, and Trust", K. Hawkins (ed.), *The Uses of Discretion*. New York: Oxford University Press, 331-60.

Hesse, M. (1980), *Revolution and Reconstruction in Philosophy of Science*. Bloomington: Indiana University Press.

James, W. (1975), *Pragmatism and the Meaning of Truth*. Cambridge: Harvard University Press.

Kuhn, T.S. (1962), *The Structure of Scientific Revolutions* Chicago: University of Chicago Press.

Manheim, K (1985), *Ideology and Utopia: An Introduction to the Sociology of Knowledge*. New York: Harcourt, Brace, Janovich Publishers.
Maniacs, P.T. (1987), *A History and Philosophy of the Social Sciences*. Oxford: Basil Blackwell.
McLellan, D. (1986), *Ideology*. Minneapolis: University of Minnesota Press.
Norris, C. (1997), *Against Relativism: Philosophy of Science, Destruction and Critical Theory*. Oxford: Blackwell Publishers.
Pashukanis, E. (1989), *Law and Marxism: A General Theory*. Worchester: Pluto Publishing.
Putnam, H. (1995), *Pragmatism: An Open Question*. Cambridge: Harvard University Press.
Quine, W.V.O. (1953), *From a Logical Point of View*. Cambridge: Harvard University Press.
Rorty, R. (1975), *Philosophy and the Mirror of Nature*. Princeton: Princeton University Press.
Special Issue (1988), "Law and Ideology", *Law and Society Review*, vol. 22, No. 4.
Tamanaha, B.Z. (1997), *Realistic Socio-Legal Theory: Pragmatism and a Social Theory of Law*. Oxford: Clarendon Press.
Thompson, J.D. (1990), *Ideology and Modern Culture*. Stanford: Stanford University Press.
Trubek, D.M. (1984), "Where the Action Is: Critical Legal Studies and Empiricism", *Stanford Law Review*, vol. 36, pp. 575-622.
Trubek, D.M. and Esser, J.P. (1990), "'From Scientism Without Determinism' to 'Interpretation Without Politics': A Reply to Sarat Harrington and Yugvesson", *Law and Social Inquiry*, vol. 15, pp. 171-80.
Wachterhauser, B. (1994), "Gadamer's Realism: The 'Belongingness' of Word and Reality" in B. Wachterhauser (ed.) *Hermeneutics and Truth*. Evanston, Ill.: Northwestern University Press.
Winch, P. (1964), "Understanding: Primitive Society", *American Philosophical Quarterly*, vol. 1, pp. 307-24.

4 Pragmatic Legal Norms[1]

Murray J. Leaf

Which "norms" would be more normative: policies strongly urged by some but deplored by others, or rules accepted as common sense by almost everyone? Alternatively, is our behavior properly guided by what we are told we ought to do, or by what we believe the nature of a situation requires?

Introduction

It seems to be widely believed that pragmatism is less normatively potent than critical legal studies (henceforth CLS) or postmodernism on the political left or law and economics on the political right. As Tamanaha has paraphrased it, "Pragmatism has nothing affirmative to offer precisely at the point at which the hard questions begin, when we are called upon to make and justify judgments about good and bad, right and wrong" (1997: 246). This has been a recurrent claim throughout the history of pragmatism and seems to me to mistake harshness for power. It is not an accident that pragmatism, when given a relatively clear field for implementation, has yielded some of the most successful social reform programs in recent history, including the legislation of the New Deal and the political and legal reconstruction of post-war Germany and Japan. Nor, on the other hand, is it accidental that Marxism, positivism and laissez faire economics, when given comparable free reign, have produced some of our greatest disasters, including but by no means limited to the Nazi and Soviet states and the abuses of monopoly capitalism when it has not been controlled by effective public regulation.

Pragmatism is grounded in a specific model of human reasoning. This is not, however, anything so simple as a prescriptive model for deductive reasoning akin to Aristotelian or symbolic logic. It is rather a descriptive model of reasoning based on experience, the most fully articulated and established form of which is taken to be scientific experimentalism. Although the pragmatic model incorporates an analysis of the limits of formal deductive reasoning, it does not stop there but goes on to develop an empirically grounded analysis of what is done when those limits are reached. Virtually every major pragmatic writer produced a variant of the analysis, or a part of it, with little if any basic disagreement. It is what we see in Peirce's *How to Make our Ideas Clear*, Dewey's *The Quest for Certainty* and *How We Think* (among others), James' functional psychology and Mead's emergent evolutionism. For law, it is most importantly what is embodied in Holmes' distinction between "mathematics", or "logic", and "experience" in *The Common Law* (first published in 1881) and his often-quoted 1897 *The Path of the Law*.

Holmes' conception of experience carries on through Cardozo, Pound and such important pragmatic thinkers of the 1930s as Thurman Arnold and Morris Raphael Cohen. It can be separated into two main components: a conception of the nature of reasoning as such, and a conception of the nature of the social situation that it reflects and within which it occurs.

Pragmatism is an extension of skepticism, ultimately rooted in Greek sophism. Skeptical thinkers from the beginning have recognized that individuals in a community work in a world of interacting perspectives and multiple and conflicting values. Judges work in a legal microcosm within that world. Their aim has been to account for this world rather than try to escape from it or transcend it. Their conception of what they are about is, therefore, fundamentally descriptive. Precisely because it is descriptive, it is and always has been also powerfully normative, not in the sense that it is phrased with words like "ought", but in the sense that it provides actual guidance. Although the skeptical approach precludes a search for monolithic standards such as CLS and the other positions seem to seek, it nevertheless produces a very clear set of entailments about how laws work and how judges should decide cases. Pragmatic social and legal theory does not affirm or urge some purported rule of fairness that decisions should impose and certainly does not say that one ought to impose one's own taste in the absence of such a rule. It says how the responsibility to decide is structured and what, given that, a good decision should take into account and how a bad decision can be identified.

Holmes' Mathematics versus Holmes' Experience

Although Holmes did not say in any one phrase what he took "mathematics" to be, there should be little doubt about what he meant when we take him in his historical and jurisprudential context and in the context of the way he linked the idea of "experience" to the way law is transformed through the largely unconscious consideration of "policy" (1923: 35). Holmes' stated purpose is to bring these unconscious criteria out into the open (1923: 35, 469).

The historical and jurisprudential context took two main argumentative forms, one concerning the British Common Law, the second concerning continental civil law. In the Common Law context, Holmes took the side of those like Maitland and Pollock who saw the traditional divisions and distinctions of the Common Law as responding to historically different interests that needed to be understood, rather than as simply an illogical mass that needed to be cleared up by some sort of Austinian or Benthamite rewriting. In Civil Law he supported the parallel position descending from von Savigny that law grew "from the life of the people" as opposed to the "Romanist" and other positions he often characterized simply as "German" that had to be imposed from above, on the model of the imperial codes, the Reception, and the Code Napoleon.

The two jurisprudential debates were in reality two versions of a single argument that had its roots in the ancient conflict between republican and imperial conceptions of Roman law. Both systems defined law, most basically, as the will of Gods. Hence, for us mortals something that necessarily would have existed before our birth would continue after our death, and is something found and not made. The implication is that law is the repository of stability. The conflict turned on views of how to find it. The constitutional principle of the republic was VOX POPULI VOX DEI. For the empire, the claim was that the emperor was the voice of the law. The republican principle meant that the will of the Gods was manifested by the people in the assemblies that elected their magistrates. For the empire, it was what the emperor said—although this was not taken as meaning that the emperor could say anything whatsoever. His legitimacy depended on the notion that what he spoke for was in fact the law. The idea of the universality and necessity of logic entered Roman legal thought in the imperial period in support of the way emperors tried to implement their claim by having teams of scholars chop up the republican legal material and use the Aristotelian idea of a class-inclusion hierarchy to reorder it into successive codes. It was obviously important in this process, given the fundamental conservatism of the idea of law itself, to claim that the codification did not change anything in substance, that the law was still the law. To say or suggest otherwise would have undermined both the idea that the law was the same and the idea that the law justified the emperor's uses of it—that the emperor administered the law according to the law.[2] The idea that such a logic was purely formal and not substantive was an essential part of this reassurance. With such codification, it was constantly claimed, gaps in the law would be filled and the whole would attain a fixed and universal form and endure, thereafter, with no confusion. In fact, each codification was either abandoned or altered soon after it was promulgated.

There had been no such codification by exogenous principles during the four hundred year history of the republic, but rather a process of slow and steady accretion and evolution. The substance of the law predated the republic. The republic began with making it a public thing (*res publica*), available to all, rather than a private thing, available only to the ruling elite. Given that, in the early republic, magistrates would say what they would enforce when standing for election; in effect, the law was chosen with the magistrates. Later, as magistrates accepted laws that had found favor from their predecessors while rejecting those that had not (with the associated case materials), these gradually accumulated, became fixed, and at the same time expanded in power and flexibility.

For the Common Law, on Maitland's analysis (1981: 8-9), a parallel choice was offered between the Romanized codification of English law offered by Bracton and the ordering of procedural devices, the forms of action, by Glanvill. The former would have organized substantive law in the manner of Justinian's *Institutes* (Güterbock, 1866: 35). The latter specified almost nothing in substantive law, but set up a system for submitting and referring cases back and forth in part according to their subject matter and in part by choice of the parties concerned (since within limits that quickly began to expand, it was up to them to say what that subject matter was, and also to elect to pay what were initially the higher fees of the king's courts as against local courts).[3] Although both approaches were aimed at producing a coherent national system, the basic strategies and long-run consequences were radically different: one presuming that the institution would flow from the substantive law, and the other allowing the substantive law to be developed by the institution in response to practical demands. The latter was adopted and set the preconditions for what became an evolving marketplace of remedies in which the kinds of disturbances that attended the ossification and replacement of the imperial codes would not only be unnecessary, but actually all but inconceivable. Holmes clearly had the highest regard for Maitland[4] and agreed with the analysis. It is precisely this view of the way Common Law courts have developed their law and the essential conservatism of the process that led Holmes to insist, in *The Path of the Law*, that the study of law is the study of history. At the same time Holmes cautions against the "pitfall of antiquarianism" and reminds his audience that "for our purposes our only interest in the past is for the light it throws upon the present" (1897: 475).

What is wrong with the idea of law as a deductive system, from a skeptical perspective, is that the idea of universal logical premises and universal rules of deduction is a fantasy. We cannot find such things. We can talk about statements being more or less general, but except for narrowly contrived examples, we cannot actually distinguish such degrees of generality and most clearly, as G. H. Mead pointed out, we cannot find a "particular" concept.

> You cannot say anything that is absolutely particular; anything you say that has any meaning at all is universal. You are saying something that calls out a specific response in anybody else provided that the symbol exists for him in his experience as it does for you (1934: 146-147).

Thought is *inherently* abstract. We do not designate specific, individual objects by using words whose meanings are somehow equally specific, but by concatenating universals: this man here with the pug nose and piggy eyes. The symbol "Socrates", defined by such abstractions, is every bit as universal as the symbol "man" or "mortal". It follows directly that the choice of premises for any logical deduction is always arbitrary. The failure of efforts like those of Russell and Whitehead to make good on the Aristotelian promise by producing a general integration of logic and mathematics and the modern development of multiple logics make it clear that what is true for the premises of deductive systems is also true for their deductive rules. And finally, there is the perhaps less obvious point that if we start with premises and rules that we hold to be detached from experience, there is no way later to attach them to experience except, again, arbitrarily by violating our initial stipulation. In short, the idea of a universal and all encompassing logical is a dualistic will-o'-the-wisp. A purely mechanical logic that could contain an entire legal argument and be sufficient ground for rendering a proper legal judgment would have to be entirely self-contained, in the sense that the rules of the logic would have to specify everything necessary to reach the conclusions. Many arguments for the possibility of such a logic have been proposed in the long line from Aristotle to, for example, Max Weber, but none have stood as a complete system and all such snippets have had to be defended and explained with surrounding arguments that in fact use quite different kinds of forms of argument and hence stand as de facto refutation of what they claim to prove.

The sophistic, skeptical, Kantian, and now pragmatic conception has consistently involved both a larger and more social view of that which provides the necessary framework for reasoning and a much more minimal and manipulable view of its internal structure. The framework is interacting human purposes. Argument and decision-making are social processes aimed at arriving at a basis for action. Their logic begins with that aim. The internal structure of arguments takes shape partly from this purpose, and partly from a kind of core rule according to which specific rules can be constructed more or less on the fly. It does not consist in an elaborate system of rules already set somewhere, firm and fixed for all time, only to be invoked (after they have been discovered). The core rule is very simply the law of contradiction, nothing more. The law of the excluded middle, as a law, is doubtful. The Aristotelian forms of syllogism are schoolbook exercises that no responsible person of "good sense" (Holmes 1923: 36) would let an important decision turn on. It is an easy matter to find examples where such logical forms cannot be relied on to yield a true conclusion from true premises; all you have to do is implicitly call attention to the limitations or ambiguities of the underlying ideas of things, classes, and universes. This is precisely the sort of thing the original sophists and skeptics delighted in showing, and precisely what Platonists and Aristoteleans apparently found so distressing. *Tant pis* for them. That is the way it is.

Moreover, skeptics and pragmatists do not, as a rule, see even the law of contradiction as a freestanding universal of thought, but as a consequence of trying to accomplish some end. After all, how do we know if something is a self-contradiction? Apart from simple cases when the contradiction is verbally patent, we know when it undermines or confuses the sense or aim of other things we have said which we judge from its effect.

The different conceptions of reasoning in the two traditions are closely associated with different conceptions of the social setting within which reasoning occurs. The Aristotelian vision of a single universal logic was meant to support the monolithic conception of society as a logical-cum-social hierarchy, controlled from the top, that goes back to Plato's *Republic.* If logic is monolithic and society has a single ruling principle or purpose, then how could society not be monolithic as well? This is the idea that runs down through the imperial codes to Canon Law and Aquinas and from Aquinas to legal positivism. Weber's conception of a bureaucrat-made and pro-capitalist "rational" legal system (Rheinstein and Shils 1954: 303-308, 351-353) and the Marxist-Stalinist ideas of the dictatorship of the proletariat, are among myriad others. Since Unger (1986) and Trubek describe CLS as a synthesis of Marx and Weber, what is true of Marx and Weber should be true of CLS, although exactly how it is true cannot be said until someone on behalf of CLS can say how this synthesis is to be affected. Just naming a pleasing bit from here and a pleasing bit from over there from two such sharply opposed schemes is not enough; it is also necessary that they fit together. Such an account will be particularly interesting given what Unger describes as the discovery that there is no "metaorder" (1983: 108)—since a metaorder is about the one thing Marx and Weber were most keen to agree on, along with their disdain for pluralist democracy. For law and economics, it seems reasonably clear that Coase's and Ackerman's arguments make little sense if one does not assume that an economy is naturally or by itself a fully integrated and monolithic system underlying all social relations and all exchanges, in which, *á la* Milton Friedman, all costs and benefits would be equally and equitably distributed if only the market would be allowed to work without interference or distortion. Posner seems to agree.

The pragmatic conception of society contrasts with these views on every important point. Society is not one thing but several, and none of these are what Weber or Marx or CLS or the law and economics arguments suggest. They are not self-subsistent things or thing-like. They are what we most commonly have in mind when we cleave to the word "institution" in contrast with group, organization, or structure, but it is necessary to be careful about what this is taken to mean. It is not anything people are "in" so much as something they construct or institute. In addition, when we have recourse to the notion of an institution to describe something of this sort it is usually because we actually cannot be very clear or definite about what that constructed thing is. A court is an organization; a bar is an organization; a law school is an organization, but all of them taken together are *part* of law as a social institution. Organizations are constructions that consist in systems of mutual expectations created through the purposive utilization of organizational ideas and other cultural resources, and in turn generally also reproduce those ideas and resources. Institutions are generic categories under which we group sets of organizations we recognize as related.

Exactly what these ideas and resources that organizations, and, hence institutions, are constructed from cannot be described in detail here without taking us much too far afield. Basically they are what anthropologists call the "material culture" of society along with the established definitions of reciprocal systems of social roles: the relations of kinship, of government, of religion, trades and occupations, and so on, each coherent within itself and separate from the others. In America, the cultural definition of the relation uncle-nephew is logically linked to the definitions of such other kinship concepts as the relation father-brother and father-son, but not to the cultural definitions of the relation priest-layperson or buyer-seller. Yet, in each institutional area social relations are constructed in precisely the same way: by using the cultural idea in conversation and constructing a mutual agreement in its terms. Applied *en mass*, what this process produces in a community is a series of logically separate sets of patterned social relations: kinship, governmental, religious, and/or whatever else the social ideas present might define. Montesquieu's *Spirit of the Laws* has the picture about right. Modern writers in anthropology and the anthropology of law who recognize the same basic features begin with Bronislaw Malinowski and include Raymond Firth, F. G. Bailey, Frederik Barth, Sally Falk Moore, Sally Engle Merry, and Nicholas Hopkins.

Organizations and institutions are not analytic stipulations. My definitions (or Weber's or Unger's) cannot create other peoples' realities. They are built from within by those who construe their relations as within them, reflecting their strategies and their purposes. Of course there are constitutive ideas, but they are the ideas used by the participants in the systems of action. Of course there are material means of production, but they are what the participants have made them and as the participants establish the patterns of their utilization. For Unger the lack of a metaorder seems to have come as a liberating but unpleasant surprise, the dethroning of what he regarded "up to now to be the sole coherent alternative to naive historiography" (1986: 108) —by which he apparently meant Marxism and structuralism (1986: 107). For pragmatists and skeptics, of whom he seems to be completely and unashamedly unaware, it has long been recognized as a basic fact with considerable explanatory power.

The Decision Context

Multiple institutions do much more than provide checks and balances that preserve or support liberty at the societal level. Much more fundamentally, they provide our main impetus to rational action at the individual level—not the *means* for rational action, but the *impetus* to it. Paradoxically, this comes about precisely because of what Weber and Austin, for example, regarded as serious social defects in need of repair; they impose multiple and conflicting demands while at the same time they provide us with ideas that can be used to form effective institutional insulation against those demands. The effect is to assure that the resolution of the conflict cannot be according to some social or cultural rule, but must reflect a situated calculus of needs. It defines the burden of rationality, assigns it to the decision-making individual, and assures that the individual cannot pass it on.

The empirical form of multiple and conflicting demands should be easy enough for any reader to recognize. We have family obligations, professional obligations, obligations as citizens, and so on. We recognize that they are different, that they can be in conflict. Tithing is a religious obligation; fulfilling it brings standing in the religious community and the promise of reward in heaven (for some at least). Paying for the medical needs of one's children is a kinship obligation, and fulfilling it assures their health and loyalty; serving in the military may be an obligation for a citizen, but carrying it out assures security of the state, standing in the political community, and avoidance of punishment. Getting an extended post-doctoral grant prepares one to advance in science. Earning money is the way to get ahead economically, and so on.

Institutional insulation means that if we are faced with what we see as a destructive imposition in one system, we can have recourse to another. And there is no *logical* way, in terms of the accepted cultural definitions, that we can be pursued across the borders. Yes, you are my cousin, but lending money is a business matter. Yes, the church needs a new roof, but my child needs surgery. Yes, I should earn money, but I need the experience of a post-doctoral grant, and so on.

If we lived in monolithic systems of roles, relations, and values, there would not only be no basis for using institutional insulation, it would be very difficult to conceive of a reason to. If I had only one set of commitments and all my resources were in the nature of the case wholly dedicated to those commitments, how could I think to hold something back when a demand was made on those resources? If I had only one set of relations, what could count as a reasonable or unreasonable demand in the name of those relations, so long as it was not self-destructive? This is why arguments for totalitarianism invariably include arguments for unitary societies.

The way these features of multiple institutional systems produce the impetus to rationality hinges on two additional points. First, all of the different roles and relations impinge on the same physical person. Second, while the conceptual definitions of the role relations and obligations cannot be transferred from one system to another, physical resources very often can be. I may take a dozen roles in the course of a day, but I am one body. Time I save in one system can be spent in others; money I earn in one can be spent in others; physical resources I obtain in one system can very often (within limits) be deployed in others. I would have to be very dense indeed not to recognize this, and it follows from this recognition that the general strategy I should follow is to combine my various activities in such a way as to provide the most useful overall mix of returns. In short, while each of the different systems defines ways to employ means to attain ends, it is the joint pressure from incommensurable relations framed in multiple and conflicting systems combined with the fungibility of physical resources that forces us to economize (in the general sense) in doing so. But note the problem that this involves: the requirement in each system that its rules be followed necessarily becomes in aggregate a requirement that all rules must be violated. Since they cannot be wholly violated, this forces the person (or a group acting as a person) at the nexus of a specific set of systems into an internal dialogue that runs like this:

> Q: To what extent should I follow this rule and to what extent that?
> A: To whatever extent is necessary.
> Q: How will I know what this is?
> A: You can only do what is best for you and those around you.
> Q: What is that?

A: It depends on the consequences.

In sum, each individual system defines interests and the means of attaining them within the framework of that system, and such definitions provide standards for rational action in the sense of ways to relate means to ends. But if a person has only one standard of rational action, there is no way to know if that standard is itself being applied rationally—that is, in the most efficient and economic way possible. This is done only by the demands made by multiple systems, as they require each individual to subordinate these several standards to one standard of *personally situated* interest, to consider how all the demands can be met jointly. At the same time, the fungibility of physical resources between institutions requires that this individual judgment be based on some general standard of efficiency. However, such general individual standards do not exist in any established way. The only standards actually established are those of several systems. Hence it is up to each individual to construct them, and virtually the only way they can do this is to combine the standards from the several systems adventitiously as best they can to fit their own times, places and circumstances. Thus, paradoxically, the most general standard of efficiency each of us has to adhere to is also the most idiosyncratic. It is something each of us must develop to pursue our perceived concatenation of obligations, demands and opportunities, and his or her individual interests, which is precisely what all mature people recognize as the need to subordinate conventional or stereotypic rationality to practical, situated, and contextual rationality.

Legal Decisions

The same conception underlies the pragmatic analysis of legal decision making where it serves as both a description of what a judge does and a prescription for what a judge should do. The link between the "is" and the "ought" is that while any given judge might not act this way at any given time, if judges as a body did not do so in the long run, and on the whole, the judicial system itself would not have evolved as it has or serve the enormous and seemingly ever-expanding range of needs that it does.

The pragmatic view of legal decision making has six discernable elements. The first two are the same as the general view: multiple frames of reference and individual purpose. The difference is that the legal conception has to recognize multiple frames of reference at two levels simultaneously, and because of this the entire picture is necessarily more complex. First, it recognizes that cases that come to court—particularly what Tamanaha calls the "hard cases"—usually reflect situations in which more than one set of standards have been applied; what is in dispute is not any one standard, but the way they have been balanced. Second, it recognizes that the social structure of the judge's decision is the same as anyone else's decision. The judge, too, is faced with multiple and conflicting *legal* standards, and is not permitted to decide on the basis of only one, but must therefore arrive at a balance. That being so, the judge, too, is impelled to analyze the situation by framing it in a personally situated purpose—a view that cannot just ask what "the law" is, but must also ask what the purpose of this decision must be. This seems to be where most of the confusion regarding pragmatism has arisen.

The common perception at the present time seems to be that in the pragmatic view the purpose of a judge in deciding a case may or must be *merely* personal or subjective. This is the view that "the core of Realism is, indeed, a certain sort of descriptive claim about how judges decide cases, according to which judges rationalize, after the fact, decisions reached on other grounds" (Leiter 1997: 268). Posner seems to construe his own position as pragmatic on the same grounds: "pragmatist's real interest is not in truth at all but in belief justified by social need" (1990: 464), which he implies can be identified extra-judicially. This is clearly not what Holmes said, and I will argue that it is also not what he meant. It is substantially the same position that Pound rejected in his attack on the "new" realists in 1931, saying that they overemphasized the subjective aspects of judgment and failed to realize that the judge's ideas of what "ought" to be done in a case are not just personal, but "institutional" (1931: 699-700). I think Pound understood and agreed with Holmes.

Holmes and Pound were quite clear that this personal purpose was a personal *judicial* purpose, the choice the judge was required to make of the particular way to redress an injury or a wrong appropriate to the particular kinds of interests and particular kinds of evidence that can be expected in particular kinds of cases, with "kind" being what experience has provided as the effective groupings: criminality, tort, or contract, the relation of landlord to tenant; relations among servants in a household; relations among workers in a shop, hauling cargo on a road; ferrying a vehicle hauling cargo across a river, or whatever. The basic point was that there was no principle for law as a whole from which subordinate principles might be deduced, but rather there were decisions recorded in cases, and usually opposed principles offered to explain them. *The Common Law* begins with a survey of historically important examples. Is the purpose of a judgment vengeance or redress? Is compensation a substitute for vengeance or something different? Is an employer liable for damage done by an employee in his service because the employer must have been negligent in hiring such a person, or because the employer is able to pay? Can a ship be held forfeit for injuries it has caused because it is a kind animate being, or because it is available? Is the sense or meaning of a right in property that one can have unlimited use of the thing, control the use of the thing, or simply exclude others from control or use of the thing? Is a person responsible for all harm that might result from his action, or only for foreseeable harm? While each of these questions may seem to require a general answer and while various legal "theories" have often seemed to provide such general answers, in fact, quite different principles reign in different bodies of law as different balances are struck in dealing with different sets of problems. Thus, in criminal cases the principle is revenge, but for the law of torts, the most important concern is "to fix the dividing lines between those cases in which a man is liable for harm which he has done, and those in which he is not" (1923: 79). Again, in tort cases the question of foreseeable consequences is crucial, but intent is not. However, for the law of possession, an entirely different set of concerns is dominant, revolving around the idea of exclusion. This idea of intent becomes central:

> If what the law does is to exclude others from interfering with the object, it would seem that the intent which the law should require is an intent to exclude others. I believe that such an intent is all that the Common Law deems needful, and that on principle no more should be required (1923: 220).

Holmes' most universally recognized explicit thesis was that general principles change over time in a kind of ongoing dialogue with cases in which a rule originally designed for one set of circumstances comes to be applied to new situations, old cases get reinterpreted in the light of new cases, and what eventuates becomes formalized as an entirely different rule. But the deeper argument, where his most basic conception of judicial decision making lies, concerns the nature of "policy" as what guides this process.

What Holmes meant by policy was "considerations of what is expedient for the community concerned" (cf. 1923: 35). The first question is whether the idea that such considerations influence decisions is *ad hoc* or evidentiary. The answer is that it is evidentiary but complex. If I can put it more flatly than Holmes did, it consists in two main points. The first is his massive documentation of the existence of conflicting theories to explain any given decision, and the second is his repeated demonstration that because the relationships between cases and theories are circular, the choice of theories can never depend wholly on the cases, nor can the choice of cases depend on theories. What this means is that the system is internally indeterminate. Neither theories nor decisions *nor theories and decisions together* can determine the course of legal evolution. There is a visible trend, more or less, but no Hegelian inner logic, or any other sort of inner logic that compels it. So if the guiding pressures are not internal, they must be external. I suppose this might be what Leiter and Posner see as arguing for the inevitability of the judges' private prejudices or biases, but it does not follow. Why should individual prejudice lead to anything but randomness? What Holmes is trying to show is a consistent movement in certain long-recognized directions. The cause of trends of this sort can only lie in something else equally directional, and this, in fact, in terms of his argument, can only lie in the external "social exigencies" that the judges, as people of "common sense", are responding to. That is, the ultimate pragmatic explanation is not only that the judges are applying their views of what will work to achieve a solution within the framework of the law, but that they are doing so rightly: that the solutions work in fact, that it is on that account that they eventually become accepted, and that they change the law itself.

By the same token, *The Common Law* is also aimed at showing not only that individual legal principles and bodies of cases evolve, but that the entire body of such contrasting principles in the several branches taken together make up a many-sided and subtle approach to problems that closely reflects what actually can be evidentiary which is at the same time more comprehensive, elegant, and appropriate than anything that has been proposed in its stead on the basis of deductive schemas. Again the question Holmes obviously expects us to ask and answer for ourselves is how this can happen, and again the answer cannot possibly lie in individual prejudice acting in myriad cases on diverse matters in diverse places and even in diverse legal systems (since he argues for parallel changes in

Roman, Civil, and Common Law). It can only be practical, real, albeit intuitive, recognition of what real circumstances will really support.

Of course there is Holmes' often-quoted statement, "For the rational study of the law, the black-letter man may be the man of the present, but the man of the future is the man of statistics and the master of economics. It is revolting to have no better reason for a rule of law that so it was laid down in the time of Henry IV" (1897: 470). Posner's and Leiter's positions imply that we cannot give this a reading consistent with the notion that the criteria for a legal decision lie within the law rather than outside it. I cannot agree. What could possibly be the sense of Holmes' admonition to study "this body of dogma or systematized prediction which we call the law" in order to "prophesy" what judges would decide (1897: 459) if he did not mean that it did actually control, and should continue to control what judges would decide? The "black letter man" is obviously the same person whom Holmes characterizes as making policy considerations intuitively and unconsciously. What the statistics and economics would do is not change the fact of making such considerations within the framework of legal reasoning (Holmes is not saying the past reasoning was not legal), but would only change their character. It would bring the reasoning out into the light of day and make it evidentiary—which is not only Holmes' expressed intent, but also clearly what he sees as one of the major parameters of legal progress generally, along with expanding breadth, flexibility, and predictability. This clearly rules out Leiter's "unfettered" and "after the fact" reading on its face. The bearing on Posner may be less obvious.

The key point for Posner's reading is that he seems to want to use "pragmatism" to include the imposition of an extralegal ideology whereas Holmes clearly means that looking to consequences must be factual and not ideological. Facts fit within the legal framework as evidence, ideology does not. It would be quite inconsistent with Holmes' basic arguments to suggest that he meant to urge that a judge should knowingly replace what he or she understood to be the recognized sense of a legal principle with something distinct and different in order to alter some social condition. How would such reasoning be different from the application of the kind of *a priori* theories he always rejected? What he meant—as exemplified by what he cited as landmark cases—was something much more microscopic: having to make new adjustments when looking to consequences of *these* (plural) particular legal purposes represented in these past cases as they work together in *this* particular present case to avoid a consequence that would violate what he describes simply as "common sense", meaning generally a consequence that would in the long or short run be perverse or destructive of either good social order or the effectiveness of the law itself. In short, the pragmatic view of legal judgment is that legal judgment is pragmatic.

Elaborating the basic analysis in terms of multiple systems and individual (judicial) purpose, the third element in the pragmatic conception of judicial decision-making is recognition that decision making is further constrained by the requirement that one has to assess the effects of one's decision through applying a logic of reciprocity, again at two levels. At the level of the immediate decision, one applies the ancient test of fairness in asking if, on the evidence, the decision might have gone the same way if the two people appearing were in the reverse roles, and if indeed the judge were in one position or the other. In this sense, reciprocity is an aspect of equality and equality is a hallmark of legal neutrality and fairness. Second, beyond the immediate decision, the way one looks to the social consequences is not to ask, in effect, "what will happen if everyone conforms to this principle", but rather "What will be the consequences of the uses people are likely to make of this principle in dealing with one another?". And in traditional Roman analyses as well as in pragmatic analyses such as we see, not so much in Holmes, but in the Brandeis, Cardozo, and Pound, this is specifically taken as meaning that one should look at how it will affect the relative advantages and disadvantages of the different interests that the case might represent. Does it decrease the likelihood that an injured worker will find compensation (and if so what would be the effect on public welfare agencies)? Does it increase or decrease the likelihood that employers will face costs that might stunt the growth of industry?

A fourth element is the idea already noted in passing of the court system as providing a legal marketplace that is made concrete in Maitland's analysis of the forms of action and Holmes' analyses of the evolution of early forms of liability into modern forms. This is directly connected to Holmes' evolutionism described by Weaver in this volume. It does not, however, begin with Darwin, but goes back to the legal evolutionism of Savigny's historical jurisprudence and, indeed, to the original Roman jurisconsults. In a system that permits a choice of ways to construe an action such that it provides a choice of courts and legal procedures, those that are chosen will be perpetuated and developed while those that are not will wither and drop out.

A fifth element, also with its roots in the historical jurisprudence, is captured by Savigny's dictum that "law grows out of the life of the people", Ehrlich's conception of the relation between the courts and the living law, Holmes' conception of policy, and Pound's view of courts as concerned with the reconciliation of interests. Formally constituted legal institutions and the legal profession exist in the context of a vast array of private agreements that it is their job to support, not supplant or even simply permit.

Finally, the sixth element is that this model is not merely *about* law, it is *in* the law. It is the model of law repeatedly adverted to in the main stream of the Western legal tradition, by which I mean what I think Holmes would: the line of democratic legal theories that extends from the sophists of Pericles' Athens and the jurisconsults of the Roman republic through the republican stream of Roman law in renaissance humanism to what John Merryman describes as the civil law tradition (1969), and the English and American Common Law. The model, in this sense, is not describable as *either* normative *or* descriptive, but both. It is in fact the norm of the system, and it is the norm because in the long run and on the whole it is the way judges need to decide order to assure that the system remains flexible and fitted to the needs of those who appeal to it.

Can judges act otherwise? Can they act as Leiter says, deciding on the basis of their preconceptions and rationalizing it after the fact? Of course they can in some private way. But if they do so on the record and it is appealed, an appellate court would be under great pressure to overturn, and if it became blatant that a judge did this regularly, there would be further action to consider. It is improper. Leiter knows it is improper, but is saying that judges do it anyway. Doubtless some do, but that is not what the pragmatists, beginning with Holmes, have tried to argue. The pragmatic argument is to explain where this sense of wrongness derives from and to explicate its consequences.

Conclusion

Does this have as much normative content as the CLS position or Posner's or Ackerman's? If you want to argue that "normative" requires a conspicuously hortatory language, we might have to debate it. But with regard to content, there is no comparison. Pragmatism is where the action really is.

Notes

1 This was first read in a panel entitled Pragmatism in Theory and Policy at the Annual Meetings of the Law and Society Association, Miami Beach, May 1999. The present argument has benefitted substantially from comments by Brian Tamanaha at that panel, and Alfonso Morales and Bill Weaver since.

2 The Roman emperors did not claim that the law sprang from sovereignty, but rather that sovereignty sprang from law.

3 For my understanding of the history of the Common Law, I follow Milsom (1981).

4 See, for example, the Holmes-Pollock letters for March 4, 1888 and January 17, 1891 (Howe 1941:31).

References

Ackerman, Bruce A. (1983), *Reconstructing American Law*. Cambridge: Harvard University Press.

Austin, John. (1861), *The Province of Jurisprudence Determined*. 2nd. ed. 1970 Rpt. New York: Burt Franklin.

Güterbock, Carl (1866), *Bracton: His Relation to the Roman Law*. Translated by Brinton Coxe. Philadelphia: Lippincott and Co.

Holmes, Oliver Wendell Jr. (1897), "The Path of the Law", *Harvard Law Review*, Vol. 8, pp. 458-479.

Holmes, Oliver Wendell Jr. (1923), *The Common Law*. Boston: Little Brown and Co. First pub. 1881.

Howe, Mark DeWolfe, ed. (1941), *Holmes-Pollock Letters*. Two Volumes. Cambridge: Harvard University Press.

Leiter, Brian. (1997), "Rethinking Legal Realism: Toward a Naturalized Jurisprudence". *Texas Law Review*, vol. 2, pp. 267-315.

Maitland, F. W. (1936), *The Forms of Action at Common Law, a Course of Lectures*. First published posthumously in 1909. First published separately in 1936. Reset and reprinted, 1969. Reprint of 1981. Cambridge: Cambridge University Press.

Mead, George Herbert. (1934), *Mind, Self and Society*. Chicago: University of Chicago Press.

Merryman, John Henry. (1969), *The Civil Law Tradition*. Stanford: The Stanford University Press.

Milsom, S. F. C. (1981), *Historical Foundations of the Common Law, second edition*. (First edition, 1969). London: Butterworth's.

Posner, Richard A. (1990), *The Problems of Jurisprudence*. Cambridge: Harvard University Press.

Pound, Roscoe. (1931), "The Call for a Realist Jurisprudence". *Harvard Law Review*, vol. 4, pp. 4697-711.

Rheinstein, Max (translator and editor), and Edward Shils (translator) (1954), "Max Weber on Law" *in Economy and Society*. Cambridge: Harvard University Press.

Unger, Roberto Mangabeira. (1986), *The Critical Legal Studies Movement*. First published 1983. Cambridge: Harvard University Press.

Tamanaha, Brian Z. (1997), *Realistic Socio-Legal Theory*. Oxford: Clarendon Press.

PART II

UPDATING PRAGMATIST INFORMED METHODS OF INQUIRY

5 Ethnography and Pragmatism

Murray J. Leaf[1]

There are, broadly, three major approaches to legal and socio-legal argument: data-independent, data-relevant, and data-driven. Examples of the first are ratiocinative system-building such as we see in legal positivism and Habermas' postmodernism. Examples of the second are determinist and reductionist theories such as we see in positivism, Marxism, and now law and economics. The third is mainly represented by empirical studies of law in action or legal institutions such as we see in the continental tradition of legal sociology represented by Eugen Ehrlich, American pragmatic jurisprudence as it crystallized with O. W. Holmes, and a wide variety of modern studies in the pragmatic tradition from Bronislaw Malinowski's Crime and Punishment in Savage Society and C. K. Meek's study of Nigerian law (1937) through Kalven and Zeisel's studies of the American use of juries (1966) and Sally Engle Merry's study of popular American legal consciousness (Merry, 1990). Ratiocinative systems and the various types of reductionism all have their philosophical roots in the long debate between idealism and materialism that began with Plato and Aristotle and continues into postmodernism. Empiricism has its roots in Greek and Roman sophism and skepticism, and continues through Kant and American pragmatism. The two traditions differ fundamentally; one cannot be understood in terms of the other.

Empiricism and ethnography are often spoken of as though they were just some sort of naïve, theory-less, bumbling. Pragmatism is often described as though it were nothing more than unprincipled opportunism. Idealistic and materialistic arguments, including the arguments of Marxists, positivists, and legal positivists, on the other hand, are equally often commonly described, or justified, as grounded in accepted philosophical principles. It should not be difficult to guess which side such characterizations originate from, and they are not to be taken at face value.

The idealist and materialist philosophical rationales for deductive and reductionist methods have been repeatedly shown to be unsound by both their own stated standards and by commonly accepted general standards, such as internal consistency, while those of empiricism are more consistent logically and far more consistent with experience. Indeed, this consistency with experience is often exactly what makes the basic assumptions of empiricism especially hard to show to those who do not already understand them. Precisely because the methodological and theoretical assumptions of empiricism lead to facts, they tend to be replaced by those facts when the final account is written. When an astronomer detects a wobble in a star that suggests the presence of a planet, he or she does not describe in detail the construction of all the instruments used and the fundamental principles that lie behind them, but concentrates on the wobble. Similarly, when a field ethnologist succeeds in developing a series of observational techniques that lead him or her to find a series of powerfully interconnected facts, it is the facts and not the techniques that will appear most prominently in the final report.

Once you have facts, calling a great deal of attention to how they were generated rarely makes the argument seem stronger and often seems to cloud it. Nor, beyond a certain minimum, does elaborate methodological discussion make an argument more attractive to publishers or manuscript referees. The exigencies of publishing, if nothing else, virtually force you to "let the facts speak for themselves" – which is to write by pushing the results to the foreground and the means of obtaining them to the background. It is only if you do not have assumptions generative of facts that you have to claim the authority of "pure" theory or philosophical first principles alone.

Of course not all good field researchers can articulate their assumptions in philosophical terms, just as all not all good empirical philosophical writers are good fieldworkers. Kant was not Malinowski. Kant produced an enormously consistent system of explanations of the assumptions of empirical fieldwork but went virtually nowhere, relying instead on wide reading and relentlessly close examination of his own thought and behavior. Malinowski spent the entire duration of World War I in the Trobriand Islands and produced a series of powerfully consistent ethnographies based on his experience there, but in the end was unable to explain how they were related to one another in general terms. Yet whatever their powers of philosophical explanation, no one can produce a consistent ethnography without a consistent and fairly sophisticated notion at a working level of what there is to look for and how to find it.

"What to look for" and "how to find it" are shorthand questions whose answers represent the relationship between data, method and theory. These answers vary enormously between scholars who adhere to the assumptions of positivism, Marxism, and postmodernism, on the one hand, and skepticism and pragmatism on the other. The most striking difference is that for the former group the assumptions are primarily theoretical and stated in such a way as to be immune to empirical correction. They may be "about" fieldwork in some general sense, but they are not dependent on it. In the pragmatic view, by contrast, the assumptions are most directly about precisely what that field experience will involve, and only secondly about what sorts of conclusions will emerge from it.

The touchstone of empiricism has always been experimental demonstration, which goes back at least to the ancient Greeks. Greek and Roman skepticism was an effort to build systems of analysis only on knowledge of this sort, avoiding claims that skeptics considered "dogmatic", which meant claims about matters beyond experience and prior to demonstration. The still stronger idea of a rigorous, complete and coherent experimental *system* of knowledge, rather than just demonstrations here and there, begins in its present form only with Galileo (see Settle, 1967), and it is this latter development that is articulated in Kantian analysis and in pragmatism. Kant and the pragmatists, each in their own way and in the language of their own times, attempted to build general approaches to the long-standing questions of philosophy by incorporating the results of experimental science and using the fundamentally experimental method that pragmatists have described as "testing by consequences".

Skeptics, Kantians, and pragmatists have never drawn a sharp line between the physical sciences and what we would now take as the social sciences—including law, ethics, and psychology, sociology and anthropology. In the physical sciences since Galileo, one does not go from theory to experiment and then start over as though anew, but from experiment to experiment to experiment in an unending and ever-expanding series of variations. The aim is much less to create theory in the positivist sense of a priori or quasi-definitional "generalized knowledge" or "law-like-statements" than to eliminate it. What one wants in the end are absolutely clean and tight connections between what is shown in one experiment and what is shown in others. Experimental knowledge is inherently situated knowledge. It is always knowledge in context. An experimental sequence takes form by varying the conditions of observation in a situation in such a way as to systematically rule in or rule out possible alternative understandings until one arrives at the point where the consequences of further variations will be precisely predictable. It does not matter whether one is trying to map and explain the motion of moons around a planet or the process of filing and pursuing a case in court.

Galileo's conception of the development of physical knowledge readily admitted a parallelism with legal knowledge and could easily have been based on it – that is, he seems to view the accumulation of physical knowledge through the progression of physical trials on the model of the way judges view the accumulation of legal knowledge through the accumulation of legal trials and the settling of appeals such that gaps in the law are identified and eliminated. *The Dialogue Concerning the Two Chief World-Systems* was written as much in a legal style (concerned with a weighing of evidence on both sides of an issue) as a physical style (concerned with exposing a principle by a single unambiguous experiment), and Galileo's correspondence about it was as much about law as physics and with as much a view toward his legal vulnerability as to his status as a natural philosopher.

We see the same parallelism and overlap of perspective in Bacon and Montaigne, Kant, and the pragmatists. Kant's *Critique of Pure Reason* provided and analyses of what "objectivity" is in our perceptions of physical objects. His *Critique of Practical Reason* did the same for our perception of the behavior of other human beings. The pragmatists applied, or perhaps better validated, these analyses in systematizing and articulating the subject matters of the key disciplines of 19th century empirical physical and social science, including law. It was not an accident that the founders of pragmatism included both lawyers and working chemists and biologists, or that Dewey wrote as much about physical science as about law, psychology and education. It was essential in order to demonstrate their most basic point – that they all involve knowledge of the same fundamental kind.

Central Pragmatic Assumptions

At the present time, and particularly with reference to law and socio-legal studies, the clearest philosophical expression of experimentalism is that central line of American pragmatism that begins with O. W. Holmes and Chauncey Wright and carries through Cardozo, Pound, Dewey, G. H. Mead, and most of the writings of Charles Morris. This is the pragmatism that roots itself equally in the broad tradition of empirical science, the Kantian critiques that articulated a way to carry this tradition into epistemology, Adam Smith's economics of self-interest, the *Historical Jurisprudence of Von Savigny*, and the psychological analyses of Humbolt, Fechner, and Wundt at the beginning of the last century that converted that Kantian vision into a set of working practices. It is the pragmatism we can see in William James if we know what to look for, although he is far from consistent. It is the pragmatism of Peirce's *How We Make Our Ideas Clear*. Although it is not his later pragmaticism which he quite accurately described as objective idealism. However, it is not what we see in W. V. O. Quine or Richard Rorty, both of whom utilize quite un-pragmatic conceptions of science that have nothing to do with interrelated experiments and of language and thought that have nothing do with empirical (and pragmatic) linguistics and psychology, but rather come directly from philosophical positivism.

The main points of connection between the experimental impulse of pragmatism and ethnographic fieldwork reflect pragmatic understanding and use of three main ideas, without which effective field work cannot be conducted: 1) an understanding of rationality as an aspect or quality of purposive behavior in a Kantian sense 2) an understanding of ideas as imaginative and symbolic tokens to differentiate possible choices, 3) an analysis of the conceptual structure of symbolic interaction in which ideas are used and through which purposes are pursued.

Purposive rationality is what Charles Morris, in his 1970 review of pragmatism was invoking when he said, "it is the thinking man, man acting intelligently, that is the center of the pragmatists' attention": (1970: 11). For Morris, this was pragmatism's core concern. It is also the central link between pragmatism as a philosophy of empiricism and pragmatism as a philosophy of democracy. The other half of that link is that for the pragmatists, such a rational person was the normal person, not just a narrow thee and me. The pragmatic opposition to privilege and appeals to authority follows. In politics as well as in science, the best decision will be the one that reflects the widest engagement of individuals acting freely on the basis of their own best judgment.

Can we actually observe purposes and people acting so as to attain them? In practice we do it all the time. There is not much that comes to us more naturally, and we do not need skeptical or pragmatic philosophy to prove this is so. But we do need skepticism and pragmatism to serve as an antidote to other kinds of philosophy that say we cannot do so, and it is also useful to call our attention to features of what we do to those whose significance we might otherwise miss.

The most prominent among the modern philosophical schools that have denied the observability of purpose and rationality is positivism. For Ernst Mach (1959), one of the two founders of logical positivism, even that most quintessentially rational of human beings, the experimental scientist performing an experiment, is engaging in little more than an elaborately staged self-deception. He interprets his experimental results through a maze of "metaphysical" assumptions about such things as objects and forces, when in fact, in Mach's view, all he really has is correlations between sensations. For Donald Black (1972), science must be "value free" and value free means not only that you do not impose your own values. It also means that you do not, or cannot, try to observe the values of others – or their ideas or purpose. Philip Nonet (1976) has described the contradictions and practical impossibilities of Black's position. There is no point repeating his arguments, although Black continues to ignore them. The question here concerns what pragmatists see differently and what that implies for fieldwork practice.

What Mach noticed was that whenever we focus on a situation or event as problematic, there are some aspects that we take as non-problematic. To him, such assumptions were "metaphysical" and this was tantamount to saying that we were not absolutely or completely rational. For pragmatists, it is the opposite. On their analysis, it is not possible to make everything problematic at once. The idea is a practical self-contradiction. Observation is situated. To make everything problematic would be to make the observation un-situated, and this simply cannot be. You cannot have an observation that is not somewhere and somewhen, and hence limited by that somewhere and somewhen. Accordingly, we must nest what is problematic, for the moment, in what Morris describes as the "pragmatic non-problematic" (1970: 4). This is what is taken as non-problematic for the issue in hand, but always subject to its own test later. This is an observable feature of the way rational problem solving works, and precisely why Galileo had to see experimental knowledge as a continuing process. It is foolish to say that because this is in fact the character of rational judgments, such judgments are unreal and we must confine ourselves to deductions from arbitrary posits instead. You may as well say that since swimming takes effort, the logical thing to do is sink. Given that we do in fact make such judgments and they do in fact produce powerful and predictable results, our problem is to observe ourselves and each other making them and set down what we find. This is what empirical philosophy helps us do.

Philosophical analyses in the empirical tradition, from ancient skepticism to modern pragmatism, has never been or claimed to be any sort of doctrine or recipe to follow in order to do with empiricism but rather an attempt to describe in the most basic way possible what empirical observation can be empirically observed to involve. Ultimately, empirical knowledge is imbedded knowledge. It is found in the world that it is intended to reflect. Philosophy cannot replace that world and cannot even fully describe it, just as a photograph cannot fully describe a three dimensional object. But it can point us toward it and provide guidance in how we can put ourselves in the way of coming to grips with it.

Rationality is an imbedded phenomenon. It does not make any difference whether we are speaking of the rationality of those we are trying to understand, or of ourselves. It follows that the only way to understand "their" rationality is to put ourselves in "their" place, to integrate and interrelate the two contexts. To do this, it is obviously helpful to understand what the imbedding process itself is, and of course in applying this knowledge we are also testing it.

Philosophical Assumptions and the Interpretation of Method

The main method anthropologists employ to observe the way people relate their activities to their purposes is what is usually called "participant observation." More exactly, it is the specific tradition of participant observation initiated by Bronislaw Malinowski under the often misrepresented heading of "functionalism." Malinowski deliberately chose the term to suggest a link to pragmatic philosophy and functional psychology.

The core idea of Malinowski's functionalism was connections through purpose. You start with any object or usage that you can observe and see what it is intended to accomplish. Then you trace all those things that this purpose leads it to be associated with. You see a kind of shell bracelet. You observe it is used to mark trading partners in a specific, named, pattern of trade. So you trace out that pattern of trade and find all the other things also involved. The result is a functional complex, a set of interrelated ideas, organizations, and usages. One such complex provided the subject matter of each of Malinowski's major monographs: gardening in *The Coral Gardens and their Magic*, trade in *Argonauts of the Western Pacific*, law in *Crime and Custom in Savage Society*, and so on. The idea apparently goes back to Karl Bucher, a prominent economic historian whom Malinowski went to study under along with Wundt, immediately after he decided to shift his career interests from physics to anthropology. Bucher's famous *Rhytmus und Arbiet* (Rhythm and Work) had argued that the original function of music, particularly rhythm, was to organize collective effort in agricultural work (Gross, 1986: 559).

Malinowski's functionalism has different philosophical foundations and is conceptually entirely distinct from A. R. Radcliffe-Brown's "structural functionalism", and the subsequent position of Talcott Parsons and many others under the same head, which were explicitly positivistic and reductionist. Nor is functionalist ethnography the same as "interpretation" in Clifford Geertz's sense, which is also fundamentally reductionist although in slightly different way, which Paul Friedrich rightly characterizes as "cryptopositivism" (1992).

The most basic difference between Malinowski's method and the methods derived from positivism concerns the relation between what is considered analysis and what is considered data. In pragmatic terms, there is no difference: field elicitation not separable from field analysis just as "collecting data" in a physical laboratory is not separable from laboratory analysis. Fieldwork is a series of predictions; the description one winds up with is a system of results from such predictions. In the process, one puts one's own perceptions and analysis on an even footing with those one is trying to understand, literally making the analysis subject to their reactions to it. In ordinary life, if you wanted to be sure that you understood somebody you would ask them, in various ways. In fieldwork, it is the same (with all the nuances this should suggest).

In the positivistic frame of reference, by contrast, data and data collection is one thing, analysis quite another, something done after the fact and quite out of the reach of those one claims to be explaining. For Malinowski, one traces out connections in the field. For Geertz, as an example, one instead collects stories in the field but one then interprets them in an entirely different context to an entirely different audience. In the introduction to *The Interpretation of Culture*, Geertz sites a story about a conflict between a merchant, two groups of Berbers, and the French authorities in North Africa and then argued that each of these different groups represented a different culture and the seemingly bizarre or unaccountable aspects of the story he related represented a "confusion of tongues" which is the anthropologist's task to decipher (1973: 9, 27). At other times Geertz has represented law (1983), ideology (1964), and religion (1966) as cultural systems in the same way, but in all of this the idea that a culture might be other than total and people might be "in" more than one at one time has never been part of his consideration.

Like Radcliffe-Brown's and Talcott Parson's structural-functionalism, Geertz's argument is not experimental but metaphoric. He does not have a method for finding what culture is, but an analogy to suggest what it is like. For Radcliffe-Brown it was an organism and for Parsons a machine. For Geertz it is a text. But while culture may in some respects be *like* a text, it is not a text in fact. There are at least three main differences.

First, texts are written or at least writable, and they are fixed. They are artifacts, not actions. They do not do things. They simply exist and their author's intent and the original situations in which they were created are only to be guessed at, and by the conventions of literary analysis may not be relevant to their interpretation in any case. Most of what we encounter in actual field work is very different. Even setting aside all those things that make up what anthropologists call "material culture" in favor of the more conceptual kinds of artifacts Geertz is more clearly concerned with, we may have a text "on the page" but we do not have conversations, verbal reports delivered live in real time, formal or informal agreements, cooperative action, or even public performances "on the page". To pretend that we do is to miss much of the ambiguity and multi-vocality that real-world cultural interaction is about. Second, ambiguity is not merely incidental to real-time and real-world cultural expression but essential. It is what drives conversation and interaction ahead. The reason is that the purpose of this real-time and real-world cultural expression, unlike the words we see on a page, is almost always to create or sustain mutual relations and behavioral expectations, and it is precisely in resolving ambiguity that this is done. The purpose of real-world, imbedded, cultural interpretation is, in fact, to be clear about the purposes of those doing the interpreting—which is precisely why recognizing such individual purposes is an essential part of pragmatic field method and also why Geertz, in refusing to recognize it, puts himself in the position of being unable to arrive at any interpretation but his own, inevitably not only alien and apart but unprovable.

Third, there are important assumptions of literary analysis that Geertz uses the analogy to legitimize that make no sense in field ethnography. Literary analysis often deals with texts whose authors are not available for questioning and whose circumstances of production are not available for observation. Accordingly, it may be appropriate to have a convention that one does not as a rule insist on asking the author what the text means, and one does not consult the purpose of the author to find the intent of the work if indeed one wants to admit the relevance of intent at all. The meaning can be held to lie in the words themselves, and given that assumption, it follows that how it is abstracted depends largely, perhaps even entirely, on the frame of reference the analyst applies. Good enough for literature, perhaps, but the effect of applying it to culture is to give all the interpretive control to the analyst and none to the members, to treat what they do as a fixed artifact and not an ongoing production, and to assume that what people take each other to mean is unrelated to what they take each other's purposes to be. This is enormously distorting. The experimental corrective is discussed in the next section.

As pragmatists have consistently recognized, cultural behavior, as it unfolds, is constantly subject to retrospective reinterpretation and reorganization. It is multiply and collectively authored, not singly authored. And it is essentially contextualized in the purposes and aims of these authors. In normal life one simply cannot understand what someone is doing without forming some notion of why they are doing it, what their purpose is.[2]

In a pragmatic and experimentally founded conception of fieldwork, the analyst does not stand off and witness the process as though through a one-way mirror, guess what is going on in the participants' minds, and convey those guesses to the folks back home without giving those described an opportunity to comment. Precisely as a physical scientist engages in the production of physical phenomena and then describes that process to others, the experimental ethnographer engages in, records, and then describes the production of cultural phenomena. Interpretation in Geertz sense is a rationale for analysts who would impose their views on those they describe. Field elicitation in an experimental sense is a method for restraining one's ability to impose one's own ideas and, thereby, for making what one concludes subject to the impositions of those one is studying—because, fundamentally, such imposition is precisely what is of interest and therefore what one wants to experimentally recreate.

Philosophical Assumptions and the Interpretation of Results

When describing the idea of experimental fieldwork to non-ethnologists, I have sometimes been told something like "you cannot put people in a test tube", in a tone that implies much more moral disapproval than practical advice. It is as if I proposed to treat people like laboratory mice. Perhaps this might be so if I saw human behavior on the positivist model of blind actions in response to external stimuli. As a pragmatist, however, I am sure that behavior reflects choice and purpose, and on that basis the aim of experimental fieldwork is not to control those I study but to see how they control themselves and each other. In any given situation, what choices will be viable, and why? Given a range of possible purposes, which will be chosen and why? Given a chosen purpose, how do people forge agreement in pursuing it? Answering this kind of question is in fact something all of us do in ordinary behavior all the time; we could not survive if we did not. There is no reason for our efforts to understand those around us in the situation of ethnographic field in a way that is fundamentally different. Fieldwork interaction is ordinary interaction with a higher degree of awareness and concentration. It is mainly a matter of making the interpretive methods of daily life cleaner, more conscious, and more cohesive. We participate, but we also pay special attention to observing that participation – not only what "they" do but also what we do.

In a physical laboratory, we set up an experimental program by systematically varying the components to affirm or eliminate alternative understandings of that situation. For example, we might subject a gas in cloud chamber to changes in pressure and electrical charges, and we keep on doing this until we can understand and predict the result of each new variation. As a field ethnographer, I do the same thing by going through a series of interview situations varying the questions I ask, the way I ask them, the people who I ask them of, and the circumstances of the interview until the results of further questions become predictable in the same way and to the same degree.

Experimental ethnographic fieldwork is far too complex to represent in detail in a readable ethnographic monograph – just as conventional accounts of physical experiments cannot record all the various twiddlings, false starts, and details of design and procedure that lead to the final physical results (cf. Galison 1997). What one can do is only what good ethnographers have tried to do since Malinowski set the pattern. They say enough about what they were looking for to let the reader put himself in the ethnographer's place with enough detail about how they found out to let the reader vicariously reconstruct the method on his own. One does not "abstract" or "generalize" from nature, but rather one shows how ideas and behavior are interconnected in it. The aim of the account, as of the fieldwork itself, is to embed the elements discovered in their natural contexts. It, therefore, must describe those natural contexts and allow us to see how they connect to one another.

But what, exactly, do we trace? What are the elements, and what counts as a connection between one element and another? I think most ethnographers would now agree that the things they describe are mainly of two kinds: process and structure. There are things connected to each other over time, and things that seem to be connected to each other independently of time. Processual connections can be further broken two into two main types: cause-effect, and means-ends. The difference is that in cause-effect connections the cause is either antecedent to or simultaneous with the effect, and in means-ends relations the end is a future condition the means are expected to lead to. A further difference is that cause and effect connections can be verified objectively, while means-ends relations are in the nature of the case more matters of belief and expectation. Of course they may overlap; many means-ends relationships reflect recognized causal relations, and anticipated or desired ends regularly act as antecedent causes of specific actions.

Ethnographers generally regard physical structures as non-problematic. Houses and bridges and boats are important, but describing them seems relatively straightforward and ethnographers are generally content with taking a few photographs, making a drawing, or taking down a description of the construction process and leaving serious analysis to engineers, architects, and the like. The ethnographic problematic focuses on structures of ideas, of thought, and here nothing is straightforward and virtually everything is contested. The disagreements are greatest, as one would expect, within the positivist and reductionist tradition and between this tradition and pragmatism. Among pragmatists, there is generally a high level of theoretical and methodological agreement.

I have already indicated that in the pragmatic view, ideas are generally seen as tokens or counters in behavioral interaction, ways of representing possible courses of action to oneself and others. The view of ideas that this leads to is difficult to describe in familiar terms. They come to be treated not as images or descriptions of anything very complete, but much more like elements in computer program, almost empty in themselves but more important for the other ideas they are linked to, the precise formal manner of that linkage, and the kinds of behavioral sequences that these linkages appear to be imbedded in. Ideas never occur alone, but always in patterned sets or groups. As far as I can see, an idea in complete isolate is virtually unthinkable. With respect to those ideas that define social relations and values, the differences between these sets or groups play out in behavior as the differences between kinds of situations or contexts while the relations within the ideas in each group play out as the ways each distinctive type of situation can be organized. We have ideas of government, in which the various contrasting entities, offices and powers are defined in relation to each other: government as a whole, its several branches, the difference between the legislative power and executive power, and the like. We have ideas of religion, in which the various entities, offices, and powers are defined in relation to each other: God and the world, immortal and mortal, priest, nun, acolyte, and congregant, and so on. We have ideas of kinship: family, clan, tribe; relational pairs like father-son, brother-sister, uncle-niece, rules of inheritance and marriage, and so on. We also have idea systems that describe technologies, meaning that they do not define parts of systems of social relationships but parts of things: tools and techniques and the aforementioned bridges, houses and the like, and these are pluralistic as well.

Within each system, relations are defined; across systems they are not. If you are my father I must be your child. If you are my father, we may or may not be working for the government. If I sit a judge over you in a case, it is a legal situation. Our relations will be made to reflect or enact the conventional definitions of the judge-defendant relation and the relation of priest-supplicant or father-son will be utterly irrelevant. If I am your father and you are my child, then it is a kinship situation and our employment relations are irrelevant. Basic cultural definitions are usually far too formal and abstract to control actual behavior in any detail, but they do control the ways behavior can be discussed and agreed to. Defined relations allow one kind of symbolic conversation, undefined relations allow others. This is a core finding of pragmatic symbolic interactionism, and it is an extremely powerfull idea that not only informs pragmatic field method but also produces a powerful integration between pragmatic social analysis, social psychological analysis, and psychological analyses.

The same ideas that define social roles also define the social "selves" that take them. If we look for our basic sense of self, what we find is that we literally cannot give it any content except as that which *we feel* must underlie and unify all the much more concrete socially defined selves we enact. Since I am a professor, a husband, a bank customer, a fisherman, a buyer and seller, a precinct captain in the Democratic party in Texas, a citizen, a writer, and so on, there must be an "I" to me even though I cannot say what its attributes are beside those shown in all these various other capacities. This inability to define my "I" can be summed up as a situated unpredictability of self, and stands for how social life is unendingly generative of options, contexts, experiences and purposes. There is no inherent logical limit to this generative power, although it does have an inherent logical structure. The pragmatic analysis of the logical structure of the social construction of the self begins with Montesquieu's recognition that "reason" in social relations must be reciprocal – I cannot define a relation for you and me unless what I define about my position is logically reciprocal with what I say about you. You cannot be my superior if I am not your inferior; I cannot owe you if you are not my creditor, and so on. Through Kant's idea of self, universe and series as general organizing principles of thought (the transcendental categories of the understanding), this led to C. S. Peirce's and Martin Buber's analysis of perception in terms of the basic relation of I-thou-it[3] and eventually to Mead's analysis of the relation between the formation of the self and the idea of the generalized other. This was the idea that in order to have a fully developed sense of self you must also have a fully developed sense that you can put yourself in the place of another. Finally, this analysis has been expanded still further with synthesis of Piaget's developmental psychology and the more contextually oriented developmental psychology of Mikhail Bakhtin, L. S. Vygotsky and A. N. Leont'ev, producing what is sometimes called "cultural psychology" (Cole, Engestrom, and Vasquez, 1997). The systems of cultural ideas that one elicits by means of a Malinowskian experimental field method are what provide the content of this general process of self-construction. The process of defining specific selves and the underlying self that they seem to refer to and the process of defining social situations and the larger social world that seems to encompass them are two sides of one and the same coin, two faces of one single process of symbolic interaction.

Since the interconnections between the social definitions are the basis of orderly social relationships, it is absolutely essential to have a clear and reliable criterion for finding which ideas are connected to each other in the field and which are not. The obvious place to start is with the most rigorous criterion we can think of, since if we pick a weak criterion we will never find strong and well defined systems. The most rigorous criterion for whether or not two ideas are in the same system is invariant association in the sense defined in terms of what linguists call "frame analysis". In this, two or more elements are considered to be invariantly associated if, in an identifiable context, they occur together or near one another, if they occur contrastively, or if they occur in complementary distribution. Semantically, what these criteria mean is that to be related, ideas must closely imply or entail one another such that one is the "same thing" as the other or the negation of the other, or if they alternate with or substitute for one another. The opposite of such relations, by which we would judge two elements not to be in the same system, is random distribution – if the presence of one did not allow to predict in any reliable way the presence or absence of the other. If I am someone's father they must be my child and cannot be my sibling, invariably. If I am someone's father they may or may not be my accountant or in the same political party.

The criterion of invariant association implies that structures will be elicited in a step-wise procedure. That is, you start with a given element and probe for what is linked to it. Then you take that and ask the same question, and so on. You cannot start with some kind of list or grab bag and ask if all the elements in it are invariantly associated with one another. This question is not answerable in practice, in part because it is very difficult to think of an orderly method by which it could be answered at all (how could you simultaneously consider all the elements at once?), and in part because no conceivable method of answering it would correspond to the way such systems appear in nature – which is to say in the normal flow of social intercourse. As a kinsman, what one encounters is not the entire kinship system but this relation and that. As a religionist what one encounters is not everything about one's religion but this idea or set of ideas on this occasion, that other set of ideas on some other occasion.

The first and most basic question of my own first fieldwork was whether such a firm criterion for association was workable. Were culturally systems really this well organized, this definite and this discrete? Would I get results that formed intelligible patterns, or would I get a notebook full of tiny little isolated bits? If the criterion worked, the next question would be what the systems were, and finally we could then see how many there were and consider why. The answers were that the method worked, that the systems were this well organized and discrete, and in the community I studied there were just six of them in substantially universal consensus, but many more held but just one or a few small sub-groups. These were, as could be expected, more or less what other ethnographers of South Asia had always been compelled intuitively to differentiate from one another and place in different chapter headings, even when their positivistic and other such "theories" gave them no basis for doing so – kinship, religion, factions, the system of farm management, the ecology and the economy. The difference is that with pragmatic theory the divisions are not anomalous but confirmatory. We can explain them instead of ignoring or dismissing them, and they fit into a much larger theoretical picture (Leaf 1972: 262ff).

Specific Differences in Sociolegal Studies

While positivists and to some extent Marxist and other anti-empirical perspectives have been predominant in general ethnology since about the 1930s, pragmatic approaches have continued to predominate in the ethnography of law. This is, doubtless, because of the predominance of pragmatism and its Kantian counterparts in law itself. Generally, sociolegal studies involving field observations over this period have been of three main types: positivistic, pragmatic, and mixed.

Positivistic studies began mainly in 1920s with a particular caste of legal realism advocated by Walter Wheeler Cook, Underhill Moore, Joseph Bingham, Herman Oliphant, and a few others (Schlegel: 1995). Although most of their writings were little more than programmatic sketches, an exception was Underhill Moore's meticulously decontextualized and logically circular study of "parking behavior" in New Haven. In it, he claimed to justify a stimulus-response conception of legal compliance (Moore, 1943). In fact, he had no psychological data and all that actually showed was that he could use stimulus-response phraseology to describe the relation between parking signs and the lengths of times for which cars were parked. Although admirable for Moore's sincerity and logical consistency, the result of the consistency was a kind of reduction to absurdity, and the program lost its revolutionary appeal among legal scholars soon thereafter.

Apart from these and Donald Black's call for a "pure" sociology of law in the 1960s already noted, ethnographic studies have either been pragmatic in method but something else in theory or consistently pragmatic in both method and theory. Max Gluckman and Leopold Pospisil illustrate the former; Sally Falk Moore represents the latter.

Gluckman explicitly described himself as a Marxist and a "strict Durkheimian". The reality was more complex. He accepted the positivist notion that theory was separate from description. Then, on this basis, he held two entirely different notions of what he was doing. What he considered his theory was indeed drawn from Marx and Durkheim, but his conception of what law was, which he considered merely "descriptive", was drawn from Benjamin Cardozo. Because he was true to the originals in both cases, no one provides a better example of the way pragmatic assumptions tend to disappear into the results they generate while positivistic "theory" remains separate and attracts attention.

Gluckman's idea of theory in general was both deterministic and reductionist. His aim was to show that social structure, not individual reason, purposes, values, and choice, controlled behavior. His idea of a theory of law was not a notion of how to find it but of how to "explain" it in these terms. What made his theory specifically Durkheimian was his idea that society in this sense was mentalistic, and what made it Marxist was that he held that this also had to do with the material conditions of existence. All this came together in his characterization of Barotse society as "multiplex". A multiplex society is one in which, because of the extreme simplicity of conditions of life, each individual does not deal with each other individual in just one role or capacity but usually in many, which they carefully keep separate. Gluckman did not offer a point-for-point contrast between this situation and our own, but his obvious reference was to Durkheim's stress on the fact that more advanced societies are both larger in "mass" and more specialized and differentiated, like more highly evolved organisms. Each person deals with others on just one basis, in one differentiated set of settings: dentist's offices, universities, grocery stores, etc.

Gluckman's main argument was in *The Judicial Process Among the Barotse of Northern Rhodesia* (Gluckman, 1955: 15). Because of the way the book was organized, with his conclusions mainly separated from the body of the argument and placed in the introduction, Gluckman did not put himself in the position of having to specify clearly which features of Barotse jurisprudence the idea of a multiplex society was supposed to be particularly attached to. Apparently, however, it is that their judicial processes show the same kind of purely conceptual and symbolic, rather than material, situational differentiations as the society at large. This is of course quite reasonable; how could it be otherwise? The only puzzle is why Gluckman thinks that his explanation has to be phrased in terms of what social structure causes people to do rather than the purposive and rational responses of people to their situations.

The model for Gluckman's ethnographic method could not have been more clearly and consistently pragmatic, and at this level rationality are as conspicuously prominent as they are conspicuously absent from what he takes as his theory. The bulk of the monograph was a point by point description based on Cardozo's analysis of the elements of adjudication in the common law. Like any other major pragmatic definition this was not just some arbitrary classification but rather a description of a process that amounted to following cases through the system. Gluckman described Barotse rules of law as counterparts of judicial conceptions of rational behavior in tort and civil law. He viewed cases from the point of view of their pre-judicial status and origin, the way they were re-cast for purposes of adjudication and the vocabulary of legal debate that was applied. He attended and described what any jurisprudent would recognize as trials, where opposing claimants met before recognized authorities in a public forum following clearly established procedures for presenting evidence and arguing its consequences, and he looked at the consequences of the resolution. In short, he understood the jurisprudential ideas he was using and was clearly guided by them through the entire process of observation, analysis, and description. The only thing he did not do was regard his description as "theory". It was simply that Cardozo, being a lawyer, had defined law and Gluckman, being an ethnologist, had used that definition in the field.

Gluckman's theory explains nothing in the way he thinks it does because it differentiates nothing in the way he thinks it does. Barotse do not differentiate roles as they do because their social structure is of a peculiar sort, but because it is not *a* structure in a monolithic and all-encompassing Durkheimian sense at all. The Barotse have multiple structures that are used to organize multiple systems of roles and relations just as all other communities do, including ours. The only real difference is that the purely cognitive component is clearer because they have so little in the way of material possessions. When we, Westerners, change roles we often change clothing and physical settings as well. They do not have as much clothing or as many types of physical settings. Yet we can just as readily dispense with physical accouterments as the Barotse if we must, with no greater difficulty. A trial does not have to occur in a purpose-designed courtroom and a judge does not have to have a robe. A family quarrel does not have to occur in a private residence. If I meet a student in the waiting room of a dentist's office, we will have no difficulty having both fellow-patient relations and student-teacher relations and keeping them separate. The basic organizational principles in both societies are the same, not different. Gluckman's ethnography shows it, but his empirically ungrounded idea of theory keeps him from acknowledging it.

Leopold Pospisil's specific arguments differed, but the effect was the same. Instead of trying to promote positivist ideas of social determinism, Pospisil argued for positivist conceptions of theory: the necessity for *a priori* definition of law and legal process as the basis of comparative sociolegal studies. You could not just be clear about your methods and see what they led to. Yet his methods were consistently and thoroughly pragmatic and, in the end, so was his actual definition of law, even though he would not recognize it.

Pospisil was trained in continental jurisprudence descended from Savigny, particularly the sociological jurisprudence of Ehrlich that is closely allied to the pragmatic jurisprudence that Gluckman drew upon. Like Gluckman, he applied the ideas of law from this tradition directly in the analysis of the social organization of a non-western community, and also like Gluckman while he clearly showed that such an application was legitimate, he completely ignored the importance of what this shows about law in general and human nature in general. Instead, he defined the "theoretical" significance of his work in wholly unrelated terms. His *Kapauku Papuans and Their Law* (1958) was divided in four parts. The first described basic Kapauku conceptions of the world and the individual, as represented in mythology, conventional stories, and the main events of an individual life cycle. Part two described the political structure, organizations, and patterns of leadership of the particular group he was concerned with, the Ijaaj-Pigome confederacy. Part three dealt with 'Rules and Disputes in Kapauku Society', and turned to what we could consider law proper, actual cases decided by actual people. Those most extensively discussed were witnessed by Pospisil in person, while reports of others filled out the argument.

The analytic headings draw on 19th century analyses of Roman law: Offences against Persons, Offenses against Rights in Things, Ownership of Movables, Contract, and Offences Against and by an Authority. Sale was considered under contract as was barter, giving four general attributes of the legal process through which all cases passed, again with evident Roman roots. The attributes were authority, intention of universal application, obligation (the imposition of an authority external to the dispute itself), and sanction (pp. 257-272). The method of applying the definition was processual. Like Gluckman, he traced cases through the process of inception, removal from their initial context to their adjudicative context, adjudication, resolution, and reinsertion.

The most interesting thing about the definition was that it worked. The attributes were present in a clear, direct, and non-circular way, even though one could hardly imagine a society more alien to the theory's original home. Legal decisions were rendered by several authorities, but mainly "big men", local informal leaders. Pospisil described them and took particular care to say just how they come to be authorities from the point of view of the options available to the individuals concerned. He describes what motivates them to do it (they gain from it), and what motivates others to come to them (they also gain, in comparison to settling the disputes on their own). He leaves no doubt that their legal function is recognized, that people do indeed take matters to them for decision, and that they do indeed make and enforce such decisions. The terms of the analysis retained the sense they had in the jurisprudential literature but also had clear empirical saliency in the New Guinea setting.

Pospisil took his argument as supporting the positivist claim that comparison depended on *a priori* definitions. In fact it proves the opposite, because in the last analysis Pospisil's definitions are not *a priori* at all but thoroughly grounded in the long haul of juridical experience beginning in the Republic of Rome and recaptured and redeveloped in Europe and the liberal democracies.

Sally Falk Moore's conception of law is derived from the same continental and pragmatic traditions of jurisprudence and legal analysis as Gluckman's and Pospisil's. Unlike them, however, she recognizes this pragmatism as a full scale juridical and social analytic tradition. It is not description and method rather than theory but description and method that is theory. In consequence, she immediately sees her legal results as instances of much more general social processes without having to strain for artificial and extraneous "theoretical" arguments to make a connection.

The aim of Moore's ethnography is not to provide something to apply social theory to but rather to develop social theory in. It is not to provide something to "explain" as an artifact of something external to it, but a setting in which she can make her own contributions to the established pragmatic analyses of social process.

Although the difference between social structure and social process is well established, it is still far from well-described. Social process is one of the easiest things in the world for us to do, but one of the hardest for us to think. This is what Moore has contributed to. Her legal perspective has led her to conceptions of structure and process in legal contexts that apply equally well to all other contexts. Her ideas of structure appear mainly in her analyses of ceremony, which develop Malinowski's idea of a "social charter". For process, her core insight is her isolation of the "transaction" as the basic building block of social relations.

Moore describes a transaction as the reciprocal assertion and transformation of a relationship (1978: 7). It is, therefore, not something reductionist like a stimulus and a response or a manifestation of intersubjectivity. It is not something imposed on raw individuals by something over and above them like *the* social structure or *the* culture. It is certainly not her private analytic construction to be imputed to individuals apart from what they think themselves. It is a modification of something already there by those already involved. People create transactions, but they do not do so out of thin air. They do it out of what they had before.

Like most powerful perceptions, the simplicity of the idea of transactions is deceptive. Once you see it you can hardly realize that a moment before you could not have thought of it if your life depended on it. More to point, you can hardly realize that what Moore is showing is precisely what Gluckman, Pospisil, and so many others were denying, or at least avoiding – apparently because they could not see a way to give it "cross cultural" or "theoretical" significance. It is not what imposes order from above but what lets it grow from below, and it is not something beyond perception and mysterious but observable and clear. Yet once you do see it, it is not difficult to recognize that transactions are the building blocks of organizations and usually do not occur without entailing or projecting a sense of an institution. A transaction is what we are doing, the organization is what we are doing it in title of, and the institution is what seems to lie behind the organization.

In pragmatic analysis, fieldwork and theory are inseparable from one another. Theory is far more importantly about what one encounters from moment to moment in cultural participation than what one might or should conclude about society or culture “as a whole”. A pragmatic perspective requires that our account of behavior be built up from experimental inquiry, from interlinked assumptions and through interlinked field experiments. We are reasonable and our actions are purposeful, and we interact with others who are reasonable and purposeful in order to understand their reasoning and their purposes. We learn from them to observe their transactions as they do. We learn how these transactions add up to organizations. We can then see how organizations produce established ways of doing things, then how established ways of doing things perpetuate culture and those who carry it. Cultures are endlessly diverse, but the processes that produce this diversity appear to be everywhere the same.

Some Other Methodological Issues

I hope I have made clear why it is difficult to say much more than I have about the field observation and elicitation of social processes and cultural systems in general terms. Just as for the experimental method in general, the details of each study must always follow the details of what it is intended to uncover and methods are constantly evolving. Nevertheless, there are three important standing misconceptions that need to be addressed. These are that 1) it is inconsistent with survey methods or other “objective” methods 2) it is inconsistent with cross cultural comparison, and 3) that it depends upon on people telling you the truth. I will take them up briefly in order.

Surveys

The most common way of designing a survey is to begin with a very large set of questions on the topic of interest based on some *a priori* scheme of logical contrasts and then go through several pretests to reject questions that do not seem to get independently patterned answers. The analyst does not ask the respondents for their interpretation of the question, or tell them the question’s purpose. The consequence is that the analyst usually has no way of knowing what the questions mean to the respondents and the respondents have no way of controlling the interpretation being placed upon their responses. This has no parallel in the way one interprets a naturally occurring conversation or in anything else that has been said above about experimental fieldwork. The "result" is whatever story goes with the best-looking statistical pattern that the analyst can find.

The problem involved in calling this kind of method "objective" ought to be obvious. The marks on the page may be objective, but the connection between them and any final imputation of meaning could not be more arbitrary. In this sense, surveys are indeed inconsistent with ethnographic elicitation. Fortunately, however, this is not the only way they can be done.

Probably the best known example of an empirically sound survey in socio-legal studies is the one incorporated in *The American Jury* (Kalven and Zeisel: 1966). There are many others. A pragmatically sound survey is an extension of a good fieldwork interview. Such a survey is one in which the interpreter and the respondent agree on each others' interpretation of the questions and the answers, and the analyst cannot only say what the respondents meant, but why they meant it. The procedures needed to construct differ from the conventional procedures in three main ways. First, the questions have to be developed with the respondents according to their notions of what issues and assumptions are relevant and the pretesting has to assure that for each question it is clear what the relevant assumptions are. Second, the questionnaire must include questions that reveal the purpose of the questionnaire itself and that ask about the purposes and concerns of those responding, so the two can be related. In my personal experience, I have found that the best way to do this is to start with relatively open-ended questions and then simplify the analysis later by careful coding of the responses in consultation with the respondents. In principle, this is also what Kalven and Zeisel did. Third, questions about purposes have to be supported with questions about concrete constraints and resources relevant to achieving them. If the questions deal with problems of farmers, do the respondents have land? If the concerns bear on diseases of children, what children are in the house? If they say they are weavers, do they have the tools for weaving? If the questions are about flooding, what floods have they experienced? This done, the answers are not only interpretable and explainable in a context of definite, known, and measurable purposes, but in a further context of known and measurable physical conditions as well.

Cross Cultural Comparison

The claim that concentrating on indigenous categories makes cross-cultural comparison impossible implicitly rejects what is sometimes called the hypothesis of the psychic unity of man. The hypothesis of psychic unity is, essentially, that we will always be able to put ourselves in the positions of those we study, and when we do so we will find, as Malinowski somewhere said, that they are "as rational as any Christian". This is empirically testable, and so far the tests have always been affirmative. Although there are very few societies left unexamined, if we find one in which this is not so, then the hypothesis will be disproved. The opposite claim, however is not testable but rather precludes such a test. To start by adopting the idea that all cross cultural comparison has to be framed only in terms of our own arbitrary preconceptions is to rule out the possibility of discovering constancies that may exist on their own. In effect, it is to say from the start that we will not let people tell us what is important to them; we will tell them what is important to us. It is not good science, and it is also not treating people as you would be treated.

Dependence on Truthful Informants

Finally, I am often asked "What happens if your informants lie?". The implication of the question is in a sense the exact opposite of the disapproval of the notion of putting people in test-tubes and in a sense the same: it is that if I do not put them under some kind of severe constraint to ensure that I am getting exactly the same kind of response in all cases, I cannot rely on or believe the information they provide. In its most general form, the question implies a rejection of participant observation as such.

The most direct response is that an informant cannot lie to a good ethnographer. This may seem naive or even absurd, but it is absolutely true. To a *good* field worker, no informant can say anything that does not convey at least some cultural information. Of course they may *intend* to lie, mislead, reveal only partial truths, or say what will be pleasing, but to a good field worker this is not really very different from a situation in which they *intend* exactly the opposite. Either way, your aim is not so much to find out who did what to whom on some occasion or another, but rather, as already said, what idea or action is normally or conventionally defined as going with what other idea or action in what context. Most people would not even begin to think of lying about such things but would rather rely on such conventions to frame whatever lies or truths they would try to tell. In fact, lies very often provide better information on such associations.

I should add, however, that in my own experience lying has never been a serious problem. If you are respectful of those around you in the field situation, have a problem that is real for them, and show a genuine interest in learning, most people most of the time make a genuine effort to teach. Again, pragmatic theory is also practical methodological guidance. People who are competent in a culture know how to put themselves in each others place. Therefore if you are to become competent, as a field ethnographer, you need to learn how to do the same, how to put yourself in their places, in all their many contexts. At first, you will misunderstand. Whether they are deliberately lying or not the effect will be the same. You will not be able to predict responses to your actions and questions. As you learn (if you learn), you will be able to put yourself in their places more effectively and also see them doing it with respect to each other, and the responses will become more predictable. Native competence is attained when they are absolutely predictable in a certain way—not that you know what exactly will be said, but that you will be able to predict the ideas that will be used to say it, and which ideas will be used with which other ideals.

Conclusion

Ethnography in socio-legal studies is not a discovery but a rediscovery, a return of socio-legal studies to its empirical and pragmatic roots. Is it to be wondered at that this method of analysis, identified with a small social science far from law, seems so apt to law? Not if we recognize that early anthropologists were drawn from law in the beginning, whether one takes that beginning to be the Roman republican jurisprudence of Montesquieu and Kant, the comparative method of Savigny and the Grimm brothers, the legal ethnography of Lewis Henry Morgan, or the pragmatic functionalism of Malinowski. The important thing is to be clear about how they worked and what they found. Accept no substitutes for seeing law as emerging from human interaction and for finding and following the trail of evidence.

Notes

1. Thanks to Alfonso Morales for extensive comments on a prior draft.

2. As Rudolph von Jhering argued, when we say "because", by way of explaining some conscious action, thought or statement of a human being, what we always mean is "in order to" (1913:9). For people, as Jhering puts it, "acting, and acting with a purpose, are synonymous" (ibid.).
3. According to Milton Singer, Peirce had used Buber's I-Thou idea in a paper written while an undergraduate at Harvard, but dropped it. The idea recurs implicitly, however, in Peirce's later "phenomenological categories" of Firstness, Secondness and Thirdness (Singer, 1984: 86) and in his view of "dialogical nature of signs" (p. 87).

References

Black, Donald. (1971), "The Social Organization of Arrest". *Stanford Law Review*, vol. 23, pp. 1087-1111.

Black, Donald. (1972), "The Boundaries of Legal Sociology". *Yale Law Review*, vol. 81, pp. 1086-1100.

Bohannan, Paul. (1957), *Justice and Judgment Among the Tiv*. London: Oxford University Press.

Cole, Michael, Yrjo Engestrom, and Olqa Vazquez. (1997), *Mind, Culture, and Activity: Seminal Papers from the Laboratory of Human Cognition.* Cambridge: Cambridge University Press.

Friedrich, Paul. (1992), "Interpretation and Vision: A Critique Cryptopositivism". *Cultural Anthropology* May, vol. 7, no. 2, pp. 211-31.

Galilei, Galileo (1632) *Dialogue Concerning The Two Chief World-Systems*

Gallison, Peter. (1997), *Image and Logic*. Chicago: University of Chicago Press.

Geertz, Clifford. (1964), "Ideology as a Cultural System". In Apter, David Ernest, ed., *Ideology and discontent*. New York: The Free Press of Glencoe.

Geertz, Clifford. (1966b), "Religion as a Cultural System". In M. Banton, ed., *Anthropological Approaches in the Study of Religion*. London: Tavistock.

Geertz, Clifford. (1973), *The Interpretation of Culture*. New York: Basic Books.

Geertz, Clifford. (1983), "Local Knowledge: Fact and Law in Comparative Perspective". In *Local Knowledge: Further Essays in Interpretive Anthropology*, pp. 167-234, New York: Basic Books.

Gluckman, Max. (1955), *The Judicial Process Among the Barotse of Northern Rhodesia*, Manchester: Manchester University Press.

Gross, Feliks. (1986), "Young Malinowski and his Later Years". *American Anthropologist*, vol. 13, no.3, pp. 556-570.

Holmes, Oliver Wendell Jr. (1923), *The Common Law*. Boston: Little Brown and Co. First Pub. 1881.

Kalven, Harry, Jr. and Hans Zeisel. (1966), *The American Jury*. Boston: Little Brown.

Kant, Immanuel. (1956), *Critique of Practical Reason*, (trans. Lewis White Beck). Indianapolis: Bobbs-Merrill.

Kant, Immanuel. (1929), *Critique of Pure Reason*, trans. Norman Kemp Smith. New York: St. Martin's Press.

Leaf, Murray J. (1972), *Information and Behavior in a Sikh Village*. Berkeley and Los Angeles: University of California Press.

__________. (1979), *Man, Mind and Science: A History of Anthropology*. New York: Columbia University Press.

Mach, Ernst. (1959), *The Analysis of Sensations and the Relation of the Physical to the Psychical.* First published 1885. Translated from the first German edition by C. M. Williams, Revised and supplemented from the fifth German edition by Sydney Waterlow, M. A. New York: Dover.

Malinowski, Bronislaw. (1922), "Argonauts of the Western Pacific: An Account of Native Enterprise and Adventure in the Archipelagoes of Melanesian New Guinea". *Studies in Economics and Political Science*, no. 65. London: Routledge and Kegan Paul.

Malinowski, Bronislaw. (1923), *Crime and Custom in Savage Society.* Paterson: Littlefield, Adams and Co.

Malinowski, Bronislaw. (1935), *Coral Gardens and Their Magic: A Study of the Methods of Tilling the Soil and of Agricultural Rites in the Trobriand Islands.* London: Allen & Unwin. 2 vols.

Meek, C. K. (1937), *Law and Authority in a Nigerian Tribe.* Oxford: Oxford University Press.

Merry, Sally Engle. (1990), *Getting Justice and Getting Even: Legal Consciousness Among Working Class Americans.* Chicago: University of Chicago Press.

Moore, Sally Falk. (1978), *Law as Process.* London: Routledge and Kegan Paul.

Morris, Charles. (1970), *The Pragmatic Movement in American Philosophy.* New York: George Braziller.

Nonet, Philippe. (1976), "For Jurisprudential Sociology". *Law and Society Review*, vol. 10, pp. 525-545.

Peirce, Charles. (Jan. 1878), "How to Make our Ideas Clear". In *Popular Science Monthly*, vol. 12, pp. 286-302

Pospisil, Leopold. (1958), *Kapauku Papuans and Their Law.* New Haven: Yale University Press.

Settle, Thomas B. (1967), "Galileo's Use of Experiment as a Tool of Investigation" in E. McMullin, ed. *Galileo Man of Science.* 1988 Reprint of 1967. Basic Books edition. Princeton Junction: The Scholar's Bookshelf. pp. 315-37.

Schlegel, John Henry. (1995), *American Legal Realism and Empirical Social Science.* London: Chapel Hill and London: University of North Carolina Press.

Singer, Milton. (1984), *Man's Glassy Essence.* Bloomington: Indiana University Press.

6 The Mathematical Metaphysics of Measurement and Metrology: Towards Meaningful Quantification in the Human Sciences

William P. Fisher Jr.

Introduction

Until recently, researchers in the history and philosophy of science have largely ignored the ways in which communities of inquirers collectively think through problems via their coordinated behaviors. This state of affairs prompted Latour (Latour, 1987, p. 247) to propose a 10-year moratorium on cognitive explanations of science and technology. As an alternative, he proposed following scientists and engineers in action to see what they do. Latour's proposals thoroughly engage with fundamental philosophical issues in much the way that Dewey (1929, p. 284) described:

> The primary problem for thinking which lays claim to be philosophic in its breadth and depth is to assist in bringing about a reconstruction of all beliefs rooted in a basic separation of knowledge and action; to develop a system of operative ideas congruous with present knowledge and with present facilities of control over natural events and energies.

To his surprise, Latour (Latour, 1995, p. 63) was able to safely lift the ban, less than ten years later upon encountering Hutchins (Hutchins, 1994) redefinition of cognition as socially distributed and coordinated mediation, a theme that has since been taken up in a number of ways in recent works in cognitive psychology (Hendriks-Jansen, 1996; Thelen and Smith, 1996; Clancey, 1997; Kelso, 1997; Clark, 1998; Port and Van

Gelder, 1998; Smith, 1998), that echoes many issues previously raised by pragmatists such as Mead (Joas, 1993, 1997).

Following through on his own proposals, Latour's science studies, and those of his colleagues (Shapin, 1989, 1991, 1994; Schaffer, 1992; Widmalm, 1995; Wise, 1988, 1995), focus on the functions of social networks of scientists and technicians in the creation and maintenance of scientific objectivity. Some of the field of science studies most important insights relevant to the methods of the human sciences follow from investigations into the practices of metrology, the science and engineering of quantitative measuring systems. The culmination of ongoing dialogues with nature in the metrological construction of objective and uniform data standards presents a previously overlooked opportunity to develop a system of operative ideas congruous with present knowledge and with present facilities of control over natural events and energies (Dewey, 1929, p. 284). Accordingly, this paper will serve several functions: 1) briefly describe metrology's two phases, through which the stubbornness of sensation (a factual experimental result) is integrated with opinion (theory) in practice 2) relate metrological practice to the broad qualitative mathematical metaphysics of science and education and locate its emergence in the history of science 3) show metrology's first phase to have been successfully undertaken in recent psychosocial research employing probabilistic conjoint (Rasch) models of fundamental measurement 4) offer an agenda for the initiation of metrology's first and second phases in psychosocial research as is necessary for the full quantification of the variables of the human sciences. The paper concludes by briefly pursuing some of the implications of fully quantifying the variables of the human sciences.

Metrology

Metrology is the science of measurement. There are two distinct phases or steps in the creation of fully quantified metrological systems (Wise, 1995; Widmalm, 1995). The first phase, intralaboratory ruggedness tests (Wernimont, 1977; Wernimont, 1978), involve what Thurstone (Thurstone, 1928) referred to as the crucial experimental test of the hypothesis that the variable of interest is quantitative. Quantitative variables exhibit stubbornly persistent and robust mathematical properties across experiments and samples when they are assessed using Thurstone's criteria. These tests are increasingly implemented in the human sciences via the application of fundamental measurement theory, especially as this is realized by Rasch's probabilistic conjoint models (Rasch, 1960, 1961, 1977; Fischer, 1974, 1989; Andersen, 1980; Andrich, 1988; Wright, 1968, 1999; Bond and Fox, 2001). The second phase, interlaboratory round robin trials (Mandel, 1977, 1978), is the means through which the results of different laboratories' ruggedness tests are brought into harmony with one another. Implementation of Thurstone's "crucial experimental test" (metrology's first, ruggedness testing phase) is rare in the human sciences (Wright, 1984; Cliff, 1992; Michell, 1990, 1997, 1999, 2000). Metrology's second phase of interlaboratory trials and the creation and monitoring of reference standard metrics is nonexistent, with only a few isolated explorations of their viability being taken up to date (Fisher 1997a, 1997b, 1999; Fisher, Harvey, Taylor, Kilgore, and Kelly, 1995).

Thus, though it is unusual for them to do so, researchers in multiple independent psychosocial labs may execute a variety of ruggedness tests by implementing methods intended to achieve parameter separation, statistical sufficiency, Guttman reproducibility, conjoint additivity, or scale- and sample-free measurement (Wright 1999). These researchers may thereby successfully calibrate their distinct versions of a type of instrument for measuring a particular variable to the desired degrees of accuracy and precision. Unfortunately, the completion of that process alone cannot result in the deployment of a standard and uniform numerical metric. The Pythagorean and positivist sense of the world as inherently numerical has led to a concept of the universe as a well of quantitatively measurable resources. But the demonstration of a variable's objective existence as a phenomenon in the world does not immediately translate into a universally accepted quantitative measurement continuum for its expression, contrary to what seems to be a widespread but mistaken notion.

The vast majority of researchers in the human sciences apparently believe that merely assigning numbers to observations according to a rule suffices for quantification. Even those who go beyond these ordinal, sample-dependent, and nonlinear methods to actually test the hypothesis that the variable is quantitative usually stop with the analysis of their own data, doing nothing to relate their experimental results with the results of other similar studies. Even when the latter is taken up, the challenge of creating a metrological network through which the variable's mathematical structure can be made the basis for quantification at the point of use remains unarticulated. The calibration and deployment of quantitative metrics that are as fully generalizable as possible will not become commonplace until standards for data quality, and metrological mechanisms for regulating it analogous to those in place for physical measures are instituted in the human sciences.

Once a construct is found to exist as an objective and robust phenomenon across a series of independently-performed intralaboratory ruggedness tests, demonstrating a stubbornly persistent, instrumentally-mediated sensation, the laboratories involved must collaborate in a series of experiments to equate their instruments so that they produce the same number for the same amount of the variable no matter which brand instrument is used on which sample by whom, where, or when. And once this equating is accomplished, a system must be implemented for the routine monitoring and maintenance of the measurement system to prevent the introduction of systematic errors. Because of the ways in which different parts manufactured by different companies have to be interrelated and coordinated in the assembly of a single product, metrology has been crucial to the development of most industries. But the industries served by the human sciences, such as education and health care, have begun only in the last few years to attempt the kinds of detailed coordinations that require metrology's reference standard metrics. These coordinations will fail to fulfill their potential as long as metrology is ignored.

Via metrology, natural phenomena first assert their independent existence across intralaboratory experiments and are then systematically coordinated so that any measure made anywhere is connected via a traceable network to a reference standard. All of the quantitative systems expressed in tables of constants and of weights and measures are created and maintained in this way. Thus, it is said that, in the natural sciences, uniform quantitative standards emerge as both agents and products of agreement (Wise, 1995; Widmalm, 1995). Standards are agents of agreement compelling recognition of their properties when independent studies conducted by different researchers in different laboratories using different instruments on different samples converge on very similar, though as yet not formally coordinated, results. When this convergence is achieved in metrology's first phase, the nonarbitrary phenomenological uniformity of the variable can be routine via interlaboratory trials, metrology's second phase. Only then is quantification complete, when the arbitrary conventions of numerical unit and range and tolerable error, are expressed as products of the participating scientists' agreement, enhancing the clarity of their communications, the interpretability of their research, and the uniformity of their commercial products and transactions.

Because language metaphorically provides a qualitative measure of meaning shared by all of those who understand it, it provides one kind of root model for successful metrology. All concepts are born as metaphors (Gadamer, 1989; Ricoeur, 1977), emerging at least sometimes, and perhaps often simultaneously at multiple independent places as part of the way that the questions of an age condense in an atmosphere saturated with particular issues. Whether the metaphor takes on a life of its own depends on its conceptual generalization which requires that local nuances of meaning attached to particular speakers and contexts be absorbed into or erased from it as it emerges as a currency for the exchange of a particular value. A similar process takes place in metrology. These issues concerning metaphor and measurement are explored in greater detail elsewhere (Fisher, 2000a).

The Metaphysics of Meaning

Qualitative and Quantitative Mathematics

Descartes (Descartes, 1961, p. 17) saw that, for the ancient Greeks, the name 'mathematics' means the same thing as learning. This general qualitative sense of the Greek category *ta mathemata* as learning or as a curriculum of what can be taught and learned is widely recognized in the mainstream of the philosophy and history of mathematics (Bochner, 1966, pp. 255, Bell, 1931: 58; Heath, 1931: 5; Dantzig, 1955: 25; Wilder, 1965: 284; Slavkov, 1973: 91; Miller, 1921: 78, 17), but is rarely pursued at any length.

Heidegger, however, focused his attention on the broad ancient Greek sense of mathematics in order to recover its wider implications for science and technology. Mathematics, as what can be taught and learned and what is learned through what is already known, structures the basic metaphysical presuppositions of academic knowledge (Heidegger, 1967). Over the entrance to the Academy, Plato put these words: “Let no one who has not grasped the mathematical enter here!”. In requiring mastery of mathematics for entrance into the study of philosophy, Plato was not demanding a kind of value-free rigor in the thinking of his students, as is sometimes desired from the study of mathematics today, and he was not interested merely in students who knew how to calculate.

Plato's main reason for linking philosophy and mathematics was philosophy's focus on a qualitative sense of what mathematical objects are. Plato understood that a student who knows enough to do a geometrical analysis of a circle knows that the analysis applies not only to the circle drawn but also to the idea of a circle that stands independent from each individual analytic example (Gadamer, 1980, p. 101). Gadamer (Gadamer, 1980, p. 100), paraphrasing Plato's Republic (510d, 527a-b) and Seventh Letter (342b), explains the following:

> Plainly no previous knowledge of the doctrine of ideas or of the dialectic of concepts is required to see that a circle is something different from the circular things which we call round, curved, oval, orbicular, etc., and which we can see with our eyes. It is clear to us that the figure, which we draw to illustrate a mathematical relationship visually, is not the mathematical relationship itself, and clearer still that the circular objects in nature are not to be confused with the circle of mathematics ...
>
> Geometry requires figures, which we draw, but its object is the circle itself ... Even he who has not yet seen all the metaphysical implications of the concept of pure thinking but only grasps something of mathematics ... knows that in a manner of speaking one looks right through the drawn circle and keeps the pure thought of the circle in mind.

It is because of the way that mathematical and geometrical figures converge with and separate from the meaning they carry that Plato required mathematical training of the students admitted to his Academy. Rather than being concerned with a mere capacity for calculation, Plato stressed mathematical training in order to keep philosophy in the closest possible contact with the things themselves which are revealed in their greatest purity via the coordination achieved between geometrical figures and their meaning – mathematically. Mundy (Mundy, 1986, p. 392) points out similar observations:

> The hallmark of a meaningless proposition is that its truth-value depends on what scale or coordinate system is employed, whereas meaningful propositions have truth-value independent of the choice of representation, within certain limits. The formal analysis of this distinction leads, in all three areas [measurement theory, geometry, and relativity], to a rather involved technical apparatus focusing upon invariance under changes of scale or changes of coordinate system.

The implication is that mathematics is a qualitative exploration of meaning as well as a matter of quantification and calculation. Mathematical generality delimits the conditions of the creation of meaning and so retains its relevance across contexts involving analyses of different kinds of metaphoric, geometric, and numeric symbolic figures. The crucial importance of sample- and scale-free measurement, of fundamental measurement theory, and of Rasch's separability theorem, therefore, is the fact that these provide models for evaluating the extent to which meaningful quantification is achieved (Fisher, 1992).

The inevitable metaphysical assumption and requirement of shared meaning put into play in all academic and scientific work is that a fundamentally mathematical coordination of symbol and meaning, of figure and sense, of text and interpretation, is achieved in the practical context of applications and relationships. Thus, the oft-repeated assertion that no field of study is scientific unless it is mathematical takes its compelling force not from the mere use of number but from deeper requirements of meaningfulness. As early as Aristotle, mathematics became immediately associated in most discourse with quantity and number because of the paradigmatic clarity with which numerical and geometrical symbols are coordinated with their meaning. Numbers are the most ideal symbols because their positions in the order exhaust all of their meaning (Gadamer, 1989, p. 413), and because they are thoroughly transparent and exhausted by their phenomenology (Derrida, 1989, p. 27).

But just because numbers embody most purely the mathematical and metaphysical coordination of figure and meaning means neither that they form the entire class of mathematical entities, nor that the symbols and signs of everyday discourse are unmathematical. Quite to the contrary, Plato's mathematical criterion for entrance into the Academy continues today to delimit the conditions for all academic knowledge claims (Heidegger, 1967, pp. 75-6). This becomes especially evident in the conduct of deconstruction and its challenges to the presuppositions of academic knowledge. In this work, the reader seeks to position her or himself at the point where "the thing signified is no longer easily separable from the signifier" (Derrida in Wood and Bernasconi, 1988, pp. 88-9), i.e., at the metaphysical and mathematical limits of meaningfulness. Deconstruction is popularly, but mistakenly, perceived as the home of academic renegades. This is so despite the fact that it has never been interested in "trying to bury the idea of 'objectivity' ... [since] it is not that texts and languages have no 'referents' or 'objectivity' but that the referent and objectivity are not what they pass themselves off to be, a pure transcendental signified" (Caputo 1997, p. 80). Latour (1987) has been similarly misunderstood, in his case, for locating objectivity in the coordinated play of metrological networks. But the point, as Latour (1994, 1999) has tried to explain, is not that there is no reality or objectivity, but that it takes a place in human affairs only to the extent that it can be embodied in a mathematically, socially, and playfully coordinated symbol system.

Metrology's Qualitative Mathematical Coordinations

What metrology does in its intralaboratory ruggedness studies and interlaboratory trials is first test for the possibility of quantitative idealization, and then realize it through the large-scale, socially networked coordination of data standards when the ruggedness tests indicate that this coordination is viable. Hutchins (Hutchins, 1994, p. 202) sense of distributed cognition develops a concept of thinking as a social process in which individuals consent to have their behavior constrained by others, who are themselves constrained by the meaningful states of representational technologies. Metrology, thus, initially coordinates within one laboratory an abstract number line with the phenomenon of interest (length, weight, temperature, electrical potential, etc.), demonstrating that the same number is obtained for the same amount, and that unit increases are of a constant size across the samples measured. The generalized application of the resulting metric does not, however, spontaneously propagate itself into the world, but requires the second metrological phase through which different instrument configurations are deliberately coordinated so as to produce common symbolic representations for the same amount measured at different times and places by different measurers.

Our positivist habits of mind blind us to the roles played by metrology and networks of technicians in the history of science (Latour, 1987; Shapin, 1989; Bud and Cozzens, 1992; O'Connell, 1993) as the very recent surge of interest in the distributed and situated concept of cognition attests. The ancient Pythagorean sense of the world as number and of the universe as inherently mathematical has overwhelmed and dominated the modern age. That is, modernity holds that the only true understanding of nature is achieved via reduction to calculable quantity.

This error and positivism's blind submission to an incomplete mathematical metaphysics became embedded in European culture in the 16th and 17th centuries as arithmetic and algebra were applied to geometry (Husserl, 1970, p. 44; Ricoeur, 1967a, p. 163). This application simultaneously did two things. First, it liberated geometry from previous concerns with actual diagrams and figures (circles, triangles, etc.), and with actual numbers and numerical relations, effecting a shift from being concretely employed exclusively for building bins for grain or measuring land, selling goods, or aiding a pilot in guiding his ship to being abstractly freed from connection with any particular existential application and use (Dewey, 1929, p. 154).

For instance, instead of having to actually draw and measure the squares incorporating each of the sides of a triangle to demonstrate or apply the Pythagorean theorem, the general relationship found to hold across all right triangles was represented simply as $a^2 + b^2 = c^2$. This abstract equation made it possible to calculate the length of any one side from measures of the other two sides, removing the need for drawing and measuring the actual square for each side. Thus, we see that it took over 2000 years, from 500 BCE to roughly 1600 CE, for Plato's sense of the transparency of geometric figures to become a layer in the embedded symbolic sediment of the culture. The algebraic expression of abstract, general geometric relationships made them easier to apply, and they proliferated rapidly across surveying, engineering, astronomy, navigation, and other fields (Crosby, 1997).

Second, the abstract arithmetization of geometry also covered over and hid the significance of the geometrical figures, since they were now replaced with symbols. Mastery of the technical manipulation of symbols eliminated the need to understand the inner workings of the processes with which the symbols were coordinated (Husserl, 1970, p. 52; Marcuse, 1974, p. 232; Ricoeur, 1967a, p. 163). By means of this process, people are able to drive automobiles or enjoy stereophonic music without understanding anything about the internal combustion engine, automatic transmissions, capacitors, or digital encoding. Though it may have been an inevitable product of his innovations, it was, nonetheless, a fateful omission that Galileo did not inquire back into the original meaning-giving achievement which, as idealization practiced on the original ground of all theoretical and practical life ... resulted in the geometrical ideal constructions (Husserl, 1970, p. 49).

Just as individuals are relieved by technology and its symbols of the need for extensive understanding of underlying empirical phenomena, so, too, was the techno scientific culture relieved by technology and mathematization of the need to understand the inner workings of symbolic techniques. The techniques work, taking on monstrous, uncontrolled proportions, whether they are understood or not. The paradox is that, though they cannot be controlled or simply rejected, it may be possible to overcome the blind domination of the mathematical coordinations of symbols and meanings embodied in technology through a better understanding and more complete tuning of these coordinations.

Mathematization is, thus, at the same time of the utmost danger while offering the greatest opportunity (Heidegger, 1977, p. 310). The danger, which Heidegger (Heidegger, 1966, p. 56) held to be greater than nuclear war, and further thought would be heightened as the danger of a third world war lessened, is that the modern and incomplete understanding of mathematical science may someday come to be accepted and practiced as the only way of thinking. The only way to liberate ourselves from this threat is, ironically, to follow mathematization through to the end, to understand it well enough to allow it to be what it is without altering humanity's poetic, meditative nature, by putting its currently incomplete state into perspective alongside other ways of thinking.

This is the widely under-appreciated point of Latour's (Latour, 1993) *We Have Never Been Modern*: not only is modernity's self-understanding grossly incomplete, but the contemporary postmodern relativisation of modern thinking is still largely incomplete and will remain so until Galileo's fateful omission is recovered. Latour shows that the social coordination and distribution of mathematical symbol systems that structure the success of modern science, but were ignored by it, completely contradict modernity's positivist and empiricist rhetoric.

So how do we follow mathematization where it leads? Can we catch a glimpse of how to routinize a method that reinvigorates the root metaphor of playfully following after (meta-) on the path (odos) of the things themselves? How do we recover what Galileo and Descartes thought too simple and self-evident to require enumeration?

Of special interest in answering these questions will be the way in which the playful dialectics of signification absorb players into language games (Gadamer 1989, pp. 101-34; Wittgenstein, 1958), lifting the burden of initiation, so that the symbol gives rise to thought (Ricoeur, 1967b). The acute significance of play is its facilitation of what Heidegger (Heidegger, 1966) calls *Gelassenheit*, usually translated as releasement, an absence of willing that lets things be what they are. It appears that technology defines and enframes the terrain and rules of a particular language game. What language, algebraic symbolization, and technology all share in common is their manner of both facilitating practice by making technical processes accessible to nontechnical users and concealing their inner workings as soon as they become effective. The mathematical coordination of figure and meaning that fully exhausts a symbol by absorbing all that it can signify from it, as occurs in full metrological quantification, is a play in the game of life that defines subjects as subjects, no matter if they are linguistic, algebraic, or technical.

The problem is how to effect the transition from being the passive subjects of whichever mathematical objects happen to emerge and absorb us to being active subjects deliberately and poetically dwelling among mathematical objects we have played an overt, conscious role in choosing and crafting, even as we admit to having no control over the paradigmatic constraints of subjectivity itself. How well might metrology serve as the medium of this transition? An initial posing of this question can begin from consideration of a remarkable coincidence in the history of the physical sciences.

Metrology in the Second Scientific Revolution of 1840

The two phases of metrology emphasize the role of instrument ruggedness testing in assuring a variable quantitative status. They also show that quantification is incomplete until different measurers equate their instruments and agree on basic conventions concerning data quality, unit size and range. Psychosocial measurement theoreticians and practitioners have experimented with forms of ruggedness testing for decades (Andrich, 1978, 1985; Engelhard, 1984, 1994; Rasch, 1960; Wright, 1968, 1984, 1997, 1999; Fischer, 1989). But this work has taken place with no acknowledgment of the crucial role played by the second phase of metrology in the successes of the natural sciences (Latour, 1987; O'Connell, 1993). That metrology as a whole, and interlaboratory trials in particular, have been systematically ignored by the human sciences that follow from philosophers and scientists' tendencies to emphasize data or theory as the primary explanations for scientific progress. Ethical, social, economic, and aesthetic explanations have become of interest only recently, as has concern with technology.

The scientific revolution of the 17th century is roughly analogous to the first phase of metrological study in which the initial viability of quantification is tested and established. In other words, the incompletely understood but, nonetheless, effective mathematical symbolizations of the 17th century constituted, via astronomy and mechanics, a kind of ruggedness test of the metaphor that the universe is mathematical. The machine-power technology [that] develops only in the second half of the eighteenth century (Heidegger, 1977, p. 304) would then be roughly analogous with the original instantiation of the second phase of metrological study, wherein the first phase's determination that the mechanistic, clockwork universe exists is generalized via practical applications distributed throughout economic and scientific networks.

That new forms of technology arrive in the wake of the scientific revolution is usually taken to mean that technology develops from scientific theory and experimental practice, but as Heidegger and others (Price, 1986, pp. 240, 248) point out, that is mistaken. Instead, technology and instrumentation drive theory and data collection (Hankins and Silverman, 1999) as is shown by the influence of the steam engine on thermodynamics and of the electric battery on chemistry. Technology seems to build on itself in a way that suggests that the birth of mathematical symbolization was a crucial event that created a context for the emergence of yet more complex mechanical extensions of itself. As Wittgenstein (Wittgenstein, 1983, p. 381) put it, mathematics teaches you not just the answer to a question, but a whole language-game with questions and answers. Algebraic symbolization allowed people to see common abstract relationships across different concrete applications, an insight that contributed to the emergence of both the concept of the mechanical, clockwork universe and the industrial age. The abstract generalization of mathematical relationships stimulated a significant amount of new and imaginative thinking. Basalla documents the emergence of playful technological fantasies and dreams published between the 15th and 19th centuries in Western Europe (Basalla, 1988, pp. 66-78) in a cultural context that increasingly rewarded novelty and the domination of nature (Basalla, 1988, pp. 129-33).

But algebraic symbolization and the emergence of new technologies in the late 18th century are insufficient markers for the full quantification of the natural sciences. In fact, the only sufficient marker for indicating the quantitative coordination of multiple laboratories would be the emergence of metrology itself as a legally sanctioned and professional discipline. In this regard, consider a passage from the work of the historian of science, Thomas Kuhn, on what he calls the second scientific revolution. In his 1961 paper on the function of measurement in the physical sciences, Kuhn (Kuhn, 1961, 1977, pp. 219-21) speculates on the reasons why the productivity and mathematical focus of these sciences seem to rapidly increase at some point between 1800 and 1850, and most notably around 1840. The role of metrology is glaring in its absence from Kuhn's speculations.

Metrology's absence is highlighted in Hacking's comments on this passage from Kuhn. Hacking (Hacking, 1983 p. 235) points out that Charles Babbage published a pamphlet in 1832 urging the compilation and dissemination of tables of physical constants. Constants of various kinds had been accumulating for some time, but Babbage can be credited with summing these up in a way that gave new voice and emphasis to the ancient Pythagorean metaphysics that the world is number, leading to modernity's virtual certainty that the universe is inherently a mathematically uniform standing reserve, or resource well.

It is important to recall in this context Latour's (Latour, 1987, pp. 251, 168) observation that constant is a nice word that simultaneously promotes and takes advantage of the unquestioned metaphysical assumption of the universe as inherently mathematical. Latour stresses that common usage of the term, thus, concealing the fact that these so remarkably invariant constants have not simply presented themselves to us fully formed, but are incredibly expensive to maintain. The U.S. annually spends more than twice as much on monitoring constants' values via metrology (6 percent of the U.S. GNP (Hunter, 1980)) as it does on research and development as a whole (less than 3 percent of the U.S. GNP, 1981 to 1994 (Subcommittee on Research, 1996)). The U.S. metrology expenditures are practically three times as much as what is allocated to non-military R and D (Subcommittee on Research, 1996).

The infrastructural support that metrology provides to scientific research prompts a question that Kuhn, Hacking, and Latour do not ask: What role might metrology have played in the consolidated mathematical physics that emerged around 1840? Historians show that its timing for having a role is perfect:

> The Imperial Weights and Measures Act [of 1824] revolutionized British metrology. All previous decrees, assizes, orders-in-council, ordinances, and statutes were repealed. Parliament broke irretrievably with the past and created a new law, one which in conjunction with the act of 1878 determined the fundamental course of British weights and measures until the seventh decade of the twentieth century (Zupko, 1977, p. 97).

Several committees meeting during the years 1819-23 drew up a series of proposals that would form the basis for the Imperial Weights and Measures Act of 1824. Additional committees were appointed thereafter (such as the Airy commission of 1838-41, which considered the relationship between physical standards and measurement units on both the decimal and duodecimal scales; the Standards Commission of 1843, responsible for the construction of new linear and weight standards in 1855; and the Select Committee of 1862, which recommended the adoption of the metric system) and they were chiefly responsible for most of the changes that occurred in imperial metrology throughout the nineteenth and twentieth centuries (Zupko, 1977, p. 96).

Parliament was also instrumental in weeding out most part-time officials from the enormous bureaucratic network of weights and measures administration and in replacing them in the late eighteenth and early nineteenth centuries with a competent, experienced, full-time, professional inspectorate (Zupko, 1977, p. 95).

In 1798, European scientists were invited to France to take part in perfecting the [metric] system. In 1799, the national legislature of France ratified the new standards. The legislation of 1799 made the metric system the sole legal pattern for measuring lengths, areas, volumes, and weights in France. Actually, however, it left a good many loopholes, and these loopholes were expanded after the coup d'etat ... [and] common people, in everyday market transactions, continued to employ the old familiar units *pouces*, *livre*, *bosseaux*, and others. In 1812, in fact, this mixed state of affairs was legalized ... Only in 1837 did France abolish the non-metric units and impose fines for their use. By then, too, the metric system had made headway in other countries (Klein, 1974, pp. 124-5).

The multiplicity of weights and measures, which afflicted, and indeed still afflicts, the world was first replaced by a logical and convenient decimal system by the French. A Report was presented to the National Assembly in 1791; the necessary measurements were finished and adopted in 1799; the system was made permissive in 1812, and compulsory in 1820 (Dampier, 1942, p. 224). The post-1830 Bourbon monarchy restored the metric system in its purity by the decree of 4, July 1837 (binding from 1, January 1840) (Kula, 1986, p. 263).

Though this evidence is not conclusive as to the effect that metrological standards may have had in the full mathematization of physics, and though, as Kuhn notes, many other changes were occurring at this time in scientific organizations, in industrial applications of science and technology, and in science education, the simultaneity is highly unlikely to be a mere coincidence. Given the acknowledged role of instruments in the creation, systematic control, public availability, and understanding of phenomena (Heelan, 1983; Price, 1986; Ihde, 1991; Bud and Cozzens, 1992; Van Helden and Hankins, 1994; Hankins and Silverman, 1999), metrological standardization is likely to have played a key role in consummating the quantification of the physical sciences, and in concomitantly concealing effective understanding of that quantification via its transparent effectiveness.

At the close of his speculations concerning the change in the character of research in the physical sciences that he supposes to have occurred around 1840, Kuhn (Kuhn, 1977, p. 221) offers the following paradox:

> The full and intimate quantification of any science is a consummation devoutly to be wished. Nevertheless, it is not a consummation that can effectively be sought by measuring. As in individual development, so in the scientific group, maturity comes most surely to those who know how to wait.

If an analogy can be made between the natural and human sciences, it is not likely, then, that the quantification of the human sciences will be achieved by simply continuing to measure. Rather, following from the stress that Kuhn (Kuhn, 1977, p. 219) himself gives the matter, because the road from scientific law to scientific measurement can rarely be traveled in the reverse direction, we must seek scientific laws, like those being discovered/created via application of Rasch's probabilistic conjoint measurement models, that are capable of supporting the construction of psychosocial metrology systems. Without the metrology systems, researchers and practitioners do not have shared expectations as to what numbers they ought to be obtaining, and they therefore necessarily do not share common frames of reference for interpreting their instrument readings.

Kuhn (Kuhn, 1977, p. 219) expands on the point: "To discover quantitative regularity one must normally know what regularity one is seeking and *one's instruments must be designed accordingly* [my emphasis]; even then nature may not yield consistent or generalizable results without a struggle". Given that different psychosocial instrument calibration experiments (intralaboratory ruggedness tests) exhibit strikingly invariant regularities (Fisher, 1997a, 1997b, 1999), perhaps the time to wait for the maturation of the human sciences is over, and the time to design instruments systematically according to the regularities required for generalizable uniform data standards has come. Indeed, for some, the time for waiting was over decades ago (Thurstone, 1926, 1928; Guttman, 1944; Loevinger, 1957; Rasch, 1960; Luce and Tukey, 1964; Choppin, 1968; Wright, 1968). As Kuhn indicates, consistent, generalizable results are not achieved without a struggle. The tools necessary for taking up the struggle are readily available, however, and their use over the last several decades has produced a number of encouraging successes.

Metaphysics and Ruggedness Tests in Psychosocial Research

Over the course of the 20th century, psychologists adopted unexamined assumptions as to why fields of study are scientific to the extent they are mathematical, resulting in a definition of measurement so inflated as to rule out none of their methods (Michell, 1990, p. 9, 1997, 1999, 2000). Michell asserts that, rather than simply accepting virtually any use of number as valid, psychologists should have treated the quantitative status of its variables as a hypothesis to be tested.

Intralaboratory ruggedness evaluations are the crucial experimental tests (Thurstone, 1928) in which the hypothesis that the variable is quantitative is tested, to appropriate Michell's (Michell, 1990) language. In the development of new instruments intended to measure a new variable, the variable must first be established as quantitative, i.e., as exhibiting the specific properties required for fundamental measurement. These properties have been specified in a number of different ways over the course of the last 100 years or more, quite possibly first by Peirce (1878; Linacre, 2000), and are effectively and efficiently expressed by Rasch's parameter separability theorem (Wright, 1999). When parameter separation is achieved in the implementation of one of Rasch's models, the rigorous independence of figure and meaning has been demonstrated, and the hypothesis that the variable is quantitative has not been falsified.

Following from the inferential requirements of Rasch's (Rasch, 1961, 1960, 1977) separability theorem, Thurstone's (Thurstone, 1928) crucial experimental test, Fisher's (Fisher, 1922) concept of statistical sufficiency, and the principle of conjoint additivity (Luce and Tukey, 1964; Krantz, Luce, Suppes and Tversky, 1971), mathematically objective quantification is achieved when the criteria of ordinality and additivity are met (Andersen, 1977, 1980; Perline, Wright and Wainer, 1979; Wright and

Stone, 1979; Wright, 1985, 1999; Michell, 1990). Simply put, a person with a higher score than another must have a higher probability of success on any test item sampled from the relevant population of items, and an item with a higher score than another must have a higher probability of provoking success for any person sampled from the relevant population of persons (Rasch, 1960). In other words, the questions included in an instrument must exhibit a unique and constant (invariant) order and spacing on the variable (the ruler, the number line) that remains the same across all persons tested within the ranges of each item's error estimate. Conversely, the persons measured must also take up an invariant order and spacing that remains the same no matter which item's responses are examined within the range of each person's error estimate.

Though this sounds like a very exacting test to pass, many instruments that were not designed to produce data meeting these requirements in fact do. And the successes achieved to date are not isolated examples internally consistent with their own requirements, but inconsistent with the results of other studies on other samples using other instruments. On the contrary, the emergent consistencies are such that it is not too early to speak of a nascent psychosocial metrology (Fisher, 2000b).

The consistent emergence and re-emergence of the same constructs across different instrument calibration studies involving different respondent samples from the same populations gives voice to phenomena as agents in the creation of uniform data standards. A series of published studies shows the remarkable consistency with which the physical functioning construct emerges across samples of assessment items, across patient self-report and clinical observation formats, and across samples of respondents.

In one study (Fisher, 1997a), eleven published Rasch calibrations of four clinician-based functional assessments were compared. Patients were universally sampled from the population of physical medicine and rehabilitation clients. Sample sizes ranged from about 50 to over 26,000. Each of the instruments assessed physical functioning in the areas of mobility and activity of daily living (ADL) skills. Patients' abilities to climb stairs, feed, dress, and bathe themselves, walk, and get in and out of chairs were rated by physical and occupational therapists. In the use of one instrument, ratings were dichotomous; the data indicated merely whether or not the patient could perform the task unassisted. Another instrument used a four-point rating system, and the two others used two different seven-point rating systems. All ratings extended from unable to perform the task to able to perform it within normal limits.

A single measurement construct emerged across all of the studies, one in which feeding was the easiest task to perform, and stair climbing the hardest. Upper extremity dressing and bathing were easier than lower extremity dressing and bathing. Getting in and out of a chair was about the same difficulty as toileting, and both were easier than walking. There was an average .93 correlation, with a mode of .98, among the 11 sets of item difficulty orders, with about seven similar items included on average across the scales. Even though these instruments were not designed to meet the rigorous requirements of fundamental measurement theory, it appears that the data they produce is sufficient or nearly sufficient for supporting a single reference standard metric for measuring physical functioning.

In a further study (Mayes, Perez, Mipro and Fisher, 1996; Qayum, et al., 1996), data were obtained from one of the instruments included in the Fisher (1997a) study from a small sample of about 100 local rehabilitation patients. The results of the small local study nearly exactly reproduced the results of the large national study with all but one of 18 item calibrations falling within an error of the position on the variable taken in the national study of 26,000 patients.

Third, a large class of studies (for instance, Choppin, 1976; Lunz and Bergstrom, 1991; Bergstrom and Lunz, 1994; Fisher, Harvey, Taylor, Kilgore and Kelly, 1995; Cella, Lloyd and Wright, 1996; Gonin, Lloyd and Cella, 1996; Grimby, et al., 1996; Adams, Wu and Macaskill, 1997; Fisher, Eubanks and Marier, 1997; Segal, Heinemann, Schall and Wright, 1997; Zhu, 1998) explores the extent to which different instruments, or collections of items from a bank, intended to measure the same variable actually do. These studies obtain data from two or more instruments on a common sample to study the relationships between the two sets of item difficulty calibrations. Results are largely positive, with different but similar items usually calibrating to within an error or two of each other. Methods for conducting these studies are readily available in the published literature (Engelhard and Osberg, 1983; Wright and Bell, 1984; Masters, 1985; Holmes, 1986; Kelderman, 1986; Glas, 1988; Smith and Kramer, 1992; Baker, 1993, 1996; Woodcock and Munoz-Sandoval, 1993; Wright, 1993; Kolen and Brennan, 1995; Wolfe, 2000).

Fourth, the item difficulty calibrations obtained from eight different samples of patients responding to a ten-item physical functioning survey (Ware, Snow, Kosinski and Gandek, 1993; Raczek, et al., 1998) were compared (Fisher, 1999). Even though the samples differed considerably in their degrees of health and illness, as well as in other demographic characteristics, there was still a .90 average correlation in item difficulties across studies. Notably, the patients self-assessed physical functioning resulted in a task difficulty order very similar to that produced by the clinicians' assessments in the first two sets of studies summarized above.

The uniformity of these results strongly suggests that these studies are providing initial glimpses into invisible but ubiquitous and leveragable mathematically abstract, objective phenomena. As these results accumulate, it will become increasingly apparent that marked enhancements in the communication and application of research results could follow from the implementation of common metric structures, or reference standards, for each of the several (20?, 200?, 2 000?) variables central to research in the human sciences. We could allow these uniformities to emerge haphazardly in their own time, or we might seize the bull by the horns and undertake a more deliberate approach to their creation in the form of a broad-based initiative analogous to the human genome project. Either way, given the deeply embedded historical and metaphysical values playing themselves out in this arena, the birth of a psychosocial metrology seems a virtual inevitability.

An Agenda for the Full Metrological Quantification of Psychosocial Variables

Scientific laws appear to take a unique form closely related to the scale-free structures of fundamental measurement (Krantz, et al., 1971), as is suggested by the fact that "scientists frequently neglect to specify the various scales entering in the equations" related to various empirical laws (Falmagne and Narens, 1983, p. 287). The implication is that we may have to await fundamental measurement before we will see any real progress in quantitative laws of behavior (Ramsay, 1975, p. 262) since scale-dependence effectively precludes obtaining the needed scientific generalizability. Contrary to early and influential opinions (Campbell, 1920; Likert, 1932; Guild, 1938) that impaired the development of psychology by binding it to the hidden and incomplete metaphysics of Galileo's fateful omission, fundamental measurement is neither theoretically impossible in the human sciences (Krantz, et al., 1971, p. 123; Luce and Tukey, 1964; Perline, et al., 1979; Wright, 1984, 1985, 1999; Andrich, 1988), nor is it so difficult as to be impractical (Wright and Stone, 1979; Wright and Masters, 1982; Fisher and Wright, 1994; Bond and Fox, 2001).

Precisely, however, because fundamental measurement is lacking, and because vulnerability to falsification of the quantitative hypothesis is seen in the human sciences as a methodological weakness rather than a strength (Michell, 1990, 1997, 1999, 2000), one approach to measurement is widely viewed as good as another. Advocates of strong measurement theory are often viewed as zealots bent on converting the heathen masses to their version of the one true religion. Consideration of the role played by metrology in actualizing the mathematical metaphysics of science, however, makes it especially apparent that the reader who believes that all that is at stake in the axiomatic treatment of measurement is a possible criterion for canonizing one scaling procedure at the expense of others is missing the point (Ramsay, 1975, p. 262).

The point has two parts. The first is that observations of abilities, attitudes, performances, and any number of other intangible measurement constructs can be arranged to satisfy the axioms of fundamental measurement theory and to add up in a manner consistent with numeric structure. The second is that quantification is not complete until measurement results in a single numeric estimate, within a range of error, for a given amount of a variable, available at the point of use, no matter which brand or configuration of an instrument type is employed, no matter who is measured by whom, or where or when the measure occurs. In order for a community of researchers to think and theorize together, they must share a common symbol system. The quantitative symbol systems of the human sciences will be significantly less meaningful than they could be, due to the scale-dependence of their truth-values (Mundy, 1986), until deliberate efforts toward the construction and maintenance of reference standard metrics are undertaken. The very strong implication of even cursory comparison of measurement quality across the natural and human sciences is that Kuhn is very probably correct in his sense of full quantification as following from established scientific laws. Given the proven capacity of fundamental measurement theory in the discovery and invention of such laws, most notably as implemented in the human sciences via Rasch's probabilistic conjoint measurement models, we should therefore deliberately and aggressively implement the following five-part agenda.

First, we must create a context in which the possibility and meaning of fully quantifying the variables of the human sciences is appreciated and understood. This will require educational efforts on the parts of professional associations aimed at end users (teachers, clinicians, human resource personnel, researchers, etc.) and the graduate training programs for professionals in the human sciences. Since it so often happens in the history of science that new technical innovations are often first adopted in business and industry (Rabkin, 1987; Rabkin, 1992), leaders in these areas should be informed of the communicative, evaluative, and competitive advantages to be gained. Their existing appreciation for uniform data standards will make this a relatively easy sale; they are, furthermore, already aware of the limitations imposed on them by existing methods and are actively searching for a new paradigm (Fitz-enz, 2000; Flamholtz, 1999).

Second, existing instruments should be leveraged for their value as initial steps into intralaboratory tests of the quantitative hypothesis. But, contrary to what is the case to date, analyses of existing data and instruments should neither remain disconnected from other analyses of similar data and instruments, nor should fairly good model fit be interpreted as an indication that the instrument need not be improved. One of the strong advantages of Rasch's probabilistic conjoint models of fundamental measurement is that instruments can be continuously quality assessed, modified and improved without making new data incommensurable with old (Wright and Stone, 1979; Holm and Kavanagh, 1985). Researchers interested in collaborating in the creation of common quantitative metrics and in approximating needed degrees of precision relative to a reference standard will need to accustom themselves to the demands of continuous quality assessment and improvement. These demands have gone unheeded in the current culture of psychosocial instrumentation because of the scale-dependency of the data; changes to the instrument necessarily make new data incommensurable with old. Probabilistic models for measurement make this unrealistically cumbersome constraint obsolete.

Third, research into reference standards for each variable will seek to identify the extreme ends of the measurement range, to find the smallest observable difference that can be consistently maintained, and to elaborate a comprehensive theory of the variable. These tasks will be accomplished through the comparison and contrast of the data/instrument reliabilities and internal consistencies obtained through different observational frameworks (performance assessment vs. self-report survey or multiple choice test, for instance). Individual applications necessarily vary in the amount of error they can tolerate. Few will need to measure at the reference standard level of detail and reliability, but the existence of that standard will make the construction of instruments exhibiting the needed properties much more systematic and efficient, largely via the implementation of item banking principles (Choppin, 1968, 1976; Wright and Bell, 1984; Masters and Evans, 1986; Van der Linden, 1986; Lunz, Bergstrom and Gershon, 1994; Revicki and Cella, 1997; McHorney, 1997; Wolfe, 2000).

Fourth, simultaneous with the development of reference standard expressions of each variable, existing, improved, and new instruments should be calibrated, in unison on common samples, with the aim of connecting them all into the reference standard's common metric. Differences and incommensurability across instruments will surely arise, concomitantly with the usual theoretical disagreements and controversies. If there is to be any difference between these arguments and existing ones that may appear to already address these issues, there will have to be an overall consensus on the value of obtaining parameter separation via the substantiation of the requirement that the raw scores are sufficient statistics. Given the values of the contemporary psychosocial measurement culture (Divgi, 1986; Goldstein, 1979, 1983; Goldstein and Blinkhorn, 1977; Hambleton, Swaminathan and Rogers, 1991; Wood, 1978; van der Linden and Hambleton, 1997), there is little reason to hope that this overall consensus will emerge any time soon. The current human sciences measurement climate supports sacrificing parameter separation, conjoint additivity, sufficiency, and the potential for trace ability to reference standards in the name of fitting ever more flexible models to whatever data happen to cross the threshold (Wright, 1968, 1984, 1997, 1999; Wilson, 1971; Wright and Linacre, 1989; Michell, 1990, 1997, 1999, 2000; Fisher, 1994; Zhu, 1996). If this attitude continues to hold sway, the needed additional constraints on the data domain that the human sciences require for more dramatic progress (Ackermann, 1985, p. 169) will not be obtained, and the metrological project will fail. If, on the other hand, the parametric convergence and separation of figure and meaning implied in the simple use of language in predication (Nagel, 1932, p. 313; Ricoeur, 1977; Fisher, 2000a) is understood for its fundamental role in the propagation of communities of researchers and the networks through which they share and exchange value, the metrological project will succeed.

Fifth, once the initial research of calibrating reference standards and connecting individual instruments to them is complete, routine methods for managing the metrology system analogous to those employed for physical variables (Pennella, 1997) will be required. Metrology's regular periodic studies of instrument functioning relative to other similar instruments and the reference standard will make it possible to maintain the accuracy and precision of the distributed process through which theory develops and the collective intelligence organizes itself. A standard procedure for creating and maintaining reference standard metrics is being drafted under the auspices of the *American Society for Testing and Materials* (Fisher, 1996).

Concluding Comments

Why does metrology matter? The answers to this question falls into two main categories relating to human and economic values. When the variables of the human sciences are effectively quantified, then psychosocial reality will be made available for humanity's self-empowerment and self-knowledge in ways never before imagined. Those who understand and act on this insight earliest will be the leaders of a new scientific and cultural revolution, one of the magnitude described by Crosby (Crosby, 1997). Crosby (Crosby, 1997, p. x) shows that the unity of mathematics and measurement in a quantitative model of the natural world is why, between 1250 and 1600, Europeans "were able to organize large collections of people and capital and to exploit physical reality for useful knowledge and for power more efficiently than any other people of the time". It can be reasonably expected that the similar unification of mathematics and measurement in a quantitative model of the psychosocial world will also enable new magnitudes of efficiency and effectiveness to be achieved in caring human relations.

Economic Reasons for Making Metrology Matter

The economic value of psychosocial metrology could be huge. The United States National Institute of Standards and Technology estimated the economic impact of 12 areas of research in metrology, in four broad areas including semiconductors, electrical calibration and testing, optical industries, and computer systems (Subcommittee on Research, 1996, Appendix C). The median rate of return in these 12 areas was 147 percent, and returns ranged from 41 to 428 percent. The report notes that these results compare favorably with those obtained in similar studies of return rates from other public and private research and development efforts. Even if psychosocial metrology produces only a small fraction of the return rate produced in physical metrology, its economic impact could still amount to billions of dollars annually.

Success in quantification of the psychosocial world on this level will raise measurement in the human sciences out of its current scale- and sample-dependent quagmire to a new kind of generality. Measures of human abilities and the effects of particular training or medical treatment programs will no longer be expressed in idiosyncratic units of measurement tied to particular collections of questions administered to particular samples of examinees or respondents. Instead, every collection, of questions purported to measure a particular variable will be linked via traceable connections to a reference standard metric, making it possible for every particular quantitative expression of that variable to share a common numeric meaning.

In the same way that amounts of commodities such as gold, wheat, milk, or electrical potential are measured in units that remain constant across businesses, consumers, investors, governments, and particular applications within any given sphere, so too job skills, mathematics and spelling ability, attitudes, performances, and physical, psychosocial, and cognitive health status be measured. The establishment of reference standard metrics for the variables of the human sciences will be tantamount to commodifying these variables. The quantitative stability of the amounts measured will lend themselves for use as common currencies for the exchange of the value expressed.

Fitz-enz (Fitz-enz, 2000), along with others writing under the headings of human resource accounting, organizational learning theory, intangibles research, knowledge management, and information capital, show that, even in the absence of psychosocial metrology, the systematic assessment of human capital can lead to knowledge powerful for its bottom-line financial implications. Fitz-enz (Fitz-enz, 2000, pp. 114-5) despairs of being able to obtain the needed direct measures of transferability, promotability, productivity, and retainability proposed by Flamholtz (Flamholtz, 1999) and others, and so proposes alternative indirect measures. The need for these alternatives will remain until psychosocial metrology is systematically instituted on a scale as broad as other metrological initiatives.

Human Reasons for Making Metrology Matter

The question of a measured, mathematically coordinated ethics cannot ask only: Why are things as they are? It must also ask why are things as they are, and not different? The concrete, ordinal, qualitative, and sample-dependent observations of individuals from which abstract, interval, quantitative, and sample-free measures are created cannot be erased, forgotten, or ignored without risking the viability of the concept of a human science as a whole. Therefore, it is significant that most readily available software programs for testing parameter separability, for example, ConQuest (Wu, Adams and Wilson, 1998), RUMM (Andrich, Lyne, Sheridan and Luo, 2000), WINSTEPS (Wright and Linacre, 1999), and FACETS (Linacre, 1995), routinely provide statistical estimates of error ranges and the internal consistency of the measures for each person and item. Thus, the phrases full mathematization or full quantification or sample-free do not in any way imply a deterministic, perfectly repeatable and reproducible, error-free, or ultimately transparent measure. Measures derived from probabilistic models demanding sufficient statistics and separable parameters facilitate understanding of the social processes that generate psychosocial data (Duncan, 1984; Rogosa, 1987), but not to the extent that any body of theory, data, or instrumentation will have the final word. Instruments are texts, and as such they are read and interpreted. Interpretation is always open to re-interpretation.

The model fit statistics, or data quality indices (Andersen, 1973; Wright and Stone, 1979; Gustafsson, 1980; Wright and Masters, 1982; Smith, 1986, 1991, 2000; Andrich, 1988; Adams and Wright, 1994), estimated for each person measured and for each test or survey item calibrated are of special importance since these, in combination with the error estimates, reveal individuality within the framework of the achieved consensus. Statistically improbable degrees of individuality preclude parameter separation and the comparison of measures, though the structure of measurement can be adapted to culturally-relevant differences via the probabilistic model's capacity to take missing data into account. Failures to obtain the anticipated confirmation of the projected mathematical structure are often the most interesting results of an experiment and have the greatest potential for provoking productive new lines of questioning (Kuhn, 1961; Wimsatt, 1981), for revealing data entry errors or idiosyncratic response styles (Wright, 1977; Wright and Stone, 1979), and for maintaining fair and just bases for the comparison of measures.

But even when anomalous responses are minimized and the goal of mathematical coordination is fairly well realized (as indicated by conformity with theoretical expectations, the ratio of variation to error or separation reliability, and model fit), the data quality indices signify the qualitative uniqueness of individuals and force us to recall that every person is more than their measure on any variable. Ballard (Ballard, 1978, p. 189) states the following:

> However useful concepts of individuals having properties in common may be, such concepts can be used in an investigative enterprise only under the shadow of a real or feigned ignorance of the individual's uniqueness. A subjectivity disciplined in the objective dialectic and skilled in the arts of measurement is also a subjectivity, which has learned to ignore uniqueness. But ignoring an individuals uniqueness may upon occasion be a major loss. The loss can be disastrous when the ignorance is real. The qualitative measure of a man by reference to a job description, to a definition of some required role, or to some moral ideal belonging to a culture is often necessary, but this measurement is justified and sophisticated only when reparation is made by recalling the uniqueness of the person measured. Otherwise, the abstraction does him violence.

Borgmann (Borgmann, 1984, p. 161), writing with much the same sentiment as Ballard, contends that a call for caring within the context of efforts aimed at reforming our relationship with technology makes sense only within a reform proposal that recognizes and fruitfully counters the technological tendency to disburden and disengage us from the care of things or each other. How can technology's inherently playful extension of language games and the interplays of mathematically coordinated signification be prevented from disengaging us from care?

Ballard provides some important clues. He (Ballard, 1978, p. 187) is explicitly concerned with a notion of the pre-mathematical numbers on which more fully mathematical measures are based, saying that such units cannot be used in counting objects but only for referring to objects before abstraction from their unique being has been made. These dialogical numbers are too variable and inconsistent to function as a basis for comparison, as Ballard recognizes. Insofar, however, as they tell both a story of each individual measured, and, via their overall consistency and calibration into an abstract variable, the story of the population of persons sampled in a measurement experiment, pre-mathematical, dialogical numbers take their place as the concrete, qualitative, ordinal observations from which abstract, quantitative, interval measures are created. The violence of abstraction is countered effectively by recalling the uniqueness of individuals via data quality indices; the previously mentioned model fit statistics reveal the sufficiency or insufficiency of the observations relative to a generalizable inference.

To the extent that psychosocial metrology contributes to the realization of the caring professions' innermost possibilities, the commodification of the variables of the human sciences will not result so much in an extension of the consumer culture as it does in a means of more effectively balancing it with alternatives. Consumption uses up an isolated entity without preparation, resonance, or consequences (Borgmann, 1984, p. 51). Fulfilled caring relations are concerned with the interrelations and connections through which we prepare for life in education, resonate with one another psychologically and socially, and deal with the consequences of life events. Insofar as improved measurement enhances our engagements with each other and our integration with the natural environment, there are strong reasons for believing that the best in human history is yet to come.

References

Ackermann, J. R. (1985), *Data, Instruments, and Theory: A Dialectical Approach to Understanding Science*. Princeton: Princeton University Press.

Adams, R. J., and Wright, B. D. (1994), "When does misfit make a difference?" In M. Wilson (Ed.), *Objective Measurement: Theory into Practice*, vol. 2, pp. 244-270. Norwood: Ablex.

Adams, R. J., Wu, M. L., and Macaskill, G. (1997), "Scaling methodology and procedures for the mathematics and science scales". In M. O. Martin and D. L. Kelly (Eds.), *Third International Mathematics and Science Study Technical Report. vol. 2: Implementation and Analysis – Primary and Middle School Years*. Boston: Center for the Study of Testing, Evaluation, and Educational Policy.

Andersen, E. B. (1973), "A goodness of fit test for the Rasch model". *Psychometrika*, vol. 38, pp. 123-140.

Andersen, E. B. (1977), "Sufficient statistics and latent trait models". *Psychometrika*, vol. 42, no. 1, pp. 69-81.

Andersen, E. B. (1980), *Discrete statistical models with social science applications*. Amsterdam: North-Holland.

Andrich, D. (1978), "Relationships between the Thurstone and Rasch approaches to item scaling". Applied Psychological Measurement, vol. 2, pp. 449-460.

Andrich, D. (1985), "An elaboration of Guttman scaling with Rasch models for measurement". In N. B. Tuma (Ed.), *Sociological methodology*, pp. 33-80. San Francisco: Jossey-Bass.

Andrich, D. (1988), "Rasch models for measurement". Sage University Paper Series on Quantitative Applications in the Social Sciences, vol. series no. 07-068. Beverly Hills, California: Sage Publications.

Andrich, D., Lyne, A., Sheridan, B., and Luo, G. (2000), *RUMM: Rasch Unidimensional Models for Measurement.* Perth, Australia: RUMM Laboratory Pty Ltd.

Baker, F. B. (1993), "Equating tests under the nominal response model". *Applied Psychological Measurement*, vol. 17, no. 3, pp. 239-251.

Baker, F. B. (1996), "An investigation of the sampling distributions of equating coefficients". *Applied Psychological Measurement*, vol. 20, no. 1, pp. 45-57.

Ballard, E. G. (1978), *Man and Technology: Toward the Measurement of a Culture.* Pittsburgh: Duquesne University Press.

Basalla, G. (1988), *The Evolution of Technology* (G. Basalla and W. Coleman, Eds.). Cambridge History of Science Series. New York: Cambridge University Press.

Bell, E. T. (1931), *The Queen of the Sciences*. Baltimore: Williams and Wilkins.

Bergstrom, B. A., and Lunz, M. E. (1994), "The equivalence of Rasch item calibrations and ability estimates across modes of administration". In M. Wilson (Ed.), *Objective Measurement: Theory into Practice*, vol. 2, pp. 122-128. Norwood: Ablex Publishing Corp.

Bochner, S. (1966), *The Role of Mathematics in the Rise of Science*. Princeton: Princeton University Press.

Bond, T., and Fox, C. (2001), *Fundamental Measurement in the Human Sciences: Applying the Rasch Model*. Hillsdale: Lawrence Erlbaum Associates.

Borgmann, A. (1984), *Technology and the Character of Contemporary Life: A Philosophical Inquiry*. Chicago: University of Chicago Press.

Bud, R., and Cozzens, S. E. (Eds). (1992), SPIE Institutes. vol 9: Invisible connections: Instruments, institutions, and science (F. Potter, Ed.) (Vol. 9). Bellingham, WA: SPIE Optical Engineering Press.

Campbell, N. R. (1920), *Physics, the Elements*. Cambridge: Cambridge University Press.

Caputo, J. D. (1997), "A commentary". In J. D. Caputo (Ed.), *Deconstruction in a Nutshell: A Conversation with Jacques Derrida* (31-202). New York: Fordham University Press.

Cella, D. F., Lloyd, S. R., and Wright, B. D. (1996), "Cross-cultural instrument equating: Current research and future directions". In B. Spilker (Ed.), *Quality of Life and Pharmacoeconomics in Clinical Trials* (2nd edition) (707-715). New York: Lippincott-Raven.

Choppin, B. (1968), "An item bank using sample-free calibration". *Nature*, vol. 219, pp. 870-872.

Choppin, B. (1976), "Recent developments in item banking". In D. N. M. DeGruitjer and L. J. van der Kamp (Eds.), *Advances in Psychological and Educational Measurement* (233-245). New York: Wiley.

Clancey, W. J. (1997), *Situated cognition: On Human Knowledge and Computer Representations*. Cambridge, England: Cambridge University Press.

Clark, A. (1998), *Being There: Putting Brain, Body, and World Together Again.* Cambridge: MIT Press.

Cliff, N. (1992), "Abstract measurement theory and the revolution that never happened". *Psychological Science*, vol. 3, pp. 186-190.

Crosby, A. W. (1997), *The Measure of Reality: Quantification and Western Society* (1250-1600). Cambridge: Cambridge University Press.

Dampier, W. C. (1942), *A History of Science and its Relations with Philosophy and Religion*. Cambridge, England: Cambridge at the University Press.

Dantzig, T. (1955), *The Bequest of the Greeks*. Macmillan: New York.

Derrida, J. (1989), *Edmund Husserl's Origin of Geometry: An Introduction*. Lincoln: University of Nebraska Press.

Descartes, R. (1961), *Rules for the Direction of the Mind*. Indianapolis: Bobbs-Merrill.

Dewey, J. (1929), *The Quest for Certainty: A Study of the Relation of Knowledge and Action*. New York: Perigee Books, G. P. Putnam's Sons.

Divgi, D. R. (1986, Winter), "Does the Rasch model really work for multiple choice items? Not if you look closely". *Journal of Educational Measurement*, vol. 23, no. 4, pp. 283-98.

Duncan, O. D. (1984), *Notes on Social Measurement: Historical and Critical*. New York: Russell Sage Foundation.

Engelhard, G., Jr. (1984), "Thorndike, Thurstone, and Rasch: A comparison of their methods of scaling psychological and educational tests". *Applied Psychological Measurement*, vol. 8, no. 1, pp. 21-38.

Engelhard, G., Jr. (1994), "Historical views of the concept of invariance in measurement theory". In M. Wilson (Ed.), *Objective Measurement: Theory into Practice*, vol. 2, pp. 73-99. Norwood, NJ: Ablex.

Engelhard, G., Jr., and Osberg, D. (1983,) "Constructing a test network with the Rasch measurement model". Applied Psychological Measurement, vol. 7, no.3, pp. 283-294.

Falmagne, J.-C. and Narens, L. (1983), "Scales and meaningfulness of quantitative laws". *Synthese*, vo. 55, pp. 287-325.

Fischer, G. H. (1974), *Einfuhrungin die theorie psychologischer tests*. Vienna: Verlag Hans Huber.

Fischer, G. H. (1989), "Applying the principles of specific objectivity and of generalizability to the measurement of change". *Psychometrika*, vol. 52, no. 4, pp. 565-587.

Fisher, R. A. (1922), On the mathematical foundations of theoretical statistics. Philosophical Transactions of the Royal Society of London, 222, 309-368.

Fisher, W. P., Jr. (1992), "Objectivity in measurement: A philosophical history of Rasch's separability theorem". In M. Wilson (Ed.), *Objective measurement: Theory into Practice*, vol. 1, pp. 29-58. Norwood: Ablex Publishing Corporation.

Fisher, W. P., Jr. (1994), "The Rasch debate: Validity and revolution in educational measurement". In *Objective Measurement: Theory Into Practice*, vol. 2 (ed. M. Wilson), pp. 36-72. Norwood: Ablex Publishing Corporation.

Fisher, W. P., Jr. (1996 Oct.), *Rating Scale Measurement Standards Relevant to ASTM 1384 on the Content and Structure of the Electronic Health r\Record*. Unpublished paper. ASTM E31 Committee on the Electronic Health Record. Washington, DC.

Fisher, W. P., Jr. (1997a), "Physical disability construct convergence across instruments: Towards a universal metric". *Journal of Outcome Measurement*, vol. 1, no. 2, pp. 87-113.

Fisher, W. P., Jr. (1997b, June), "What scale-free measurement means to health outcomes research". *Physical Medicine and Rehabilitation State of the Art Reviews*, vol. 11, no. 2, pp. 357-373.

Fisher, W. P., Jr. (1999), "Foundations for health status metrology: The stability of MOS SF-36 PF-10 calibrations across samples". *Journal of the Louisiana State Medical Society*, vol. 151, no. 11, pp. 566-578.

Fisher, W. P., Jr. (2000a), "Mathematics, measurement, metaphor, metaphysics. Parts I and II". *Journal of Theoretical and Philosophical Psychology*, in review.

Fisher, W. P., Jr. (2000b), "Objectivity in psychosocial measurement: What, why, how". *Journal of Outcome Measurement*, vol. 4, no. 2, pp. 527-563.

Fisher, W. P., Jr., and Wright, B. D. (1994), "Introduction to probabilistic conjoint measurement theory and applications". *International Journal of Educational Research*, vol. 21, no. 6, pp. 559-568.

Fisher, W. P., Jr., Eubanks, R. L., and Marier, R. L. (1997), "Equating the MOS SF36 and the LSU HSI physical functioning scales". *Journal of Outcome Measurement*, vol. 1, no. 4, pp. 329-362.

Fisher, W. P., Jr., Harvey, R. F., Taylor, P., Kilgore, K. M., and Kelly, C. K. (1995), "Rehabits: A common language of functional assessment". *Archives of Physical Medicine and Rehabilitation*, vol. 76, pp. 113-122.

Fitz-enz, J. (2000), *The ROI of Human Capital: Measuring the Economic Value of Employee Performance.* New York: AMACOM.

Flamholtz, E. G. (1999), *Human Resource Accounting: Advances in Concepts, Methods and Applications*, 3rd Edition. Boston: Kluwer Academic Publishers.

Gadamer, H.-G. (1980), *Dialogue and Dialectic: Eight Hermeneutical Studies on Plato* (P. C. Smith, trans.). New Haven: Yale University Press.

Gadamer, H.-G. (1989), *Truth and method* (J. Weinsheimer and D. G. Marshall, trans.) (Second revised edition). New York: Crossroad.

Glas, C. (1988), "Psychometric aspects of maintaining standards of examinations". *Educational Psychology*, vol. 8, no. 4, pp. 257-270.

Goldstein, H. (1979), "Consequences of using the Rasch model for educational assessment". *British Educational Research Journal*, vol. 5, no. 2, pp. 211-220.

Goldstein, H. (1983), "Measuring changes in educational attainment over time: Problems and possibilities". *Journal of Educational Measurement*, vol. 20, no. 4, pp. 369-377.

Goldstein, H., and Blinkhorn, S. (1977), "Monitoring educational standards – An inappropriate model". *Bulletin of the British Psychological Society*, vol. 30, pp. 309-311.

Gonin, R., Lloyd, S. R., and Cella, D. F. (1996, Feb.), "Establishing equivalence between scaled measures of quality of life". *Quality of Life Research*, vol. 5, no. 1, pp. 20-26.

Grimby, G., Andrén, E., Holmgren, E., Wright, B., Linacre, J. M., and Sundh, V. (1996, Nov.), "Structure of a combination of Functional Independence Measure and Instrumental Activity Measure items in community-living persons: A study of individuals with spina bifida". *Archives of Physical Medicine and Rehabilitation*, vol. 77, no. 11, pp. 1109-1114.

Guild, J. (1938), "Are sensation intensities measurable?" *British Association for the Advancement of Science*, vol. 108, pp. 296-328.

Gustafsson, J.-E. (1980), "Testing and obtaining fit of data to the Rasch model". *British Journal of Mathematical and Statistical Psychology*, vol. 33, pp. 205-233.

Guttman, L. (1944), "A basis for scaling qualitative data". *American Sociological Review*, vol. 9, pp. 139-150.

Hacking, I. (1983), *Representing and Intervening: Introductory Topics in thePphilosophy of Natural Science*. Cambridge: Cambridge University Press.

Hambleton, R. K., Swaminathan, H., and Rogers, L. (1991), *Fundamentals of Item Response Theory*. Newbury Park: Sage Publications.

Hankins, T. L., and Silverman, R. J. (1999), *Instruments and the Imagination.* Princeton: Princeton University Press.

Heath, T. L. (1931), *A Manual of Greek Mathematics*. Oxford: Oxford at the Clarendon Press.

Heelan, P. (1983, Jun.), "Natural science as a hermeneutic of instrumentation". *Philosophy of Science*, vol. 50, pp. 181-204.

Heidegger, M. (1966), *Discourse on Thinking: A Translation of Gelassenheit* (J. M. Anderson and E. H. Freund, Trans.). New York: Harper and Row.

Heidegger, M. (1967), *What is a Thing?* (W. B. Barton, Jr. and V. Deutsch, trans.). South Bend: Regnery/Gateway.

Heidegger, M. (1977), "The question concerning technology". In D. F. Krell (Ed.), *Basic Writings* (283-317). New York: Harper and Row.

Hendriks-Jansen, H. (1996), *Catching Ourselves in the Act: Situated Activity, Interactive Emergence, Evolution, and Human Thought*. Cambridge: MIT Press.

Holm, K., and Kavanagh, J. (1985), "An approach to modifying self-report instruments". *Research in Nursing and Health*, vol. 8, pp. 13-18.

Holmes, S. E. (1986, Jun.), "Test equating and credentialing examinations". *Evaluation and the Health Professions*, vol. 9, no. 2, pp. 230-249.

Hunter, J. S. (1980, Nov.), "The national system of scientific measurement". *Science*, vol. 210, no. 21, pp. 869-874.

Husserl, E. (1970), *The Crisis of European Sciences and Transcendental Phenomenology*. Evanston: Northwestern University Press.

Hutchins, E. (1994), *Cognition in the Wild*. Cambridge: MIT Press.

Ihde, D. (1991), *Instrumental Realism: The Interface Between Philosophy of Science and Philosophy of Technology. The Indiana Series in the Philosophy of Technology*. Bloomington: Indiana University Press.

Joas, H. (1993), *Pragmatism and Social Theory*. Chicago: University of Chicago Press.

Joas, H. (1997), "G.H. Mead: A contemporary re-examination of his thought" (Meyer, trans.). *Studies in Contemporary German Social Thought*. Cambridge: MIT Press.

Kelderman, H. (1986), *Common Item Equating Using the Log-linear Rasch Model*. Twente, Netherlands: Department of Education, University of Twente.

Kelso, J. A. S. (1997), *Dynamic Patterns: The Self-organization of Brain and Behavior*. Cambridge: Bradford Books.

Klein, H. A. (1974), *The World of Measurements: Masterpieces, Mysteries and Muddles of Metrology*. New York: Simon and Schuster.

Kolen, M. J., and Brennan, R. L. (1995), *Test Equating*. New York: Springer.

Krantz, D. H., Luce, R. D., Suppes, P., and Tversky, A. (1971), *Foundations of Measurement*, vol. 1: *Additive and polynomial representations*. New York: Academic Press.

Kuhn, T. S. (1961), The function of measurement in modern physical science. *Isis*, vol. 52, no. 168, pp. 161-193. In T. S. Kuhn, *The essential tension: Selected studies in scientific tradition and change*. (1977). Chicago: University of Chicago Press.

Kuhn, T. S. (1977), *The Essential Tension: Selected Studies in Scientific Tradition and Change*. Chicago: University of Chicago Press.

Kula, W. (1986), *Measures and Men* (Screter, trans.). Princeton: Princeton University Press.

Latour, B. (1987), *Science in Action: How to Follow Scientists and Engineers Through Society*. New York: Cambridge University Press.

Latour, B. (1993), *We Have Never Been Modern*. Cambridge: Harvard University Press.

Latour, B. (1994), "Pragmatogonies: A mythical account of how humans and nonhumans swap properties". *American Behavioral Scientist*, vol. 37, no. 6, pp. 791-808.

Latour, B. (1995), "Cogito ergo sumus! Or psychology swept inside out by the fresh air of the upper deck: Review of Hutchins' Cognition in the Wild". *Culture, and Activity: An International Journal*, vol. 3, no. 1, pp. 54-63.

Latour, B. (1999), *Pandora's Hope: Essays on the Reality of Science Studies*. Cambridge: Harvard University Press.

Likert, R. (1932), "A technique for the measurement of attitudes". *Archives of Psychology* vol. 140, pp. 5-55.

Linacre, J. M. (1995), *Facets Rasch Analysis Computer Program*. Chicago: MESA Press.

Linacre, J. M. (2000), *Almost the Peirce model? Rasch Measurement Transactions*, vol. 14, no. 3, pp. 756-7 [http://www.rasch.org/rmt/rmt143.htm].

Loevinger, J. (1957), "Objective tests as instruments of psychological theory". *Psychological Reports*, vol. 3, pp. 635-694.

Luce, R. D., and Tukey, J. W. (1964), "Simultaneous conjoint measurement: A new kind of fundamental measurement". *Journal of Mathematical Psychology*, vol. 1, no. 1, pp. 1-27.

Lunz, M. E., and Bergstrom, B. A. (1991), "Comparability of decision for computer adaptive and written examinations". *Journal of Allied Health*, vol. 20, no. 1, pp. 15-23.

Lunz, M. E., and Bergstrom, B. A. (1994), "An empirical study of computerized adaptive test administration conditions". *Journal of Educational Measurement*, vol. 31, no. 3, pp. 251-263.

Lunz, M. E., Bergstrom, B. A., and Gershon, R. C. (1994), "Computer adaptive testing". *International Journal of Educational Research*, vol. 21, no. 6, pp. 623-634.

Lunz, M. E., Bergstrom, B. A., and Wright, B. D. (1992, Mar.), "The effect of review on student ability and test efficiency for computerized adaptive tests". *Applied Psychological Measurement*, vol. 16, no. 1, pp. 33-40.

Mandel, J. (1977, Mar.), "The analysis of interlaboratory test data". *ASTM Standardization News*, vol. 5, pp. 17-20.

Mandel, J. (1978, Dec.), "Interlaboratory testing". *ASTM Standardization News*, vol. 6, pp. 11-12.

Marcuse, H. (1974), "On science and phenomenology". In A. Giddens (Ed.), *Positivism and Sociology* (225-236). London: Heinemann.

Masters, G. N. (1985, Mar.), "Common-person equating with the Rasch model". *Applied Psychological Measurement*, vol. 9, no. 1, pp. 73-82.

Masters, G. N., and Evans, J. (1986, Dec.), "Banking non-dichotomously scored items". *Applied Psychological Measurement*, vol. 10, no. 4, pp. 355-367.

Mayes, P., Perez, A., Mipro, R. C., Jr., and Fisher, W. P., Jr. (1996, Jun.), "Comparison of Functional Independence Measure data from the Uniform Data System and the Louisiana Rehabilitation Institute [abstract]". *LSU Deparment of Medicine, Section of Physical Medicine and Rehabilitation, Residents' Research Day*. New Orleans: LSU School of Medicine.

McHorney, C. A. (1997, Oct.), "Generic health measurement: Past accomplishments and a measurement paradigm for the 21st century". *Annals of Internal Medicine*, vol. 127, pp. 743-50.

Michell, J. (1990), *An Introduction to the Logic of Psychological Measurement*. Hillsdale: Lawrence Erlbaum Associates.

Michell, J. (1997), "Quantitative science and the definition of measurement in psychology". *British Journal of Psychology*, vol. 88, pp. 355-383.

Michell, J. (1999), *Measurement in Psychology: A Critical History of a Methodological Concept*. Cambridge: Cambridge University Press.

Michell, J. (2000), "Normal science, pathological science and psychometrics". *Theory and Psychology*, vol. 10, no. 5, pp. 639-667.

Miller, G. A. (1921), *Historical Introduction to the Mathematical Literature*. Macmillan: New York.

Mundy, B. (1986), "On the general theory of meaningful representation". *Synthese*, vol. 67, pp. 391-437.

Nagel, E. (1932), "Measurement". *Erkenntnis II*, vol. 22, pp. 313-333.

O'Connell, J. (1993), "Metrology: The creation of universality by the circulation of particulars". *Social Studies of Science*, vol. 23, pp. 129-173.

Peirce, C. S. (1878), "Illustration of the logic of science. Fourth paper: The probability of induction". *Popular Science Monthly*, vol. 12, pp. 705-718.

Pennella, C. R. (1997), *Managing the metrology system*. Milwaukee: ASQ Quality Press.

Perline, R., Wright, B. D., and Wainer, H. (1979), "The Rasch model as additive conjoint measurement". *Applied Psychological Measurement*, vol. 3, no. 2, pp. 237-25

Port, R. F., and Van Gelder, T. (1998), *Mind as Motion: Explorations in the Dynamics of Cognition*. Cambridge: MIT Press.

Price, D. J. d. S. (1986), *Little Science, Big Science ... and Beyond*. New York: Columbia University Press.

Qayum, M., Ortenberg, K., Morstead, R., Siddiqui, F., Mipro, R. C., Jr., and Fisher, W. P., Jr. (1996, Jun.), "Measuring functional status in rehabilitation: Louisiana Rehabilitation Institute vs. Uniform Data System [abstract]". *LSU Deparment of Medicine, Section of Physical Medicine and Rehabilitation, Residents' Research Day*. New Orleans: LSU School of Medicine.

Rabkin, Y. M. (1987), "Technological innovation in science". *Isis*, vol. 78, pp. 31-54.

Rabkin, Y. M. (1992), "Rediscovering the instrument: Research, industry, and education". In R. Bud and S. E. Cozzens (Eds.), *Invisible Connections: Instruments, Institutions, and Science* (57-82). Bellingham: SPIE Optical Engineering Press.

Raczek, A., Ware, J., Bjorner, J., Gandek, B., Haley, S., Aaronson, N., Apolone, G., Bech, P., Brazier, J., Bullinger, M., and Sullivan, M. (1998, Nov.), "Comparison of Rasch and summated rating scales constructed from SF-36 physical functioning items in seven countries: Results from the IQOLA Project. International Quality of Life Assessment". *Journal of Clinical Epidemiology*, vol. 51, no. 11, pp. 1203-14.

Ramsay, J. O. (1975), "Review of Foundations of Measurement", vol. 1, by D. H. Krantz et al. *Psychometrika*, vol. 40, pp. 257-262.

Rasch, G. (1960), *Probabilistic Models for Some Intelligence and Attainment Tests* (reprint, with Foreword and Afterword by B. D. Wright, Chicago: University of Chicago Press, 1980). Copenhagen, Denmark: Danmarks Paedogogiske Institut.

Rasch, G. (1961), *"On general laws and the meaning of measurement in psychology". In Proceedings Of The Fourth Berkeley Symposium On Mathematical Statistics And Probability* (321-333). Berkeley: University of California Press.

Rasch, G. (1977), "On specific objectivity: An attempt at formalizing the request for generality and validity of scientific statements". *Danish Yearbook of Philosophy*, vol. 14, pp. 58-94.

Revicki, D. A., and Cella, D. F. (1997, Aug.), "Health status assessment for the twenty-first century item response theory item banking and computer adaptive testing". *Quality of Life Research*, pp. 595-600.

Ricoeur, P. (1967a), *Husserl: An Analysis of his Phenomenology* (J. Wild, ed.) (E. G. Ballard and L. E. Embree, trans.). Northwestern University Studies in Phenomenology and Existential Philosophy. Evanston: Northwestern University Press.

Ricoeur, P. (1967b), *The Symbolism of Evil* (N. Anshen, ed.) (E. Buchanan, trans.). Reprinted from the Religious Perspectives Series, vol. XVII. Boston: Beacon Press.

Ricoeur, P. (1977), *The Rule Of Metaphor: Multi-Disciplinary Studies Of The Creation Of Meaning In Language* (Robert Czerny, trans.). Toronto: University of Toronto Press.

Rogosa, D. (1987), "Casual [sic] models do not support scientific conclusions: A comment in support of Freedman". *Journal of Educational Statistics*, vol. 12, no. 2, pp. 185-95.

Schaffer, S. (1992), "Late Victorian metrology and its instrumentation: A manufactory of Ohms". In R. Bud and S. E. Cozzens (Eds.), *Invisible Connections: Instruments, Institutions, and Science* (23-56). Bellingham: SPIE Optical Engineering Press.

Segal, M., Heinemann, A., Schall, R. R., and Wright, B. D. (1997, Jun.), "Extending the range of the Functional Independence Measure with SF-36 items". *Physical Medicine and Rehabilitation: State of the Art Reviews*, vol. 11, no. 2, pp. 385-396.

Shapin, S. (1989, Nov.-Dec.), "The invisible technician". *American Scientist*, pp. 554-563.

Shapin, S. (1991), "'A Scholar and a Gentleman': The problematic identity of the scientific practitioner in early modern England". *History of Science*, vol. 29, pp. 279-327.

Shapin, S. (1994), *A Social History of Truth: Civility and Science in Seventeenth-century England*. Chicago: University of Chicago Press.

Smith, B. C. (1998), *On the Origin of Objects*. Cambridge: Bradford Books.

Smith, R. M. (1986), "Person fit in the Rasch model". *Educational and Psychological Measurement*, vol. 46, pp. 359-372.

Smith, R. M. (1991), "The distributional properties of Rasch item fit statistics". *Educational and Psychological Measurement*, vol. 51, pp. 541-565.

Smith, R. M. (2000), "Fit analysis in latent trait measurement models". *Journal of Applied Measurement*, vol. 1, no. 2, pp. 199-218.

Smith, R. M., and Kramer, G. A. (1992), "A comparison of two methods of test equating in the Rasch model". *Educational and Psychological Measurement*, vol. 52, pp. 835-846.

Subcommittee on Research, C. o. F. S. (1996, Jul.), *Assessing Fundamental Science: A Report From The Subcommittee On Research, Committee On Fundamental Science*. Washington, DC: National Science and Technology Council.

Thelen, E., and Smith, L. B. (1996), *A Dynamic Systems Approach To The Development Of Cognition And Action*. Cambridge: MIT Press.

Thurstone, L. L. (1926), "The scoring of individual performance". *Journal of Educational Psychology*, vol. 17, pp. 446-457.

Thurstone, L. L. (1928), "Attitudes can be measured". *American Journal of Sociology*, vol. 33, pp. 529-544. Reprinted in L. L. Thurstone, The Measurement of Values. Midway Reprint Series. Chicago: University of Chicago Press, 1959, 215-233.

Van der Linden, W. J. (1986, Dec.), "The changing conception of measurement in education and psychology". *Applied Psychological Measurement*, vol. 10, no. 4, pp. 325-332.

Van der Linden, W. J., and Hambleton, R. K. (1997), *Item Response Theory: A Brief History. Handbook Of Modern Item Response Theory* (IRT)W. J. van der Linden and R. K. Hambleton (Eds.), (pp. 1-28). New York: Springer-Verlag.

Van Helden, A., and Hankins, T. L. (Eds.). (1994), *Instruments. Osiris: a Research Journal Devoted to the History of Science and its Cultural Influences*, vol. 9. Chicago: University of Chicago Press.

Ware, J. E., Snow, K. K., Kosinski, M., and Gandek, B. (1993), *SF-36 Health Survey: Manual and Interpretation Guide*. Boston: The Health Institute, New England Medical Center.

Wernimont, G. (1977, Mar.), "Ruggedness evaluation of test procedures". *ASTM Standardization News*, vol. 5, pp. 13-16.

Wernimont, G. (1978, Dec.), "Careful intralaboratory study must come first". *ASTM Standardization News*, vol. 6, pp. 11-12.

Widmalm, S. (1995, May 12), "On exactitude, a review of The Values of Precision", by M. Norton Wise. *Science*, vol. 268, pp. 905-6.

Wilder, R. (1965), *Introduction to the Foundations of Mathematics*. New York: Wiley.

Wilson, T. P. (1971), "Critique of ordinal variables". *Social Forces*, vol. 49, pp. 432-444.

Wimsatt, W. C. (1981), "Robustness, reliability and overdetermination". In M. B. Brewer and B. E. Collins (Eds.), *Scientific Inquiry And The Social Sciences*. San Francisco: Jossey-Bass.

Wise, M. N. (1988), "Mediating machines". *Science in Context*, vol. 2, no. 1, pp. 77-113.

Wise, M. N. (Ed.). (1995), *The Values of Precision*. Princeton: Princeton University Press.

Wittgenstein, L. (1958), *Philosophical Investigations* (G. E. M. Anscombe, trans.) (3rd Ed.). New York: Macmillan.

Wittgenstein, L. (1983), *Remarks On The Foundations Of Mathematics* (G. H. von Wright, R. Rhees, and G. E. M. Anscombe, eds.) (G. E. M. Anscombe, trans.). Cambridge: MIT Press.

Wolfe, E. W. (2000), "Equating and item banking with the Rasch model". *Journal of Applied Measurement*, vol. 1, no. 4, pp. 409-434.

Wood, D. and Bernasconi, R. (1988), *Derrida and Difference*. Evanston: Northwestern University Press.

Wood, R. (1978), "Fitting the Rasch model: A heady tale". *British Journal of Mathematical and Statistical Psychology*, vol. 31, pp. 27-32.

Woodcock, R. W., and Munoz-Sandoval, A. F. (1993), "An IRT approach to cross-language test equating and interpretation". *European Journal of Psychological Assessment*, vol. 9, no. 3, pp. 233-241.

Wright, B. D. (1968), *Sample-Free Test Calibration And Person Measurement. In Proceedings Of The 1967 Invitational Conference On Testing Problems* (85-101). Princeton: Educational Testing Service.

Wright, B. D. (1977), "Solving measurement problems with the Rasch model". *Journal of Educational Measurement*, vol. 14, no. 2, pp. 97-116.

Wright, B. D. (1984), "Despair and hope for educational measurement". *Contemporary Education Review*, vol. 3, no. 1, pp. 281-288.

Wright, B. D. (1985), "Additivity in psychological measurement". In E. Roskam (Ed.), *Measurement and Personality Assessment*. North Holland: Elsevier Science Ltd.

Wright, B. D. (1993, Summer), "Equitable test equating". *Rasch Measurement Transactions*, vol. 7, no. 2, pp. 298-299.

Wright, B. D. (1997, Winter), "A history of social science measurement". *Educational Measurement: Issues and Practice*, vol. 16, no. 4, pp. 33-45, 52.

Wright, B. D. (1999), "Fundamental measurement for psychology". In S. E. Embretson and S. L. Hershberger (Eds.), *The New Rules of Measurement: What Every Educator and Psychologist Should Know*. Hillsdale: Lawrence Erlbaum Associates.

Wright, B. D., and Bell, S. R. (1984), "Item banks: What, why, how". *Journal of Educational Measurement*, vol. 21, no. 4, no. 331-345.

Wright, B. D. and Linacre, J. M. (1989), "Observations are always ordinal; measurements, however, must be interval". *Archives of Physical Medicine and Rehabilitation*, vol. 70, no. 12, pp. 857-867.

Wright, B. D., and Linacre, J. M. (1999), *A User's Guide to WINSTEPS Rasch-Model Computer Program*, v. 2.94. Chicago: MESA Press.

Wright, B. D., and Masters, G. N. (1982), *Rating Scale Analysis: Rasch Measurement*. Chicago: MESA Press.

Wright, B. D., and Stone, M. H. (1979), *Best Test Design: Rasch Measurement*. Chicago: MESA Press.

Wu, M. L., Adams, R. J., and Wilson, M. R. (1998), *ConQuest: Generalized Item Response Modeling Software*. Camberwell, Victoria, Australia: Australian Council for Educational Research.

Zhu, W. (1996) "Should total scores from a rating scale be used directly?" *Research Quarterly for Exercise and Sport*, vol. 67, no. 3, pp. 363-372.

Zhu, W. (1998), "Test equating: What, why, how?" *Research Quarterly for Exercise and Sport*, vol. 69, no. 1, pp. 11-23.

Zupko, R. E. (1977), *British Weights and Measures: A History from Antiquity to the Seventeenth Century*. Madison: University of Wisconsin Press.

PART III

PRAGMATISTS' PERSPECTIVES ON POLICY AND POLITICS

7 The Pragmatic Policy Analyst

Anne Larason Schneider and Helen Ingram

Introduction

Pragmatism provides an interesting and potentially powerful philosophical backdrop for an integrated theory of policy analysis that links public policy to democracy. Policy scholars seldom reference pragmatism, although it is not particularly difficult to trace the history of policy sciences and policy studies back through Dror (1971), Lasswell (1971), Lindblom (1982, 1959), Merriam (1936), and Popper (1966) to Dewey (1946). Nor is it difficult to find pragmatic themes in contemporary theorizing about public policy and policy analysis (Farr, 1999). Drawing on central principles of pragmatic philosophy, we advance an approach that incorporates the quality of American democracy as a fundamental concern of the policy analyst and that integrates scientific, political, postmodern, and critical forms of analysis.

To avoid potential confusion over terminology, we define public policy in Eastonian terms, as the "authoritative allocation of values for a society" (Easton, 1963). Policies are revealed through texts, practices, symbols, and discourse of governments and its agents (including legislatures, courts, public agencies, special districts and public officials at all levels). Policies deliver benefits and burdens through both instrumental actions and symbolic messages. Policy design refers to the content of public policies – the elements of the text or practice itself such as the goals or problems to be solved, the benefits and burdens allocated to target populations, the rules, tools, rationales, assumptions, and implementation structures. Policy designs are observable in statutes, guidelines, court rulings, and the everyday practices of street level public workers who interact with ordinary people in the delivery of public policy. Policy processes are the dynamic interactions through which policies are produced and consequences occur. Policy analysis refers to the study or analysis of public policies and publicly funded programs utilizing a wide range of methods including causal analysis, evaluation research, forecasting, cost benefit studies, interpretive studies, ethnography, narrative analysis, and field experimental studies.

The purpose of this chapter is to introduce a pragmatic policy analysis that we believe will help integrate the field and focus attention on its original mission of contributing to a democratic polity. Pragmatic policy analysis does not need to invent new methods or theories, but instead needs to incorporate as central components some research traditions that have previously been marginalized by the field. In the first section of the paper, we identify several principles of pragmatism that should guide the work of a pragmatic policy analyst and show how they apply. In the second section, we contend that public policy is expected to play at least four roles in a democratic society: solving problems efficiently and effectively, being responsive to interests and resolving conflicts, providing arenas for democratic deliberation and citizenship, and advancing the cause of justice. Problems emerge when these roles become unbalanced, and the policy arena is dominated by only one or two. For each role, we illustrate the types of research that have come to be associated with it and show how these can be utilized to study public policy. In the third section, we make the critical point of the paper which is that a pragmatic policy analysis must focus most attentively on the values that the policy is serving least well so that the policy arena can be brought back into balance. We illustrate this point by drawing examples from two very different kinds of public policy: water policy and criminal justice policy. These two policy areas reflect quite different academic traditions and hence are useful in illustrating how a pragmatic analytic approach applies in widely divergent contexts. The water example shows a policy arena that is dominated by powerful political interests yet is legitimated through technical, scientific, and economic considerations. Criminal justice policy, however, is ideologically driven by powerful and opportunistic elected officials, but is legitimated through the negative social constructions of the target populations.

Pragmatic Principles of Policy Analysis

Central to our approach are several important pragmatic principles: a problem-oriented understanding of science and the process of inquiry; an eclectic and self-reflective stance about both theory and methods; a recognition of a plurality of contingent "truths" and "meanings" that are grounded in concrete experience rather than absolute or fundamental truths; an avoidance of dichotomies and uni-dimensional approaches and an explicit incorporation of democratic ideals in both the outcomes (goals) of public policy, and in the way that policy analysis itself is conducted.

A problem-oriented approach to policy analysis begins with an understanding of how the issues have been framed and the contextual conditions that shape the social construction of the issue itself. The way the problem is framed establishes the entire stage upon which the policy debate will take place, including the kind of language that will be used (e.g., scientific or political), the types of power and influence that will be effective, and the credibility of different kinds of evidence. Whoever succeeds in framing the issue is able to select the range of alternatives that will be viewed as rational. Problems do not just happen; they are socially constructed. The pragmatic policy analyst needs to view the dominant construction of the issue with a skeptical eye and encourage alternative constructions that may permit broader public participation and greater opportunity for resolving conflicts or avoiding injustices. Our emphasis on the social construction of the issue should not be confused with a strict constructionist perspective as we reject the strict construction contention that there are never any empirical or close-to-the-ground conditions from which policies are produced. Our position here is that of the contextual constructionists who recognize that socially constructed phenomena may emerge from a context that contains material conditions, personal experiences, and agreed-upon facts (Best, 1993).

The context within which a policy operates is not a neutral ground. A form of policy analysis that is respected and widely accepted in one context may be rejected in another. Policies that work well in one city may fail elsewhere. Policies developed through deductive theorizing or even through experimentation in one context may have quite different consequences in another. The development of policy designs that will produce desirable results for democracy requires a continuing process of diagnosis, analysis, experimentation, and redesign within context.

Science is a process of observing, testing, and searching for meaning that contributes to an ever-changing body of knowledge and tentative theorizing. Facts are important and have a central role in policy arguments and analysis, but the social construction of facts is as much a part of understanding the issues, policy, and context, as are "bare facts". Furthermore, "bare facts" exist only to the extent that people who are confronted with the same empirical information and experiences agree that these are "bare facts". Knowledge about policy can be cumulated, but will always remain contingent upon such a wide array of contextual conditions, that fundamental truths (across all times and all places) are difficult to find and probably do not exist. To cumulate policy knowledge requires attention to the internal validity of the study above all (that is, the instrumental and symbolic aspects of the policy within the context where it is operating). In different contexts, the policy almost certainly will produce different – perhaps radically different – results. The pragmatic approach to policy analysis, then, begins with a deep immersion in the context where the policy operates, seeking to understand how the issues have been framed and why.

The pragmatic policy analyst draws on methods that are appropriate to producing useful knowledge within the context where the policy operates and does not have an ideological commitment to any particular methodology. On this point we are in significant agreement with Tamanaha (1997) that selected aspects of many different methodological/theoretical traditions are necessary for policy analysis, including behavioral, interpretive, critical, economic, positivist and post modern. Methods useful in policy analysis range from random assignment experiments in field situations to ethnographic and narrative analysis. Textual analysis, survey research, in-depth interviews, highly structured decision making analysis, benefit cost studies – all of these are part of the pragmatic policy analyst's repertoire.

The use of mixed or multiple methods has gained considerable respect in many social science disciplines over the past decade, but an eclectic approach to theory has been more problematic. In contrast with those who think of theory as a world view that inexorably shapes everything one encounters, we contend that pragmatic policy analysts should be able to understand a variety of alternative theories, including more than one "grand" theory and several mid level or narrow theories more specific to the subject matter of the policy. Policy analysts need to see the world through multiple perspectives, recognizing that different approaches generate different insights. No one, of course, can completely escape from the culture, context, values, and "reality" in which we exist. That is, we are never free of "theory" in the sense of the cumulative experience and knowledge we bring to a situation. Nevertheless, the best protection against theoretical narrowness is an eclectic approach that sparks innovative and creative ideas about how the world might be even if none of us have experienced it exactly that way.

The pragmatic policy analyst also should be self reflective about theories and methods: able to recognize that policy analysis itself contributes to the context within which policy is developed, implemented, and meanings constructed. The self reflective analyst does not set himself/herself apart from others in a democratic form of policy analysis, but becomes a facilitator of a more democratic process at the same time that he or she maintains a stance with respect to the various claims that bring unbiased and objective information forward. Pragmatic policy analysts understand that they should not bias their information so that it favors one or another of the contesting groups, but they also must recognize how their work may be influenced by the politics of their academic disciplines (Morales, 1998; Diesing, 1991). Academic disciplines sometimes privilege particular methodologies or theories and attempt to marginalize others. These sorts of academic fashions need to be avoided as the choice of theory and methods needs to be based on what is most likely to produce useful information.

Truth and meaning in pragmatic policy analysis are contingent, not foundational. Meaning is grounded in concrete experiences, but it can be understood more broadly through qualitative research methods such as narrative analysis and natural language ethnography. On the other hand, there is respect for the traditional scientific methods including field experiments, survey research, comparative case studies, time series analysis and the statistics associated with these, provided that they are directed toward solving important societal problems rather than focused on an illusive search for general or universal laws. There is respect for the standards of evidence associated with scientific research. Scientific policy analysis produces information or captures information in a way intended to avoid certain kinds of bias and subjectivity. Qualitative methods including ethnography and narrative analysis capture a different kind of information and avoid other kinds of bias and subjectivity associated with strictly instrumental approaches. The experiences that ordinary people have with policy are respected as forms of evidence that should be incorporated into the policy discourse rather than dismissed as anecdotal (and therefore unscientific and irrelevant). The meaning of science itself is socially constructed and all of the findings from scientific study are subject to various interpretations.

The final principle pertains to the connection between public policy and democracy. Democracy was a fundamental concern of Dewey and many other pragmatists (Dewey, 1946; Bohman, 1999; Smiley, 1999; Morris, 1999; Siegfried, 1999; MacGilvray, 1999). Dewey (1946) conceptualized democracy as a process of continual experimentation carried out by communities of inquirers each of whom brings only a partial perspective to bear. He recognized that science is commonly used by political regimes for oppressive purposes and argued that deliberative, communicative forms of collective action are needed for a true democracy. Yet Dewey constantly emphasized experimentation as the way individuals learn from their own experiences and, by extension, the essence of a pragmatic scientific (and democratic) mode of inquiry. Experimentation with policies and programs, along with the scientific studies of their instrumental and symbolic results, should be central to the process of democratic inquiry. Policy experiments, however, often go awry, at least partly because policy scientists who rely on them tend to view the role of public policy in a society in strictly instrumental terms and fail to recognize the multiple roles policy must serve. Head start policies, for example, were pronounced a dismal failure only a short time after they began when the reading scores of students in head start programs did not improve dramatically. Later studies have found numerous positive effects including increased political participation and efficacy among both the participants and the parents of head start participants (Fischer, 1997).

Pragmatic principles can play an important role in legitimating a more diversified, more open, more useful and more democratic form of policy analysis. Rather than adopting just one tradition of scholarship, the pragmatic analyst should choose from a broad array of traditions, methods, and theories; selecting those that will be most useful in a given context.

Multiple Roles of Policy in Democracy

In contemporary American society, public policy is expected to play at least four critical roles: problem solving, responsiveness, providing arenas for citizen discourse, and advancing justice. Public policy is expected to be an effective and efficient problem solver through its causal impacts on behavior and on technical relationships. Policy must be responsive to interests and public opinion, with self-correcting mechanisms such as the pluralists envision so that if policy is not working properly in its allocation of benefits and burdens, public discontent will lead to changes through the political system. In a democratic society, policy must move beyond politics and expertise to involve and engage citizens so that they can perform the critical roles of citizenship. Policy should serve justice in insuring that all members of the society are adequately cared for in a supportive and empathetic environment. To advance democracy, these divergent roles need to be balanced so that the policy enjoys general acceptance across these and perhaps other dimensions.

In some public policy arenas, however, one or another of these purposes may come to dominate the policy process, and such an imbalance has serious impacts. Unfortunately, policy analysis has also become quite uni-dimensional in its view of the role of public policy and has become largely dominated by technical and economic approaches, or by narrowly construed evaluation studies that focus on behavioral changes most closely linked to the policy's instrumental goals. Thus, narrowly construed policy analysis actually contributes to the imbalances that it should be correcting. Pragmatic policy analysis, however, should focus attention on the values that are being served least well, and utilize methodologies that will contribute to a better balance across the multiple roles policy is expected to perform.

Solving Problems

Policy scientists and evaluation researchers are most familiar with public policy's role in the achievement of instrumental goals and objectives or in alleviation of problems toward which the policy is directed. In water policy, sufficient water delivered at a reasonable price to serve human needs is the foundation from which policy analysis proceeds. In criminal justice policy, behavioral change is expected to occur which will result in crime rates declining. The *Personal Responsibility and Welfare Reform Act* of 1995 established sanctions for continued welfare "dependency" that were expected to produce behavioral changes, including a reduction in illegitimate births, more mothers in the work force, and a decline in the number of people on welfare. Environmental policy is expected to protect environmental quality and insure clean water for drinking.

As a problem-solving enterprise, the policy process is conceptualized as a logical sequence of events that begins with the definition of a problem or goal, the identification of alternatives that have the causal levers and behavioral incentives needed to produce the desired change, selection of the optimal alternative, implementation, evaluation, and redesign as needed. Policy scientists see themselves as playing a critical part at each stage. Policy analysts frame the issues in terms most consistent with the theories of their disciplines. Engineers understand the problem of having residential development in a flood plane, to be one of building another dam. To a city planner, the problem is one of enforcing zoning laws. To a psychologist, the problem should be framed in terms of the decision-making heuristics of individuals. n economist would consider raising the costs of insurance until people could not afford to live in the flood plain. Alternatives for solving problems depend fundamentally on how the issue has been framed in the first place. Those who understand the "welfare problem" as an issue of justice develop alternatives for reducing the number of people who live below the poverty level. Those who see it as an issue of morality develop incentive systems or sanction systems to reduce illegitimate births.

Policy analysts assist decision makers in setting priorities from among alternatives by estimating the positive and negative consequences of various actions. They help structure an action agenda through monitoring of important indicators. Water scientists, for example, determine the salinity level at which salt in the Colorado River becomes a significant problem. Poverty researchers establish a standard poverty level and track the proportion of individuals, families, and children who are below it. Scientific studies search for the root causes of problems and analyze the impact of alternative strategies. Once a policy is put into place, further analysis determines whether goals are being reached and if not, what adjustments might be helpful. The standard against which a policy is judged is that it achieves goals effectively and efficiently.

Policy subsystems emerge, usually comprised of specialists and experts who conduct research in the policy arena, and who often have advanced degrees in the policy field. Such persons are located in bureaucracies, congressional staffs, universities, think tanks, and consulting firms. In some policy arenas there is a professional network that understands the jargon and has a shared perception of how the problems in this policy arena should be understood.

The pragmatic policy analyst must take seriously this role as expert. Regimes cannot survive continued public policy failures as was so vividly illustrated in the Soviet Union where mounting practical problems of poor economy and degraded environment contributed significantly to undercutting the legitimacy of the regime itself. Even so, the scientific and utilitarian perspective is at best a partial view of what public policy in a democracy must do; therefore, it is only a partial view of what a policy analyst must do.

Reflecting Interests and Public Opinion

The second role of policy pertains to the policy-making process itself. This perspective builds from pluralist theories of democracies and focuses on policy as a reflection of the exercise of political power. Contending coalitions compete with one another to define the issue in terms most favorable to the outcome they prefer. Within any particular understanding of the issue, groups coalesce around alternatives that will maximize their benefits and minimize their losses. In addition to intensive direct lobbying of policy makers, organized groups mobilize grass-roots interest to buttress their claims. Policies emerge from contests in which people have much to gain or lose. Some policy arenas have long-standing oppositional coalitions, such as those found between economic interests and environmental interests. Much of the history of water policy since 1970 consists of the struggle between those who profit from economic progress and those associated with the environmental movement. Labor and business interests have collided throughout the industrial period in all western nations. Conservatives have contested every advance in the social welfare system of the United States and with the 1996 welfare reform law, enjoyed a major victory that for the first time in the history of the United States actually ended a federal entitlement.

Pluralist theory makes it clear that policy making is almost never finished. Each statute, executive order, regulation, or court ruling marks a temporary balance among contending powers. Good policies are not judged by their instrumental impacts, but rather are judged by the process that produced them and their acceptability to the public. Good policies are those that are produced by a fair, open, and competitive political process. Such policies are expected to enjoy acceptance, even if not agreement. Contending factions simply retreat to fight again another day, or in an arena more conducive to the types of power they enjoy. In some instances, public policies may succeed in reconciling contending interests and produce results that gain such wide acceptance that the policy is no longer contested at all-- such as seems to be the case with Social Security.

Underlying this role of policy is the theory of pluralist democracy which holds that policy makers should be accountable and responsive to public preferences, reflect majority interests, and reconcile conflicts. Political scientists are most comfortable with the types of policy analysis that emerge from pluralist theory. Lasswell – who many credit with the modern-day invention of policy analysis – also coined the phrase that has for decades served as the central focal point for political science as the study of "who gets what, when and how?" (Lasswell, 1936). Many studies since the 1950s have sought to determine the structure of power in communities and to determine (as if it could be determined, once and for all) whether the American political system is pluralist or elitist (Stone, 1989). There also is a long tradition of case studies of particular policy struggles focusing on the power of various coalitions and why one lost and the other won. The role of public opinion in public policy has been studied for more than 50 years and continues to be an important form of policy analysis (Sharp, 1999). Comparative state policy studies use the states as a unit of analysis and seek to determine why they have adopted different policies. Implementation studies examine how statutory intentions are often deflected at lower levels of government, as interests that lost at one point re-emerge to win at another. The popularity of rational choice theories from the 1970s onward has produced literally hundreds of studies that begin with the presumption of a self-interested utility maximizing individual (or institution). The principal-agent theory of implementation, for example, contends that pluralist democracy depends on "agents" (such as persons in government bureaucracies) carrying out the wishes of the "principal" (such as the will of Congress as reflected in statutes). The advocacy coalition framework developed by Sabatier and Jenkins Smith treats policies as the results of long-standing belief systems and coalitions that form around core beliefs. They have produced a long list of hypotheses in an attempt to continue development of a positive theory of policy change (Sabatier and Jenkins Smith, 1993).

Technically oriented policy scientists trained in the theories and methods of positive science often have nothing but disdain for the pluralist political process and most view it as the major factor in producing flawed public policy. Many policy analysts and evaluation researchers believe there are instrumentally correct answers to instrumentally framed problems; hence, compromises, negotiations, or "pandering" to public opinion only produce policy problems – not policy solutions. Policy has failed in an important aspect of its mission in a democracy, however, when it is produced through undemocratic or unfair processes and when it fails to structure the policy-making arena in such a way that future policies also will reflect well on democracy.

The pragmatic policy analyst should pay attention to this central role of public policy in a democracy, but must not be misled into accepting pseudo democratic exercises of power and influence for a legitimate, fair, open, process of competing interests and reaching compromises. Rather than seeking to overcome power simply with technically-oriented or scientific "truth", pragmatic policy analysis needs to describe the power structures, deconstruct the divisive social constructions of target populations, illustrate alternative ways to frame issues or events, de-mystify overly scientific language, bring the perspectives of marginalized populations into the policy discourse, and reveal patterns of deception, hate, manipulation, or other injustices when they occur. The policy analyst should recognize when pluralism is not working as assumed by pluralist scholarship and instead has become a destructive form of "hyper" or "degenerative" pluralism. When democratic processes are not working properly, the debate should not be over whether scientific policy analysis is "rational" and politics "irrational" (or vice versa); the effort should be to find meaningful scientific information and meaningful political participation.

Providing An Arena for Deliberation

A third aspect of policy is to provide an arena and subject matter for democratic deliberation through which citizens are enlightened, informed, and participate in the search for the public interest. Articulated today by critical theorists, postmodernists, and scholars interested in participatory democracy, this vision of policy has been espoused by some throughout the history of the United States. Thomas Jefferson, for example, firmly believed that the people themselves were capable of making decisions that affected them (Ingram and Wallace, 1996).

Democratic deliberation has been realized in some instances, but not others. Water policy, for example, has a long history of involvement, particularly where it pertains to irrigation. Maas (1978) shows that the community legislature and water court in Valencia, Spain are among the oldest democratic institutions in the world, existing even before the British parliament. These institutions allow ordinary people to make and enforce rules to ensure that water will serve community interests (Mann and Anderson, 1978). Ostrom (1990; 1992) has written extensively about long-standing self-governing institutions that protect common pool resources from the "tragedy of the commons". Michael Meyer has demonstrated that white settlers in the American west copied much of earlier Hispanic water law that allocated water above all to serve human welfare, not just to satisfy individual rights (Meyer, 1994). In criminal justice policy, alternative dispute resolution strategies have been used for several decades, allowing disputants to come together and seek a resolution of their grievance. Neighborhood juvenile justice diversion programs permit persons within the neighborhood to hold youth accountable through restitution or community service and provide an important alternative to the formalized court process.

It is apparent from these examples that people can come together and resolve conflicts. Formal, hierarchical authority is not always required and, as Ostrom points out, sometimes does more harm than good. The work of Putnam on social capital and its remarkable correlation with the capacity of states to address critical problems provides convincing evidence that arenas for civic action build trust and understanding essential to democratic deliberation (Putnam, 2000). It is apparent that people can learn to defer self interest in favor of the collective good – whether one views this as altruistic behavior or "long term" self interest is not as important as the fact that people are able to create and maintain institutions that serve a collective interest. Most public policy today, however, does not show much confidence in people's ability to participate in the search for common solutions. The history of many social policies in the United States has been one of gradually disempowering those who are to receive help and transferring authority to specialists in schools, government agencies or non profits, many of whom must be licensed.

It should be obvious to any reasonable observer that there are numerous examples of how policy is failing in its role as an enhancer of democratic deliberation. In recent surveys most people have said they distrust their governments more than any other institution. While many see government as an active threat to their rights, others simply view the acts of government as irrelevant to their lives. Others understand government as that collection of agencies that they must manipulate to obtain that which is rightly theirs. Many actions by governments and the policies produced are greeted with alienation, cynicism, or disinterest.

Postmodern and critical theorists are most comfortable with the forms of policy analysis that are built on communicative rationality rather than instrumental rationality (Yanow, 1998; Fischer, 1999; deLeon, 1997; Forester, 1985, 1988; Fox, 1996; Rosenau, 1992). Reality is socially constructed and fragmented; images and symbols are more important than objective or empirical phenomenon. Narrative analysis seeks to communicate alternative perspectives and experiences of people in their own words. Deconstruction of hegemonic belief systems or power structures strips them of their presumed legitimacy and reveals basic contradictions or alternatives that could become widely accepted. Studies of discourse and argument reveal underlying interests and assumptions that are built into racism, sexism, and capitalism.

The issues with postmodern and critical analysis begin when their claims of truth and correctness rival those of the positivist perspectives they seek to replace (Tamanaha, 1997). When pursued from a strict constructionist perspective (in which there are no underlying empirical conditions), interpretive analysis is unable to deal with raw political power resources, differences in material conditions, physical or emotional pain. "Marital rape" was a real and painful problem for women even when it was socially constructed as being simply a normal part of marriage. Material conditions are real for those who experience them – the pain, humiliation, and happiness – are understood through experience even if the contemporary social construction is quite different. Strict constructionism is especially risky or even dangerous in politics as it implies that any construction is as legitimate as any other. In some situations this results in a perspective being dismissed as irrelevant ("after all, it is just a social construction") as if long-held historical beliefs can simply be replaced with new and more useful constructions. In other situations, it prevents arguments that are closer to the ground in terms of factual accuracy from being considered legitimate contenders that could help unmask a particular construction. Not all postmodernists or all critical theorists advocate such stringent forms of constructionism, however, and offer very useful ideas for the pragmatic policy analysis.

Advancing Justice

The fourth role of policy in a democracy is to serve justice. The relevant questions here pertain to fairness in decision processes and allocation decisions as well as issues of respect for people and the natural environment. Policies that appear to be quite effective and efficient may have highly differential impacts on various social groups or may destroy the environment for future generations. Some groups are disproportionately represented in favorable decisions and others are systematically on the losing site. Issues about justice have become so prominent in environmental policy, for example, that an entire field of study called "environmental justice" has emerged. In other policy arenas, such as criminal justice, "justice" has taken on a very narrow meaning focused on retribution that has produced extremely long sentences even for "victimless" crimes such as violation of drug laws. Issues of justice were virtually ignored in the welfare reform of 1995. Cost benefit studies often do not examine differential impacts of policies in terms of race, gender, or socio-economic class even though they could do so. The case studies of contending coalitions that focus on who won from among those in contention often do not recognize that some interests were not even in contention, and that the problems of some groups that one could argue (from a justice point of view) should be addressed by public policy are not even on the agenda at all. The history of water rights and water allocation in the west shows the systematic disadvantage of Indian tribes.

Concern with justice is most central to critical theory and to the role of policy in perpetuating oppressive institutions and life styles. Critical theorists, generally speaking, do not view public policy in a favorable light but tend to see it as part of the state, which, along with capitalist economic systems, is oppressive in terms of race, gender, and social class. Pragmatic analysts need to identify limitations and oppressiveness of public policy; but in contrast with the most radical critical perspectives, we believe that democratic public policy offers the most promising means for collective action that will serve broad-based public interests. Policy analysis always needs to have a comparative focus:

if not this, then what? And to tear down without seeking better collective solutions is destructive as Tamanaha (1997) pointed out:

> Critical scholars have harmed their cause far more so than advanced it ... [when they] make the mistake of attacking everything about law from every conceivable angle ... The first consequence is that the failure to be judicious in the critique led to a failure to recognize that law does much good for many people ... the second consequence is that...there was no basis upon which to build (p. 253).

Balancing these partially conflicting roles is essential to good public policy. Finding the appropriate balance requires analysis and democratic deliberation within the context of particular policies at particular times. When public policy in any area is single minded in its purpose and pursues instrumental rationality, pluralist political balance, democratic and civic participation, or justice to the exclusion of all else, policy undermines rather than supports democracy. Where imbalance occurs, action needs to be taken to bring the various roles of policy into better balance. And this, then, is the task of a pragmatic policy analyst.

Examples of Imbalance in Water Policy

It is not difficult to find examples in water resource policy where one or more roles of policy have not been fulfilled. Sol Resnick, the former Director of the Arizona Water Resource Center, has told a story about his experiences as a hydrologic advisor in a developing country where the state of deliberative democracy and sense of justice were quite advanced, but which was technically backward (Ingram and Schneider, 1998). Villagers met to decide where to put a new well. After debating the advantages of various placements, they finally agreed on a site and remained completely committed to it in spite of Resnick's efforts to explain that the depth to ground water was far too great at that particular place. Digging began anyway, but they reached only sand. According to Resnick's story, the villagers blamed him rather than their decision making process. In this instance, democracy and democratic deliberation were overbalanced compared with utilitarian and technical expertise.

The 1922 Colorado River Basin Compact represents a political context in which interests were satisfied, but which lacked important scientific information, was inattentive to issues of justice, and did not provide for democratic deliberation. The delegates to each of the basin states who met at Bishops Lodge outside Santa Fe represented all of the powerful interests, but were certainly not democratic decision makers. They met behind closed doors and carved up the Colorado River, parceling it out among the states as if they both had the power of mother nature and were omnipotent about the public interest. Their elite meetings were far from democratic deliberations, and the interests of Native Americans were poorly represented. Further, their science was flawed and their assumptions that the Colorado River would flow dependably at more than 15 million acre-feet a year was significantly off the mark. The flawed policy that emerged led to a sense of injustice and prolonged conflict over who would bear the shortages (Weatherford and Brown, 1986).

Contemporary water policy is imbalanced in a different way. The kind of imbalance can best be described as dominance of political power that is technically legitimated. Policy choices reflect political competition among powerful interests that are legitimized by appeals to scientific and technical arguments. Interests, including those found in bureaucracies, contend with one another in a context where participants disguise their concerns with scientific and technical arguments that appear credible, although not chosen on scientific grounds, but because they serve specific interests. Elected leaders fear appearing at cross-purposes with experts on water. They take positions depending on whether they can find experts who will give them convincing technical rationales. This kind of imbalance leads to policies that are destructive to justice and to deliberative democracy. Further, such politics and policy ultimately discredit science.

The impulse to disguise water policy in technical terms can be traced to the progressive era during which the power of expertise to fashion policies was elevated above the politics of powerful interests. John Wesley Powell, for instance, contended that the federal government and the Department of Interior should create scientifically based water and land policy for the West. Earlier reclamation policy promised to make the deserts and agrarian democracy bloom through projects that were planned and constructed by experts in centralized bureaucracies. Local interests challenged and often prevailed against centralized experts, but the notion that there was a scientifically right way to handle water resources became firmly imbedded in the public mind.

The linkage of science to government is reinforced by the technically oriented missions provided to federal natural resource agencies. There is a natural affinity of science, technology, and bureaucracy because of shared values, such as a belief in hiring based on merit and specialization rather than kinship, friendship, or patronage. Management specialists are being replaced by disciplinary specialists who have advanced degrees in one or another scientific field. Scientific rationalizations provide a powerful legitimation to policy proposals and actions emerging from agencies.

Despite the veneer of science and scientific rationality, the politics of interests, including professional, bureaucratic, geographic, economic, and environmental is clearly the driving force. Utilitarian reasoning and science are brought in as very junior partners in the combination. Science is more used (abused) than listened to in contemporary water policy. That is, only those scientific and technical arguments that support policy options favorable to interests are made. The unfettered consideration of all possibilities does not take place.

In interest dominated, technically justified water policy, issues are socially constructed as technical questions that only technicians can answer. Most issues are subject to a variety of constructions; water issues tend to become defined narrowly and technically. Contamination is described as parts per million of an alphabet soup list of chemicals that only chemists understand. Possible health effects are discussed in terms that communicate only with a toxicologist. While the debate sounds highly technical, most research scientists view it as superficial. Under such definitions, a broader focus is absent, and issues such as the sustainability of water systems into the future is not usually part of the discussion.

Social construction of issues in narrow technical terms also leaves out important social justice concerns in water policy. There is little focus on fairness or on who wins and loses. Seldom discussed are questions about which industries receive subsidized water rates, how present users have to pay for future expansion, and what may happen to trees and other greenery as a result of water rate changes. Science is presented as politically neutral. The technical nature of the discussion eliminates real participation by the lay public. If the public becomes part of the discussion, attention usually focuses on how little they know and how they need to be educated before they can speak rationally about water policy. Instead of policies providing arenas for citizen discussion, policy designs tend to do what experts like best: study, gather data, employ additional researchers, plan, evaluate, and write reports. Little distinction is made between what is good for the experts and what is good for the public interest. Experts prosper whether or not projects are built and there seems to be endless calls for additional research.

Examples of Imbalance in Criminal Justice Policy

Criminal justice policy also suffers from imbalances, but these are different in important respects from water policy. Consider, for example, the evolution of punishment policy and the establishment of prisons in the United States (Schneider, 1999). From the colonial period through the early 1900s, prison policy in the United States was dominated by political power, justified through humanitarian and economic reasoning. Beginning in the late 1600s, prisons gradually replaced death sentences, mutilation, and flogging due to a convergence of interests among humanitarian reformers, public officials, and local businesses. Humanitarians believed that prisons were more humane than inflicting physical pain or death on a person. Public officials believed prisons could be self supporting or even profitable. Western states such as Oklahoma and Arizona viewed prisons as essential to the economic development of the state and as a way to show the eastern business establishment that these new frontiers were "safe" and "civilized". Businesses thought they could share in the profits from cheap prison labor. Prisons eventually failed on both counts. They were not humane enough for the reformers and they did not produce profits for business. The imbalance in this example is a lack of effectiveness and efficiency in producing the desired instrumental consequences. As a failed venture in humanity and profit-making, the state was left on its own, without either its economic or humanitarian justifications, to operate an expensive system of prisons.

Contemporary criminal justice policy is dominated by political elites and legitimated through the negative social constructions of persons who break the law. People who break the law are socially constructed as "deviant", "violent", "dangerous" and "undeserving" (Schneider and Ingram, 1993, 1997). From 1925 to 1975 there were virtually no increases in the rate of incarceration per 100,000 persons in the United States (Schneider, 1997). Beginning about 1974, however, there has been a dramatic shift in U.S. criminal justice policy in which the rehabilitative ideal has been largely abandoned in favor of increasing the scope of legislation to cover a larger number of behaviors (especially drug use), a dramatic increase in the crimes for which imprisonment is mandated, and lengthier sentences (Sharp, 1999). From 1975 to 1995, incarceration rates per 100,000 quadrupled, increasing to 446 from 99. The rationale put forth by elected officials and the media is that the increasing prison population is due to an increase in violent crime. This claim, however, is refuted by the available data which show no upward pattern in the most serious violent crimes (murder). When measured by victimization surveys, violent crime has shown a slight decrease from the first survey in 1973 to the most recent (Schneider, 1999).

Political elites seldom even attempt to argue that the increased punitiveness of the criminal justice policy has reduced crime rates because the evidence for this is uneven and conflicting. Violence as measured by the victimization surveys began its long downward trend before the increases in punishment were initiated. Murder, as measured through the Uniform Crime Reports, has shown an up and down pattern, but very little overall change (9.5 murders and non negligent manslaughters per 100,000 in 1993 compared with 9.6 in 1975). Since the murder rate is the most reliable of the UCR crimes (as it is not subject to changes in victim reporting habits nor changes in definitions), it tends to be the most respected measure. On the other hand, the UCR index of violent crime has climbed steadily mainly due to the increases in forcible rape and aggravated assault. Robbery, however, has been up and down with a slight upward bias. The UCR property crime index shows some cycles but overall has not changed much (4,736 per 100,000 in 1993 compared with 4,810 in 1975).

Without benefit of logical claims of effectiveness, however, elected officials have gained considerable political capital by advocating increased punitiveness of criminal justice policy. By inflicting harsh punishment upon those who are socially constructed as violent, deviant, and undeserving, elected officials gain the accolades of the general public who have been led to believe that such punishment is deserved and necessary for publish safety, without risking the wrath of those actually receiving the punishment (prisoners) who have no credibility and no political power. Felons are not even able to vote – a practice that will eventually disenfranchise a significant proportion of all black males in the United States.

A much debated issue is whether the increased punitiveness is attributable to an increased demand for punitive policy by the general public or whether this is an example of elite manipulation of public opinion for political gain. In her work on the relationship between public opinion and criminal justice policy at the national level, Elaine Sharpe defined the relationship as a "broken thermometer" (1999). In a thermostatic model, an increase in public demand for punitiveness would be followed by more punitive policies, which would then be followed by a cessation of public demand for greater punitiveness. Instead, the pattern in criminal justice shows that public opinion changed dramatically from the mid 1960s to the mid 1970s in its belief that the courts were not harsh enough and that more should be spent on crime control. These increases persisted until the early

1980s and have remained at a very high level since that time in spite of the huge changes in policy at both the state and federal levels that have produced the dramatic increases in prison populations.

We suggest that a primary reason for the "broken thermometer" model of opinion policy linkage is because this policy arena is dominated by a particularly degenerative form of pluralism in which negative and divisive social constructions are attributed to entire social groups. Pluralism no longer reflects reasoned analysis and a balance among competing interests, but degenerates into ill-founded characterizations that set one group against another. Policy arenas dominated by this type of divisive social constructions and the political opportunism of elected officials do not serve justice, do not create arenas for public discourse, and are not held accountable in terms of effectiveness or efficiency. Without the participation of reasonable interest groups and an informed, alert public to create a balanced dialogue, the discourse about punishment policy is one-sided.

In contrast with water policy, scientific expertise has not played a significant role – even in terms of legitimating criminal justice sanctioning policy. To correct the imbalances that currently exist, well-executed studies of the impacts of prison on prisoners, ex-prisoners, crime rates, victims, and public discourse about crime should be conducted. In this arena, there is not too much scientific expertise; there is too little.

However, if we had focused attention on rehabilitative policies for offenders, such as diversion programs, probation, parole, work programs and the like, we would find that evaluation studies are routinely called for and programs that are unable to provide positive results are almost certainly doomed. Again, this is a characteristic of degenerative pluralism: accountability through the use of scientific studies is seldom called for when the policy will produce significant political capital, such as providing benefits for "advantaged" populations or punishment for those who are socially constructed as "deviant" (Schneider and Ingram, 1993, 1997). Accountability for effective and efficient results will be expected mainly when "going against the grain", providing potentially beneficial policy (such as rehabilitation or diversion) to negatively constructed target populations or attempting to impose burdens on powerful, positively constructed groups (the "advantaged").

Criminal justice punishment policy does not provide arenas for citizen discussion about crime and punishment. Even though public opinion about crime is intense, thoughtful arenas of discussion are virtually absent. Conservatives have no interest in sparking thoughtful discussion because public opinion is firmly on their side and is more likely to stay there if they can continue to convince the public that crime is increasing, that severe punishment has no immediate costs to taxpayers, and that it will be effective if it is truly severe enough. They particularly do not want to break down the negative social construction of lawbreakers with its strongly racial and class terms since it is these constructions that continue to provide significant political advantage to those who are "tough on crime". The cost consequences of rapidly increasing prison populations are being framed as a management issue with private prisons projected as the way to save money. Policies promoted by liberals seldom include arenas for discourse, either because liberals tend to be afraid that discussions will only intensive the public demand for punishment and the association of crime with racial minorities in the public eye. Unless dispassionate policy analysts take the lead on creating criminal justice policies that will include arenas for public discourse, it is not likely to happen.

Criminal justice policy also does not serve justice as well as it should. Over two million people now are incarcerated in the United States, and many scholars will argue that an injustice exists for every person whose incarceration is disproportion to their offense, or who is no longer (or never was) a threat to society or to public safety. The disproportionate representation of racial minorities and persons with poor educations and low incomes reflect deep structural issues of lack of opportunity as well as the likelihood of racist administrative practices even when such practices are believed to serve the goals of effectiveness and efficiency – such as racial profiling.

Conclusion: Towards More Appropriate Balance

Policy analysis would be improved if it paid more attention to a number of pragmatic philosophical principles. Because public policy must serve multiple roles in a society, policy analysis must attend to all of these roles which need to be generally balanced. Policy solves problems, provides arenas for citizen discourse, reflects interests and public opinion, and advances justice. Different modes of inquiry are needed to assess the extent to which each of these is being served. Rather than privilege only one form of analysis, whether it be one of the traditional scientific modes or newer forms such as narrative analysis, the pragmatic policy analyst must be familiar with a much wider range of theories and methods. Pragmatic policy analysis must focus most intently on those values that policy is serving least well within a particular context.

Policy analysts should approach the dominant social construction of issues with considerable skepticism, recognizing that the history of the issue, within context, may have produced an issue frame that is dysfunctional from the perspective of designing policies that will serve democracy. Creating arenas for discussion where alternative constructions of the issue may be heard and have an opportunity to confront dominant constructions may be a central task for policy analysts. Dominant perspectives are seldom hegemonic, and it is almost always possible to find fissures that offer the opportunity for alternative constructions. In water policy, for example, the dominant conception of water as a commodity subject to private property rights enables water to be bought and sold. The arena is conceptualized as a scientific and technical one, where decisions can be made by scientific analysis and quantitative (automatic) decision aids. There are alternative framings, however, such as water contributing to healthy ecosystems and healthy communities (Ingram, 2000). By framing the issue in terms of watersheds, community, and eco-systems, it has been possible to open discussion to citizens and others who had been largely ignored previously. In criminal justice policy, the efforts by some reformers to introduce the notion of "restorative justice", realized through restitution and community service programs has helped break down the negative social constructions that have been used so effectively in this politically manipulated policy area. By providing arenas in which persons who have broken the law are held accountable to victims and society through restitution payments and community service activities, the restorative justice movement has made it possible for law-breakers to redeem themselves through positive action rather than simply through having been punished.

Mixed methods and an eclectic approach to theory are both important aspects of pragmatic policy analysis. In policy arenas where analysis is dominated by scientific and technical experts, we urge the experts to embrace discourse and a more participatory policy analysis as part of their activity so that they may contribute scientific information – within an arena of discussion where they are not the only experts at the table, but where all voices are heard and respected. In policy arenas dominated by strategic politics, ideological rhetoric and advocacy science, we urge the policy analysts to bring information that is reliable and valid and to draw upon evaluation studies with strong designs that have greater chances of breaking down rationales used in the political and ideological debates. Policy analysts in arenas that are dominated by divisive, negative social constructions of target populations should put a "human face" on the most disadvantaged and seek to encourage a more empathetic and reasoned discourse. The discourse may succeed in unmasking the claims of the political strategists and breaking down the divisive, negative social constructions.

Acknowledgement

Thanks to Murray Leaf and Alfonso Morales for their comments on a prior draft.

References

Best, Joel. (1993), "But Seriously Folks: The Limitations of the Strict Constructionist Interpretation of Social Problems", in *Reconsidering Social Constructionism*, James Holstein and Gale Miller (Eds.), Hawthorne: Aldine de Gruyter.

Bohman, James. (1999), "Democracy as Inquiry, Inquiry as Democratic: Pragmatism, Social Science, and the Cognitive Division of Labor". *American Journal of Political Science*, vol. 43, no. 2, pp. 590-607.

Bullert, Gary. (1983), *The Politics of John Dewey*. Buffalo: Prometheus Books.

De Leon, Peter. (1997), *Democracy and the Policy Sciences*. Albany: SUNY Press.

Dewey, John. (1946), *The Public and its Problems*. Chicago: Gateway Books.

Diesing, Paul. (1991), *How Does Social Science Work? Reflections on Practice*. Pittsburgh: University of Pittsburgh Press.

Dror, Yehezkel. (1971), *Design for Policy Sciences*. New York: American Elsevier.

Easton, David. (1963), *A Systems Analysis of Political Life*. New York: John Wiley and Sons.

Farr, James. (1999), "John Dewey and American Political Science". *American Journal of Political Science*, vol. 43, no. 2, pp. 520-541.

Fischer, Frank. (1997), *Evaluating Public Policy*. Chicago: Nelson Halls.

Fischer, Frank and John Forester. (1993), *The Argumentative Turn in Policy Analysis and Planning*. Durham: Duke University Press.

Forester, John (Ed). (1985), *Critical Theory and Public Life*. Boston: Massachusetts Institute of Technology.

Forester, John. (1988), "Critical Theory and Planning Practice", in Forester, (Ed) *Critical Theory and Public Life*, Boston: MIT Press.

Fott, David. (1998), *John Dewey: America's Philosopher of Democracy*. New York: Rowman and Littlefield.

Fox, C. a.H.T.M. (1996), *Postmodern Public Administration - Toward Discourse*. Thousand Oaks: Sage.

Ingram, Helen. (2000), *The Policy Analyst and the Future of American Democracy*. Invited Presentation, University of Massachusetts.

Ingram, Helen and Anne L. Schneider. (1998), *Science, Democracy, and Water Policy. Water Resources Update*, (Elisabeth A. Graffy, U.S. Geological Survey ed.).Issue Number 113.

Ingram, Helen and Anne Schneider. (1996), *Public Policy, Science and Social Constructions*. Prepared for the 1996 annual conference of the American Political Science Association, August 31, 1996, San Francisco.

Kaufman-Osborn, Timothy V. (1991), *Politics, Sense, Experience. A Pragmatic Inquiry into the Promise of Democracy*. Ithica: Cornell University Press.

Knight, Jack and James Johnson. (1999), "Inquiry into Democracy: What Might a Pragmatist Make of Rational Choice Theories?" *American Journal of Political Science*, vol. 43, no. 2, pp. 566-589.

Lasswell, Harold. (1936), *Who Gets What, When, and How?* New York: McGraw Hill.

Lasswell, Harold. (1971), *A Preview of the Policy Sciences*. New York: American Elsevier.

Lindblom, Charles E. (1982), "Another State of Mind", *American Political Science Review*, vol. 76, pp. 9-21.

Lindblom, Charles E. (1959, Jan.), "The Science of Muddling Through, Public Administration Review", pp. 79-88.

MacGilvray, Eric. (1999), "Experience as Experiment: Some Consequences of Pragmatism for Democratic Theory". *American Journal of Political Science*, vol. 43, no. 2, pp. 542-565.

Mass, Arthur and Raymond Anderson. (1978). *And the Dessert Will Rejoice: Conflicts and Justice in Arid Lands*. Cambridge, MA: MIT Press.

Merriam, Charles. (1936), *The Role of Politics in Social Change*. New York: New York University Press.

Meyer, Michael. (1994), *Water in the Hispanic Southwest: A Social and Legal History*. Tucson: University of Arizona Press.

Morales, Alfonso. (1998), "Pragmatism's Mundanity: Epistemic Foundations for Practising Sociolegal Science". *Law and Society Review*, vol. 32, no. 2, pp. 493-515.

Morris, Debra. (1999), "How Shall We Read What We Call Reality? John Dewey's New Science of Democracy". *American Journal of Political Science*, vol. 43, no. 2, pp. 608-628.

Nelkin, Dorothy. (1992), *Controversy*. Newbury Park, NJ. Sage.

Ostrom, Elinor. (1990), *Governing the Commons*. Cambridge: Cambridge University Press.

Ostrom, Elinor. (1992), *Crafting Institutions for Self-Governing Irrigation Systems*. San Francisco: Institute for Contemporary Studies

Popper, Karl. (1966), *The Open Society and Its Enemies, Vol. I; The Spell of Plato, Vol II, The High Tide of Prophecy: Hegel, Marx and the Aftermath*. Princeton: Princeton University Press.

Putnam, Robert (2000), *Bowling Alone*. New York: Simon and Schuster.

Rein, Martin and Donald Schon. (1993), "Reframing Policy Discourse", in Fischer and Forester (Ed) *The Argumentative Turn in Policy Analysis and Planning*. Durham: Duke University Press.

Roe, E. (1994), *Narrative Policy Analysis: Theory and Practice*. Durham: Duke University Press.

Rosenau, Pauline M. (1992), *Postmodernism and the Social Sciences – Insights, Inroads and Intrusions*. Princeton: Princeton University Press.

Roth, Robert J. (1998), *Radical Pragmatism*. New York. Fordham University Press.

Sabatier, P. and Hank Jenkins Smith. (1993), *Policy Change and Learning. An Advocacy Coalition Approach*. Boulder: Westview Press.

Schneider, Anne. (1998), *Private Prisons as Public Policy*. Paper presented at the 1998 American Political Science Association Annual Conference, Boston.

Schneider, Anne. (1999), "Public-Private Partnerships in the U.S. Prison System". *American Behavioral Scientist*, vol. 43, no. 1, pp. 192-208.

Schneider, Anne and Helen Ingram. (1993), "Social Constructions and Target Populations: Implications for Politics and Policy", *American Political Science Review*, vol. 87, no. 2, pp. 334-347.

Schneider, Anne and Helen Ingram. (1997), *Policy Design for Democracy*. Kansas: University Press of Kansas.

Schneider, Anne and Helen Ingram. (1999), "'Good' Public Policy: A Policy Design and Social Construction Perspective". In Rosalyn Y. Carter and Khi V. Thai, *Current Public Policy Issues*. Philadephia: Pre-Academics Press.

Sharp, Elaine. (1999), *The Sometime Connection*. Albany: SUNY Press.

Shields, Patricia. (1996), "Pragmatism: Exploring Public Administration's Policy Imprint". *Administration and Society*, vol. 28, no. 3, pp. 390-341.

Singer, Beth J. (1999), *Pragmatism, Rights, and Democracy*. New York: Fordham University Press.

Smiley, Marion (1999), "Pragmatic Inquiry and Democratic Politics". *American Journal of Political Science*, vol. 43, no. 2, pp. 629-647.

Stuhr, John J. Ed (1993), *Philosophy and the Reconstruction of Culture Pragmatic Essays after Dewey*. Albany: SUNY Press.

Tamanaha, Brian Z. (1999), R*ealistic Socio-Legal Theory: Pragmatism and a Social Theory of Law*. New York: Oxford University Press.

Thayer, H. S. (1952), *The Logic of Pragmatism. An Examination of John Dewey's Logic*. New York: The Humanities Press.

__________. (1968), *The Philosopher of the Common Man: Essays in Honor of John Dewey*. New York: Greenwood Press.

Weatherford, Gary D. and F. Lee Brown. (1986), *New Courses for the Colorado River: Major Issues of the Next Century*. Albuquerque: University of New Mexico Press.

Yanhow, Dvora. (1995), *How Does a Policy Mean*. Washington D.C: Georgetown University Press.

8 Does Consensus Work? A Pragmatic Approach to Public Participation in the Regulatory Process

Cary Coglianese

The officials who staff regulatory agencies are not elected and yet they make more decisions than even elected legislators, decisions that can have direct and significant effects on matters such as workplace safety, environmental quality, and the cost and reliability of essential goods and services. How regulators make their decisions and what role the public plays in the regulatory process should concern all who are interested in the quality of democratic governance (Schneider and Ingram, 2002). A general commitment to democratic principles does not, however, determine the specific strategies which should be used to involve the public in the regulatory process. Regulatory officials can hold hearings or solicit comments on proposals from individuals and organizations likely to be affected by proposed regulations, or they can convene interactive dialogue groups or public workshops to engage in ongoing discussions.

Over the past several decades, regulatory officials have taken considerable interest in procedures that go even further than soliciting public feedback and gathering public input when making decisions. Regulators have begun to seek consensus among regulated industries, citizen groups, government agencies, and others before making public policy decisions. Regulatory policy created and implemented through express agreements between government and business – an approach used most extensively in the Netherlands and elsewhere in Europe – is often held up as a model for policymaking (Dana, 2000; Orts and Deketelaere, 2000). In the United States, consensus building has been institutionalized in the Negotiated Rulemaking Act and in more than two-dozen other statutes that authorize, and increasingly, require regulatory agencies to seek consensus as a basis for proposed policy decisions (Coglianese, 2000).

The ideal of consensus also looms large in intellectual discourse about the validity of knowledge as well as the legitimacy of politics (Habermas, 1996; Rawls, 1993; Kuhn, 1970). As a result, it is understandable that anyone committed to democratic principles would take an interest in consensus building as a form of public participation. Yet a commitment to democracy does not demand the attainment of consensus over policy decisions. Other means of engaging the public in deliberation, which do not hinge on the achievement of consensus, can also satisfy robust standards of democratic governance. How then should regulatory officials determine whether consensus building is an appropriate way to design the regulatory process?

In this chapter, I adopt a pragmatic approach to the question of whether organizing public participation around a search for consensus – as opposed to around a desire for public input or feedback – will contribute to effective and responsive regulatory policy. The approach I apply here draws on a classical conception of pragmatism which holds that ideas should be tested by taking into account the results of acting on them (Rescher, 2000). To the pragmatist, consensus should be the goal of public participation in the regulatory process only if its application in the world of practice is successful. The test for the ideal of consensus is whether pursuing it serves as a realistic and effective way of achieving important social goals.

How well does policy making by consensus work? Advocates of consensus-building have claimed that it serves to improve regulatory policy by enabling policy decisions to be informed by the knowledge of those in the industries that will be regulated (Harter, 1982; Dunlop, 1984; Freeman, 1997). They also assert that consensus building will reduce conflict, increase compliance, improve policy effectiveness, and promote democratic participation (e.g., Freeman and Langbein, 2000). Yet, as much as consensus may be attractive as an ideal, and as much as advocates of consensus building may assert its instrumental value, claims about the positive effects of consensus-building need to be subjected to empirical scrutiny and any potential negative effects must also be considered. Agreement should not be valued simply for its own sake.

In the next section of this chapter, I elaborate on the ideal of consensus and illustrate how it has been employed in specific regulatory contexts. In the remaining sections, I review the effects of consensus building and suggest that such an inquiry supports the conclusion that consensus is decidedly ineffectual for making sound, legitimate regulatory policy. However attractive it may be as an ideal, in practice consensus can contribute new sources of policy failure. Moreover, a search for consensus offers little by way of countervailing benefits that cannot already be achieved by other processes of public participation. Consensus may hold an abstract allure, but when put into practice it is neither a practical nor efficacious method of making regulatory decisions. Alternative methods of public participation that do not demand agreement are the more realistic strategies for democratic engagement.

I. The Ideal of Consensus in the Regulatory Process

Regulators are increasingly called upon to engage the public in making policy decisions through processes variously described as "stakeholder involvement", "partnerships", "consultation", "collaboration", "regulatory negotiation", and "consensus-building". As these different terms suggest, regulatory policy makers have numerous methods for allowing members of the public to participate in the policy process, including soliciting written comments, holding public hearings, and conducting policy dialogues. These various modes of public participation allow members of the public to share their views with agency officials as they frame policy problems and develop possible solutions. Viewpoints can be shared individually in one-on-one conversations with regulators or in group sessions such as roundtables or policy dialogues which allow multiple parties to engage each other in deliberation. According to a recent report by the United States Environmental Protection Agency (EPA), officials in that agency employ public input procedures such as "workshops, joint fact finding, conference calls, and public meetings" in more than 70 percent of their rulemakings (US EPA, 2000). These commonly used procedures allow the public a chance to share information, exchange arguments, and help regulatory officials make more informed policy choices.

More recently, interest has grown in a quite different form of public participation, which seeks unanimity or agreement – consensus-building. While consensus building does not require that everyone gets exactly what they want, it does mean minimally reaching a decision that all can accept. This is the understanding of consensus reflected in *the Negotiated Rulemaking Act* and other statutes in the United States which define consensus specifically as a "unanimous concurrence" of all the interests represented in the negotiation. This is also the understanding reflected in other settings. For example, in the early 1990s, EPA sought to reform environmental regulation in six sectors of the economy in cooperation with representatives from the different industrial sectors, citizen groups, and federal, state, and local government agencies. The committee consisting of these representatives, called the Common Sense Initiative Council, established the principle that it would "operate by consensus decision-making", which meant that decisions were "reached when all Council members at the table can accept or support a particular position" (US EPA, 1996).

Unlike other forms of public participation, consensus-building establishes a decision rule. Unanimity becomes the basis for making a policy decision. In this way, consensus-building is different from other forms of public participation because these other forms do not necessarily seek agreement nor dictate unanimity for reaching a decision. The goal of consensus building, in contrast, is not simply to engage in deliberation and gain public input in order to establish a more informed policy decision. Rather, the goal is to forge an explicit agreement among all of the participants with the expectation that this agreement will form the basis for public policy.

Over the years, agency officials and mediation consultants have urged that efforts to obtain unanimous agreement will result in numerous advantages, not the least of which is the reduction of conflict and litigation. Negotiated rulemaking, a consensus-based strategy for developing new regulations, has long been advocated as a means of reducing subsequent legal challenges to agency regulation. A senior manager within EPA recently claimed that, in addition to saving time and preventing litigation, consensus-building at the agency has resulted in policies that "were more practical and cost-efficient, contained more innovative solutions, were more technically and scientifically current, and had greater legitimacy" (Fox, 1998). As this statement suggests, those who advocate consensus building promise numerous benefits. The literature on alternative dispute resolution and regulatory negotiation is filled with such claims (e.g., Pritzker and Dalton, 1995). Although advocates sometimes acknowledge that consensus-building is no panacea, it would seem to be, if not a cure-all, at least a major advance if it in fact results in reduced conflict, increased compliance, improved public policy, and enhanced legitimacy. After all, if otherwise opposing groups can reach agreement, the resulting policy would seem intuitively to be sound. This is the allure of consensus building, for if all the affected parties can agree on a policy it is difficult to see how anyone could find fault with it. The mere fact of agreement would seem to make consensus appear to be the epitome of a successful regulatory process (Innes, 1999).

Perhaps for this reason, some advocates of consensus building argue that the various benefits attributed to consensus-based processes depend crucially a unanimity decision rule and on a commitment by the agency to following a unanimous agreement. Advocates of consensus building have argued against mere "consultative processes" by which they mean the more typical forms of public participation that do not seek the achievement of consensus. Such consultative efforts, they argue, lack many of the benefits that come from a search for consensus (Harter, 1997; Freeman and Langbein, 2000).

II. The Application of Consensus in the Regulatory Process

Despite the claims made for consensus over the years, few efforts have been made to determine whether processes organized around a search for consensus achieve their goals in practice. Most of the evidence held up in favor of consensus building has been illustrative case studies, most of them being cases which ostensibly succeeded (Weber, 1998). As a result, the attention given to consensus building in the literature has tended to be lop-sided, stressing the benefits of consensus almost to the exclusion of its downsides (Coglianese, 2001a). Yet if we approach the question from the standpoint of classical pragmatism, we need to be open to the possibility that consensus might not work well in practice and therefore seek to test out its application as systematically as we can. Does consensus-building result in the kinds of positive impacts that have been attributed to it? Moreover, are there any pitfalls of consensus building that need to be taken into account? Seeking answers to these two questions will lead to a more realistic assessment of the value of consensus in the regulatory process.

The Impact of Consensus Building

Perhaps the most intuitive impact attributed to consensus has been the reduction of conflict. If all the interested parties can come to an agreement, then presumably all subsequent conflict should be avoided. After all, affected organizations should not subsequently contest a policy in which they have concurred. Yet this intuition does not seem to be borne out in practice, in part because parties to consensus processes do still challenge the resulting policies and in part because those left out of consensus processes also raise objections.

In an earlier empirical study of negotiated rulemaking, I compared the litigation rate for U.S. environmental regulations that had been negotiated with the litigation rate for comparable regulations developed through conventional techniques. Contrary to expectations, the negotiated rules overall ended up being challenged in court more frequently than did a comparison group of rules that were not based on consensus (Coglianese, 1997). This bears out predictions that collaborative processes are as likely to result in conflict or stalemate as anything else (Moore, 1995: 181).

Consensus-based processes create new sources of conflict that do not exist with other methods of policy-making. Conflicts can arise, for example, over who participates in consensus-building proceedings. A recent set of negotiated proceedings at the Department of Housing and Urban Development, for example, spawned legal action by parties seeking to secure a spot on a negotiated rulemaking committee (Coglianese, 2000). In addition to conflicts over who gets to participate, processes structured around consensus can create conflicts over the meaning of agreements that are reached and over whether the ultimate policies comport with the agreements. Disagreements also arise over the meaning of terms in any agreement, as well as over the implications of terms or issues that are missing from the agreement. Obviously none of these additional sources of conflict can arise outside the context of processes structured around agreements.

Another asserted benefit of consensus building has been that it will save regulatory agencies time and resources. Why seeking consensus should save time is not intuitively obvious, but the theory apparently is that reaching an agreement will permit a regulatory agency to move more speedily through its internal decision making process. In practice, the results have been otherwise: consensus-building does not save time nor reduce resources. In one study, participants in negotiated rulemakings were three times more likely to complain that the process took too much time and effort than were respondents who participated in conventional rulemakings (Langbein and Kerwin, 2000). One of the most common complaints about the EPA's now-defunct *Common Sense Initiative* was that it took a long time to accomplish anything (Todd, 1997). Other EPA projects that have relied on consensus have generated similar reactions (US EPA, 1998: 41).

Of course, it really should not be surprising that these methods demand more time and energy. It takes time for everyone to present their concerns and for others to respond. Consensus demands that the deliberation continue until everyone agrees, which often will never happen

(Moore, 1995:165). No one should expect that decision-making by consensus will help speed up the policy process (Coglianese, 1997; Coglianese, 2001a; Balla and Wright, 1999).

Although consensus building neither reduces decision making time nor reduces subsequent conflict, it is supposed to have other positive impacts. For example, it is supposed to lead to better policy decisions. Harter (1997: 1418) has claimed that consensus building "forces the parties to bring an enormous amount of practical information to the table and hence expands the data base on which to build a regulation". The opportunity for government to engage in a dialogue with regulated industry and other parties is supposed to bring more accurate and detailed information to the government decision makers that should enable them to make better policy decisions. While engagement with others can lead to new ideas and even more informed decisions, consensus building is not a prerequisite for such dialogue. Workshops, policy roundtables, and advisory committees can provide similar opportunities for learning and engagement without imposing consensus as a goal.

Moreover, there is no evidence that would validate the claim that consensus-based processes yield systematically better policies. Langbein and Kerwin (2000) have reported that participants in negotiated rulemakings rate the quality of the final rules higher than do individuals who write letters to the agency in other rulemakings. However, the views of participants in innovative procedures like negotiated rulemaking are hardly an adequate basis for drawing conclusions about the actual quality of public policy (Coglianese, 2001b). Since participants have invested considerably more time and effort in consensus-based proceedings, they are less likely to think their time was wasted (Aronson, 1999). Advocates' claims about the quality of public policy that emerges from consensus-building have so far found no more support than have their claims that consensus building saves time or avoids litigation.

The Pitfalls of Consensus Building

Not only does the evidence suggest that consensus building has failed to live up to the claims of its advocates, consensus building also presents significant pitfalls that have tended to be overlooked. Although these problems with consensus have generally been neglected, a realistic appraisal of consensus building requires taking into account both its benefits as well as its drawbacks.

First, consensus building increases the likelihood that policy makers will focus more attention on tractable issues to the neglect of the issues that are most important. For example, less than one-tenth of one percent of all regulations have been established using formal consensus-based procedures (Coglianese, 1997), a select sample that clearly excludes the regulations having the largest impact on the public. After more than a decade of experience with regulatory negotiation, agencies have negotiated only five rules that were classified as "major" or "significant" (according to conventional criteria set forth under executive order) (Coglianese, 1997). Many practitioners advise only using consensus-building when it is reasonably likely that an agreement can be reached, a bias that inevitably tends to emphasize tractability over importance.

Once negotiations are under way, an emphasis on consensus can also lead to a focus on the most tractable issues rather than the most important ones. In 1996, former EPA Administrator William Ruckelshaus convened the Enterprise for the Environment initiative that brought together industry, government, and environmental leaders to forge a consensus on regulatory reform. Although the project initially sought to diagnose problems associated with the current regulatory system, it soon became apparent that the process would never result in an agreement on such a diagnosis, so the participants shifted their efforts to finding agreement on a broad vision of an ideal environmental protection system. What was really needed, of course, was first to identify and understand the existing problems, even though this was a daunting challenge. A similar experience occurred with the EPA's Common Sense Initiative, which the agency initially launched as a major effort to achieve fundamental change in the regulations affecting six industrial sectors, but after becoming bogged down in consensus-building, evolved into a vehicle for developing only modest, incremental projects (Coglianese and Allen, 2001). A emphasis on consensus pushes participants away from squarely confronting the most pressing problems and instead shifts their effort to less important problems where agreement is more likely.

A second pitfall of consensus building is its comparative exclusivity. Consensus in the regulatory process never really reflects agreement of all those affected by regulatory policy. Negotiations take place between representatives of different organizations, not between all the consumers, taxpayers, and citizens who will be affected by a policy decision (Rose-Ackerman, 1994). Furthermore, even among those relevant organizations, policy-making by consensus can lead to the relative exclusion of affected organizations from policy decision-making (Rossi,

1997; Harrison, 1998). This is simply because it tends to be easier to achieve consensus among smaller rather than larger groups. Most practitioners of negotiated rulemaking, for example, recommend that negotiating committees consist of no more than about 25 members. As a result, it is not surprising that members of negotiated rulemaking committees acknowledge that agencies exclude parties from the negotiations who should be at the bargaining table (Langbein and Kerwin, 2000). Moreover, there have been concerns that even among those groups represented in a negotiation, consensus building disadvantages smaller or less well-endowed organizations, such as citizen groups and small businesses. The disproportionate burdens that consensus-building places on different participants is a subtler, but still a notable form of exclusivity worth considering.

A third pitfall of consensus-based processes is imprecision (Mansbridge, 1980: 167). The Enterprise for the Environment initiative noted earlier is a dramatic example of the imprecision that can result from a search for consensus. The outcome of this initiative was a set of recommendations with which no one could seriously disagree, but which spoke mainly in platitudes, such as that "the environmental protection system of the next century must become as efficient and low cost as possible without compromising environmental progress" (Enterprise for the Environment, 1998: 36). It is a well-known phenomenon, reflected in the ambiguities commonly found in statutes, that negotiators can more readily reach agreement by employing imprecise language. Imprecision is almost always less controversial in policymaking than precision (Diver, 1983). Hence, one risk of consensus building is that agreements that are achieved will be forged on the basis of broad, ambiguous principles that paper over underlying conflicts.

A fourth pitfall of consensus building is the lowest common denominator effect (Rescher, 1993). In the context of international policy making, which is grounded ultimately on consensus, it is common for treaties to require no more than what is acceptable to the country with the most objections. The problem with the lowest common denominator, of course, is that such a minimally acceptable outcome will not be enough when a more dramatic decision is needed. In a recent study of negotiated rulemaking, Caldart and Ashford (1999: 201) found that because industry will not likely agree to regulations that would compel firms to make dramatic changes, "negotiated rulemaking's focus on consensus can effectively remove the potential to spur innovation".

Finally, by making consensus the goal of participatory processes, policy makers contribute to a fifth pitfall: the creation of unrealistic and counterproductive expectations. Even if a broad consensus can be forged, holding fast to that agreement, without allowing even minor changes to be made in the resulting regulatory policy, can prove to be extremely difficult. Actors not party to the agreement, such as legislators, other interest groups, and executive branch officials, will undoubtedly try to affect the policy decision (Kagan, 1997). When this happens and the resulting outcome diverges from the agreement even modestly, participants in the consensus proceeding will naturally have certain expectations disappointed, expectations that would have been much less likely to have developed had the process simply sought public input rather than an agreement. In a recent study of consensus building at the National Marine Fisheries Service, it was reported that 60 percent of the participants were dissatisfied with the results of the consensus-based process (Resolve, 1999). The study's authors concluded that much of the dissatisfaction arose because participants expected to dictate the results more than the agency could legally allow. To the extent that government officials enact policies that depart even modestly from what those involved in policy negotiations thought they had agreed to or hoped to achieve, consensus-based processes can foster expectations that will eventually be unfulfilled.

III. Some Pragmatism about Public Participation

For the pragmatist, the validity of consensus building as a regulatory procedure depends not on its theoretical possibility of achieving "win-win" solutions, but on the efficacy of consensus building in its application. Pragmatism holds that the ideas and principles "which prove to be most successful in the course of utilization and application ... are (for that very reason) to be taken to be optimal. Practice, in sum, is to monitor theory: theory is to be evidentiated through its capacity to provide for successful product" (Rescher, 2000: 60). If consensus-building does not fulfill the promises that have been made for it, and if it also adds a series of new pitfalls to the regulatory process, then it fails the kind of practical test contemplated by a classical conception of pragmatism and is hardly something that regulators should be urged to use.

Of course, if consensus did achieve some of the goals that have been set out for it, it might well be worth taking the risk of some of the pitfalls if it was the only means of achieving these goals. But a search for consensus is not needed to reduce conflict, improve policy, or expand public participation (even assuming it could achieve these results). In practice, other forms of public participation, which rely on consultative or deliberative policy processes that do not seek unanimity, can achieve these same benefits and do so more efficaciously.

First, seeking consensus is not the only way to avoid conflict. Conflicts emerge when policies do not satisfy affected individuals and groups. Government officials can avoid conflict by listening carefully to the various parties and seeking to make decisions that respond to their interests. Most sophisticated government officials already do this on a regular basis. That helps explain why most policy decisions never prompt a legal challenge (Coglianese, 1997). To avoid litigated conflict, government officials need not fully satisfy all the interests of all affected individuals and organizations. Such a task is almost always impossible anyway. However, interest groups ordinarily do not pursue each conflict they have with an agency. Disagreement over regulatory policy must rise to a level that justifies making a legal challenge. Conflict and litigation can be minimized if regulatory officials listen to the views expressed by affected parties and seek to craft policies that, while not based on any agreement, nevertheless, are reasonably responsive to public input while at the same time effective in achieving policy goals (Moore, 1995: 189).

Second, consensus is not needed to make policy makers better informed and make policy more sensible. The pitfalls that can afflict consensus-based processes obviously detract from its ability to achieve effective policy results. Moreover, the fact that a negotiating group seeks agreement may actually inhibit some participants from raising important issues. Unanimity may well result from conformity rather than a deliberate agreement (Elster, 1989: 117). In his study of groupthink in policy making, Paul Hart (1994: 293) writes that some participants in consensual processes hesitate to express all their concerns either due to peer pressure or in order to keep from disrupting the group process. When agreement is not the sole object of a deliberation, individuals may express themselves more openly. An EPA official told me, for example, that he knew industry was overlooking a key issue in a consensus-based process to develop new air pollution regulations, but that he never raised the issue during the negotiations (Coglianese, 1997). Similarly, a member of another EPA consensus-building committee reportedly came to agreement only reluctantly after "feeling pressure from all sides" (US EPA, 1999: Appendix 1). This is troubling because a pluralistic airing of differences can often better illuminate policy issues and informs decisions than a discussion that is truncated because individuals feel pressured to reach an agreement.

Finally, although advocates of consensus sometimes suggest that the prospect of an agreement is needed in order to attract people to participate, this is certainly not true. Aiming for an agreement is not the only or even best way of motivating individuals to deliberate over regulatory policy. The possibility of influencing policy decisions drives participation in policy-making – with or without consensus – as is evidenced by the rapid growth in interest group participation in Washington, D.C. in recent decades (King and Walker, 1991). Somewhat ironically, consensus building can in practice sometimes dampen participation. Some of the participants in EPA's Common Sense Initiative, for example, detached themselves from this consensus-based initiative once they could see that the discussions were headed virtually nowhere due to the stringent demands of consensus (Todd, 1997). Government officials can most effectively motivate groups and individuals to participate by sincerely demonstrating their willingness to listen and learn from members of the public (Heifitz, 1994: 123-24).

Given the emphasis within pragmatism on democratic deliberation and public participation (Kaufman-Osborn, 1992), it is important to recognize that participation can still be effectively achieved in settings which allow for dialogue without making consensus the goal. Agencies can promote participation by demonstrating their willingness to listen as best they can while still pursuing their overarching public mandates to incorporate what they learn into their decisions. Indeed, when consensus is abandoned as the goal of public participation, agencies can expand public participation by reaching out to broader and more diverse segments of the population. Avoiding consensus as the goal can also avoid creating unrealistic expectations about what an agency is able or willing to deliver. When these expectations are dashed, as they inevitably will be in some cases, it can lead to cynicism on the part of the public about future consensus-building efforts and less willingness to engage in public deliberations. The best way for an agency to motivate outside groups to participate in policy deliberations would therefore seem to be to set realistic expectations, meet them, and demonstrate consistently that public input affects – even if it does not fully determine – regulatory decisions. Agency practices that take public input seriously, even though not designed around a search for agreement, prove themselves more efficacious.

Policy making by agreement is simply unrealistic as a general strategy for public participation. Even the most extensive and respectful efforts at democratic deliberation will, in practice, still leave important disagreements unresolved (Ferejohn, 2000; Gutmann and Thompson, 1996). If consensus is often unachievable, it only makes sense to accept consultative or deliberative approaches to public participation without requiring regulators to secure agreement before making their decisions. Rescher (1993: 192) argues that pragmatism does not demand full agreement as a basis for policy decisions, but merely seeks to minimize "the overall extent to which people are seriously dissatisfied by its adoption". Eugene Bardach (1999) makes a similar argument in favor of a concept he terms "sufficient consensus" which does not dictate unanimity but simply seeks an adequate degree of political support to ensure that an effective policy decision can move forward. Although Charlene Siegfried (1996: 275), writing from a pragmatic feminist perspective, advances a similar conception of consensus, she makes plain that this "does not mean avoiding conflicts or denying differences". A search for consensus, defined as it has been in the regulatory context as demanding unanimity, should be well recognized as an unrealistic strategy for making policy decisions.

A pragmatic approach to public participation tests the validity of ideas through their efficacy in practice. Formal efforts at consensus building have overall tended to fail that test and are, therefore, not appropriate as a general model for the regulatory process. Public input can be more effectively pursued using public meetings, policy dialogue sessions, informal consultations, and other methods that do not seek to achieve unanimous agreement.

Conclusion

Pragmatism "strives not for the unattainable unanimous agreement" demanded of consensus-based theories of regulatory policy making (Rescher, 1993: 192-93). Searching for consensus fosters unrealistic expectations, increases decision-making time and resources, makes a lowest common denominator outcome more likely, encourages imprecision, and favors tractability over importance. Moreover, consensus is simply not needed in order to ensure democratic legitimacy and effective public policy because alternative forms of public participation can yield the same kinds of benefits while avoiding the new sources of conflict and policy failure created by a fixation on consensus. Designers of regulatory processes should therefore not engage in wishful thinking about consensus-based processes, nor succumb to a unrealistic vision of democratic decision making that demands unanimity. Those who are considering whether to require agencies to engage in consensus-based processes or pursue other contractual forms of regulatory policy making should consider whether consensus really works. Since the purported benefits of consensus building can be achieved through other participatory processes, which do not aim for consensus, and since consensus-based decision-making introduces new sources of policy failure, pragmatic observers of the regulatory process are likely to conclude that calls for the expansion of consensus building are unwarranted.

Acknowledgement

I am grateful to Alfonso Morales and Kenneth Winston for their helpful comments on an earlier version of this chapter and to Travis LeBlanc for his excellent research assistance.

References

Aronson, E. (1999), "Dissonance, Hypocrisy, and the Self Concept". In E. Harmon-Jones and J. Mills (eds), *Cognitive Dissonance: Progress on a Pivotal Theory in Social Psychology*, American Psychological Association.

Balla, S. and Wright, J. (1999), "Consensual Rulemaking and the Time it Takes to Develop Rules", paper presented at the fifth National Public Management Research Conference, College Station, Texas.

Bardach, E. (1999), *Getting Agencies to Work Together: The Practice and Theory of Managerial Craftsmanship.* Washington, D.C: Brookings Institution Press.

Caldart, C. and Ashford, N. (1999), "Negotiation as a Means of Developing and Implementing Environmental and Occupational Health and Safety Policy" *Harvard Environmental Law Review*, vol. 23, pp. 141-202.

Coglianese, C. (1997), "Assessing Consensus: The Promise and Performance of Negotiated Rulemaking", *Duke Law Journal*, vol. 46, pp. 1255-1349.

Coglianese, C. (2000), "Is Consensus an Appropriate Basis for Regulatory Policy?' In E. Orts and K. Deketelaere (eds), *Environmental Contracts: Comparative Approaches to Regulatory Innovation in the United States and Europe*. Kluwer Law International.

Coglianese, C. (2001a), "Assessing the Advocacy of Negotiated Rulemaking", *New York University Environmental Law Journal*, vol. 9.

Coglianese, C. (2001b), "Is Satisfaction Success? Evaluting Public Participation in Regulatory Policy Making", paper presented at the Maxwell School/Indiana Conflict Resolution Institute conference on "Evaluating Environmental and Public Policy Dispute Resolution Programs and Policies", Washington, D.C., March 8-9, 2001.

Coglianese, C. and Allen, L. (2001), "Building Sector-Based Consensus: A Review of the U.S. EPA Common Sense Initiative,' paper presented at the Kennedy School of Government workshop on 'Voluntary, Collaborative, and Information-Based Policies", Cambridge, May 10-11, 2001.

Dana, D. (2000), "The New 'Contractarian' Paradigm in Environmental Regulation", *University of Illinois Law Review*, vol. 20, pp. 35-59.

Diver, C. (1983), "The Optimal Precision of Administrative Rules", *Yale Law Journal*, vol. 93, pp. 65-109

Dunlop, J. (1984), *Dispute Resolution: Negotiation and Consensus Building*. Dover: Auburn Publishing.

Elster, J. (1989), "The Market and the Forum: Three Varieties of Political Theory". in J. Elster and A. Hylland (eds), *Foundations of Social Choice Theory*. Cambridge: Cambridge University Press.

Enterprise for the Environment (1998), *The Environmental Protection System in Transition: Toward a More Desirable Future*. Washington, D.C.: The Center for Strategic and International Studies Press.

Ferejohn, J. (2000), "Instituting Deliberative Democracy", in I. Shapiro and S. Macedo (eds), *Designing Democratic Institutions*. New York: New York University Press.

Fox, J.C. (1998), "A Real Public Role". *The Environmental Forum*, vol. 15, pp. 18-30.

Freeman, J. (1997), "Collaborative Governance in the Administrative State", *UCLA Law Review*, vol. 45, pp. 1-98.

Freeman, J. and Langbein, L. (2000), "Regulatory Negotiation and the Legitimacy Benefit" *New York University Environmental Law Journal*, vol. 9, pp. 60-151.

Gutmann, A. and Thompson, D. (1996), *Democracy and Disagreement*. Cambridge: Harvard University Press.

Habermas, J. (1996), *Between Facts and Norms: Contributions to a Discourse Theory of Law and Democracy*. Cambridge: Massachusetts Institute of Technology Press.

Harrison, K. (1998), "Talking with the Donkey: Cooperative Approaches to Environmental Protection", *Journal of Industrial Ecology*, vol. 2, pp. 51-72.

Hart, P. (1994), *Groupthink in Government: A Study of Small Groups and Policy Failure*. Baltimore: Johns Hopkins University Press.

Harter, P. (1982), "Negotiating Regulations: A Cure for Malaise", *Georgetown Law Journal*, vol. 71, pp. 1-113.

Harter, P. (1997), "Fear of Commitment: An Affliction of Adolescents", *Duke Law Journal*, vol. 46, pp. 1389-1423.

Heifitz, R. (1994), *Leadership Without Easy Answers*. Cambridge: Harvard University Press.

Innes, J. (2000), "Evaluating Consensus-Building". In L. Susskind, S. McKearnan, and J. Thomas-Larmer (eds), *The Consensus-Building Handbook*, Sage Publications.

Kagan, R. (1997), "Political and Legal Obstacles to Collaborative Ecosystem Planning" *Ecology Law Quarterly*, vol. 24, pp. 871-5.

Kaufman-Osborn, T. (1992), "Pragmatism, Policy Science, and the State". In J.E. Tiles (ed), *John Dewey: Critical Assessments* (vol. II), Routledge Press.

King, D. and Walker, J. (1991), "An Ecology of Interest Groups in America". In J. Walker, *Mobilizing Interest Groups in America: Patrons, Professions, and Social Movements*. Ann Arbor: University of Michigan Press.

Kuhn, T. (1970), *The Structure of Scientific Revolutions*. Chicago: University of Chicago Press.

Langbein, L. and Kerwin, C. (2000), "Regulatory Negotiation Versus Conventional Rulemaking: Claims, Counter-Claims, and Empirical Evidence", *Journal of Public Administration Research and Theory*, vol. 10, pp. 599-632.

Mansbridge, J. (1980), *Beyond Adversary Democracy*. Chicago: University of Chicago Press.

Moore, M. (1995), *Creating Public Value: Strategic Management in Government*. Cambridge: Harvard University Press.

Orts, E. and Deketelaere, K. (2000), *Environmental Contracts: Comparative Approaches to Regulatory Innovation in the United States and Europe*, Kluwer Law International.

Pritzker, D. and Dalton, D. (1995), *Negotiated Rulemaking Sourcebook*, Administrative Conference of the United States, Washington, D.C.

Rawls, J. (1993), *Political Liberalism*. New York: Columbia University Press.

Rescher, N. (1993), *Pluralism: Against the Demand for Consensus*. Oxford: Clarendon Press.

Rescher, N. (2000), *Realistic Pragmatism: An Introduction to Pragmatic Philosophy*. Albany: SUNY Press.

Resolve, Inc. (1999), *The National Marine Fisheries Service Take Reduction Team Negotiation Process Evaluation*, National Marine Fisheries Service, Washington, D.C.

Rose-Ackerman, S. (1994), "Consensus versus Incentives: A Skeptical Look at Regulatory Negotiation", *Duke Law Journal*, vol. 43, pp. 1206-20.

Rossi, J. (1997), "Participation Run Amok: The Costs of Mass Participation for Deliberative Agency Decisionmaking", *Northwestern University Law Review*, vol. 92, pp. 173-249.

Schneider, A. and Ingram, H. (2002), "The Pragmatic Policy Analyst". In A. Morales (ed), *Renascent Pragmatism: Studies in Law and Social Science*. London: Ashgate Press.

Siegfried, C. (1996), *Pragmatism and Feminism*. Chicago: University of Chicago Press.

Todd, J. (1997), *Review of the Common Sense Initiative*, U.S. Environmental Protection Agency, Washington, D.C.

U.S. Environmental Protection Agency (1996), *Operating Principles of the U.S. Environmental Protection Agency Common Sense Initiative Council*, Washington, D.C.

U.S. Environmental Protection Agency (1998), *Evaluation of Project XL Stakeholder Processes: Final Report*, Washington, D.C.

U.S. Environmental Protection Agency (1999), *Constructive Engagement Resource Guide: Practical Advice for Dialogue Among Facilities, Workers, Communities and Regulators*, Washington, D.C.

U.S. Environmental Protection Agency (2000), *Engaging the American People: A Review of EPA's Public Participation Policy and Regulations with Recommendations for Action*, Washington, D.C.

Weber, E. (1998), *Pluralism by the Rules: Conflict and Cooperation in Environmental Regulation*. Washington, D.C: Georgetown University Press.

PART IV

EMPIRICAL STUDIES FROM PRAGMATIST PERSPECTIVES

9 A Pragmatist Theory of Social Movement Leadership

Alfonso Morales and Robert R. Jimenez

Introduction

Current social movement literature on the management of social movement organizations is grounded in conceptual dualisms: professional/formal and entrepreneurial/informal approaches (Staggenborg, [1988] 1997, 1989; Poster, 1995; Edwards and Marullo, 1995; Hutchinson et al., [n.d.]). Analysts create these mutually exclusive categories and sort social movement leaders by the conceptual scheme. Leaders incompletely captured by a category are ignored, considered unimportant or simply mislabeled in some way, for instance when a social movement leader behaves inconsistently, switching between formal and informal tactics. The claim, often left implicit, is that the essences expressed by the conceptual scheme capture and serve as an account of SML behavior. Focusing on social movement activity in east Los Angeles, this work critiques the essentialist assumptions of this approach (Leaf 1979) distinguishing it from a pragmatist approach, which explains social movement leaders' (SMLs) behavior as a contingent and relational process.

Social movement leaders (SMLs), acting through their community-based organizations (CBOs) in east Los Angeles, engage in a government sponsored "request for proposal" (RFP) cycle. They engage in the RFP cycle to develop and attempt to fund community/client-oriented programs organized by their CBO. There are two basic approaches to understanding SML behavior (essentialist and pragmatic): understanding by way of categorizing and understanding by way of contextualizing.

The essentialist position is to categorize SMLs as either professional or entrepreneurial, and each category (according to Staggenborg), is understood to have its own exclusive techniques for organizing and operating the Social Movement Organization (SMO). Essentialists uncritically accept the idea that leadership style overlaps with organizational structure without explaining why that should be so, and what to do when it is not the case. The analyst assumes that SMLs distinct management techniques overlap with the organization of the SMO. For instance, an SML categorized as using professional leadership techniques will have an organization characterized by formal structures, and, in contrast, entrepreneurial leadership techniques are uncritically thought to overlap with the existence of informal organizational structures. However, the data discussed in this paper indicate that categorization overly simplifies the reality of a complex social process. We find that SMLs vary in the way they mix professional and entrepreneurial management styles; subsequently, few SMO conform to analysts' ideal-typical conceptual schemes. In short, our thesis is that to understand SMLs leadership practices and choices, the analyst must theorize the social process SMLs practice. SML behavior is better explained with reference to their perspectives and attending to those perspectives uncovers and comprehends behavioral regularities.

In brief, we elaborate this argument by examining the behavior of SML engaged in a six month long, and longer, request for proposal (RFP) process in which the SML are part of a complex web of relationships and activities. In this funding environment, inclusive of city sanctioned community based needs assessments, a variety of other organizations and actors, academic, city, community based, and others, SMLs attend and organize many sorts of meetings and activities. However, the essentialist observer attending these activities and predicting behavior on the basis of professional/entrepreneurial categories could hardly recognize the same SML from one activity to the next. Inconsistency in behavior from the essentialist perspective reins even in observed consistency of purpose.

For instance, in City sanctioned needs assessments SMLs are considered experts in the identification of community problems and needs and the observer finds SMLs taciturn and technical as much as aggressive and aroused. In meetings with the community, the SML might become charismatic, mobilizing clients for demonstrations, or other disruptive behavior but then revert to being a careful technician in letter writing campaigns or gauging support from clients. With fellow SMLs, the SML is Machiavellian, measuring strengths against needs and dependencies, knowing well that within an RFP process all are seeking part of limited funds. Understanding the importance of time and place and utilizing past experience, SMLs adopt behavior suitable to the situation. In short, the essentialist impulse to categorize does not explain SML behavior. But the essentialist might respond that when SMLs are called to work with the City to meet the community's needs, they act professionally. When advocating on behalf of community needs, they act entrepreneurally. However, this is not the case. SML behavior is not attributable to simple categorization. To explain SML behavior by categorization belies the complexity of SML responses to processes and circumstances. Furthermore, categorization does not capture learned responses to particular relationships and contexts, nor does it comprehend SML capacity to change behavior and so modify the rules of the "language game" that is being played in those contexts. Ultimately, what is required to understand SML behavior is to locate the behavior as an aspect of situation and process. To understand behavior requires that analysts adopt behavioral assumptions which capture the dynamic aspects of SML behavior instead of trying to fix the behavior by some essentialist scheme.

A Brief Literature Review

Our interest in understanding social movement leaders can be traced to McCarthy and Zald (1973) as they argued then that movement activity was becoming more professionally and formally managed. These new management and tactical SMOs would eschew informal practices adopting profiles analogous to large businesses (McCarthy and Zald, 1977). Since then, analysts have identified and reified the formal/informal distinction (But see Aminzade, 1995). Thus, Staggenborg's ([1988] 1989, 1997) study of the pro-choice movement established and grounded formal/professional and informal/entrepreneurial as the essentialist (or dualist, Leaf 1979) conceptual apparatus with which to understand and explain the management of social movements and the subsequent success or demise of its organization(s) or practice(s).

Staggenborg ([1988] 1989, 1997) uses an essentialist approach to explain SML behavior. Her key distinction is between professional and entrepreneurial SMLs. Leaders are characterized by leadership style and form of organization, and the latter follows from the former. She describes a typical professional SML, "professional managers tend to formalize the organizations that they lead" ([1988] 1997: 428). She continues, "Formalized SMOs engage in fewer disruptive tactics of the sort that pressure government authorities and other elites to make concessions or provide support than do informal SMOs" ([1988] 1997: 437). By contrast the typical entrepreneurial SMLs, "prefer informal structures that enable them to maintain personal control" ([1988] 1997: 428). She continues to describe informal SMOs, "Informal SMOs, with their more flexible structures, are more likely to innovate direct-action tactics" ([1988] 1997: 437). In sum, Staggenborg argues that SML behavior is either professional or entrepreneurial; this distinction is essential to the individual, a characteristic of the individual, and, furthermore, that each organization is managed according to whichever type of leader they are.

Despite her argument that some SMLs make a transition from entrepreneurial to professional in order to keep the SMO they manage alive ([1988] 1997), her conceptual apparatus is not suited to account for this transitional process. In other words, for Staggenborg and other similar analysts, SMLs spring into the world as entrepreneurial or professional and why they are only one and not the other is unexplained, nor do we have the tools to understand how an SML might change from one behavior to another. Why SMLs (or anyone) behave consistently is a question not resolvable by labeling their behavior, and, furthermore, the labeling itself, besides being ambiguous, is no substitute for an explanation.

Poster (1995), Edwards and Marullo (1995), and Hutchinson et al. (n.d.) use Staggenborg's classification system to analyze SMO and in use they uncover some of its difficulties. Poster (1995) suggests that class, gender and race usefully modify Staggenborg's classification system. Poster argues that women of color and of poorer economic class constitute the entrepreneurial leadership and clients of the informal SMO on the periphery of a broader social movement. These people have more to gain from informal tactics, and they assume a radical position in the movement and produce a "Radical Flank Effect" (Haines, [1984] 1997) in an effort to achieve their aims or broaden the movement. One obvious question is why attribute informal behavioral characteristics and movement tactics to the poor or persons of color? Since Staggenborg identifies 'informal' leadership with 'unsuccessful' movements, this identification may reify stereotypes grounded in popular culture. Are there no SMLs of color who utilize tactics appropriate to circumstance?

Edwards and Marullo (1995) also modify the classification system. They argue that when SMOs adopt several issues or causes in addition to a leadership style they tend to survive. However, this claim is ambiguous, and can be seen as powerful evidence against categorically limiting SML behavior to professional or entrepreneurial.

On the other hand, Hutchinson, et al. (unpublished) argue that SMLs mobilizing their SMOs at the local level do not display a tendency towards formalization or professionalization. They state, "the core leadership of Derechos Humanos never founded a formal organization in their 20 years of activism to pursue collective action" (n.d.: 31). Although, Hutchinson et al. (n.d.) argues against Staggenborg's transitional phase—from entrepreneurial/informal to professional/formal—that they, nonetheless, view SMLs and SMOs in terms of Staggenborg's classification system: either entrepreneurial/informal or professional/formal. In the end, these analysts uncritically utilize Staggenborg's essentialist conceptual apparatus.

Staggenborg's approach pervades the literature on SMLs. Our review illustrates that Staggenborg's classification of SMLs is grounded on the analyst interpreting their behavior as either professional or entrepreneurial, and assuming they behave consistently so. Analysts following the essentialist approach to understanding the dynamics of social movement management will misunderstand, ignore, or incompletely explain SML behavior.

The Pragmatist Approach

The dualist perspective for theory creation has it that the analyst creates or develops a set of concepts and arranges them in some logical sequence, linking them to predictions about some aspect of social life. In the above cast, the "professional" SML is always and only part of "formal" SMO. The pragmatist perspective prescribes that analysts learn the concepts used by people in some activity, describe what she has learned, and then to test the description, use the concepts to predict what the people will do next or to predict what will happen if some aspect of the system is changed. What is important here is answering the question: what is the analyst assuming about people's behavior in this activity? Essentialism leads to abstraction, pragmatism to understanding the ways language games or ideas-in-practice are constituted and change, and the concrete experimental and empirical understanding of how people learn and change particular social activities.

Following the pragmatist approach our theory of SML is not of leadership as such, it is about understanding the *contingent process* of leadership. Processes are social in origin and outcome, and in this approach we assume leaders (and others) are communicative, habitual, reciprocal in orientation and purposeful (Dewey and Mead). We will discuss each assumption in turn. A key problem in understanding the behavior of SML (or people in any social activity) is to understand how to identify and relate the processes that are producing and modifying interpersonal relationships.

The pragmatist approach focuses on communicative processes and begins with Mead's insight regarding the development of the self. The self is made possible by interaction and communication and grows in the processes of learning roles. Reciprocity is important here. The capacity for role-taking and subsequent appreciation of the consequences of action-communication produces reciprocity for orienting ongoing interaction. The accumulation of shared meaning/behavior is the context for purpose and the creation of habits, but habits and purposes are not forever unchanging. New problems or opportunities are the conditions for new usages and modifications of purposes and habitual ideas-in-practice. Finally, this notion of purpose undergirds the development of self and separates utilitarian approaches from the pragmatist position. Purpose itself is organized by the ideas people have about any given situation, ideas that help define who counts in any given circumstance and how actors might behave toward each other.

For us, the Request for Proposals (RFP) process enacts interrelated social definitions: roles, mutual obligations, expectations and dependencies in the course of purposeful behavior. Those who accept roles accept responsibilities. Those who accept roles are compelled to interpret and practice the role in a fashion to enable ongoing interaction. This is not without challenge and modification, but the SML we examined demonstrably behave within limits of roles and consequent responsibilities. And so, SMLs are consistently oriented by purpose and mutual understanding even when they vary by tactics.

Pragmatism is distinct from essentialist position in two key ways. First, categories are not reified, every behavior observed is potentially, (but not always) important because behavior is contingent on process, purpose and circumstances. Second, the description of the meaning/behavior observed is a theory of that behavior. The theory is predicated on the behavioral assumptions, and these are observed in different degrees in distinct situations. So to apply the perspective briefly, first we do not assume people are going to behave consistently, we can see why SMLs would behave differently but understandably by way of the common behavioral assumptions. Concepts like "professional" and "entrepreneurial" are now *situational* instead of transcendent descriptions of behavior. Instead of privileging concepts and associated definitions, pragmatists use concepts to describe SML behavior evidently selected according to context, purpose and experience.

So the pragmatist approach has two elements: (1) the language game learned, enacted, developed and changing in the practice of a collective activity and (2) those people socialized into the practice of that game. Together we can call these elements a leadership meaning system (LMS) (see Tamanaha 1997; Leaf 1994 for examples of this approach in other empirical contexts). Our claim is twofold: first, that this method is inclusive, demanding only sharp skills of observation from anyone interested in how leadership is present in a given situation, and second, that the theory will produce informative descriptions that get to the facts of the matter about leadership and the behavior of SML.

Methods and Data

In order to understand SML behavior we need to understand the various actors in their relationships to SML and the resultant LMS. So we gathered data from various sources and cross-examined these data to maximize validity. Fourteen different community leaders were interviewed in addition to three governmental officials. These interviews were open-ended and conversational. The questions addressed the political process that community leaders engage in their community-based organization's (CBO's) structure and culture, their definition of key terms (such as self-sufficiency identified and used among CBOs, their CBO's purpose, and their CBO's history including some autobiographies. Five additional SMLs were identified either through newspaper accounts or through observations of CBO or City sponsored events. All together we interviewed, often multiple times, a total of eight female leaders and eleven male leaders for a total of nineteen community leaders, of which one was black, five were white, and thirteen were Hispanic.

Internal and/or external documents of nineteen different CBOs were analyzed. City documents from the City's Community Development Department (CDD), Community Action Board (CAB), the Mayor's Office, and the Commission on Children, Youth, and Families were collected and analyzed. Local newspapers including the *Los Angeles Times, Eastside Journal*, *Northeast Sun*, and *The Wave* were also collected and examined for evidence about the behavior of SML and the organization and practice of the LMS. Participation and observations of various CBOs and governmental functions were also analyzed to help with interviewing the SML and integrating other data. In addition, Federal Regulatory Acts were assessed to understand some of the broader context.

Key ideas-in-practice and behavior were identified from these various sources of data: ideas/behavior that constitute the LMS for securing funding through the RFP process. Below we will discuss these ideas/behaviors-in-practice and note circumstantial variation in the LMS by different SMLs. We will also note how SML experience and beliefs is a source of variation in their approach to the RFP process.

Findings

In this section of the chapter we will discuss the RFP LMS in which SMLs find themselves. This includes aspects of how SMLs/CBOs understand and respond to the RFP process. The process has two core elements, the identification of community needs and the transformation of needs into RFP.

Our data illustrate that in order for SMLs to compete effectively in an RFP process and secure funding for their CBOs, they must be able to use several distinct leadership tools. But to understand why this is so we must understand the RFP cycle. Both the tools and the cycle are elements of the LMS. The RFP process is initiated by the City and has two major components: (1) the process of identifying community needs (2) the transformation of community needs into community action plans (CAP) or consolidated plans (CP) and proposals responsive to the RFP. While stated simply, the behavior associated with each is rather more complex, but is bounded by shared goals and constraints we call the LMS. Both components have subsections, which describe them below. SMLs use considerable amounts of time engaging in the government sponsored RFP process. It is roughly estimated that in a RFP cycle (six-nine months) SMLs spend no less than 50 percent of their time on the RFP process.[1] Examining the RFP process reveals the complexity of SML's behavior by indicating that SMLs vary in how and when they relate to other SMLs/SMOs, the "community", and the "City". It is precisely this heterogeneity that essentialist theory fails to theorize adequately.

In order to play the RFP game an SML must learn the LMS, inclusive of who the players are, and the formal and informal aspects of the RFP process. To be successful in the RFP process, the SML plays the game, using various tactics we might describe as professional or entrepreneurial, establishing relationships, modifying these, and, in sum, working to produce a proposal responsive to the RFP. In terms of the RFP, the city's Community Development Department (CDD) makes the first move and coordinates and oversees directly or indirectly all the phases surrounding a RFP cycle. Essentially, the CDD facilitates the context in which SMOs perceive and act upon "official" sources of information regarding an RFP. In this sense the CDD is a central source of information in the LMS. SMLs organize relationships and activities and orient themselves to CDD pronouncements.

The essentialist theoretical strategy would ignore the CDD (we do not need it to understand the professional/entrepreneurial distinction) or homogenize it with regard to SMLs (all SML are treated *essentially* the same way by the CDD). On the other hand, the pragmatist strategy is to ask about the ideas/behavior found in the LMS and how these are adopted, modified and/or rejected in the course of participants working toward their interests with their unique capacities and opportunities. All the participants in the LMS, SMLs included, contingently interpret and act on the ideas learned and modified in the LMS.

Identifying Needs

In the RFP process the city's Community Development Department (CDD) seeks to facilitate a consensus among willing SMLs on how to approach community needs. The mechanism of this facilitation is the CAP (Community Action Plan). Below the plan is quoted to illustrate the sort of ideas/behavior expected within and between CBOs in the practice of the RFP process that eventually produces public programs:

> The Family Self-Sufficiency approach requires trained and caring staff, coupled with the creative use of resources. It involves intensive and challenging work by a professional, specialized staff. Building an agreement among line staff and management about the effectiveness and validity of this process [which] results in a program without the drag of doubt and dissension in the future. Reaching true agreement with collaborating agencies about the scope and focus of the program prevents turf wars later [amongst CBOs] (City of Los Angeles' Community Development Department, 9).

Implicitly the CDD's statement recognizes a reality: that conflict exists within and between CBOs. The ambiguous wording, which could not be otherwise, is the vehicle for multiple responses from participants in the LMS. The reality the LMS represents is complex, a world of conflict and cohesion, but a world oriented to producing programs. But, to produce programs some agreements must be established, roles reciprocated, and goals reached. To encourage these ends the CDD implicitly rewards those CBOs who participate in the consensual creation of what is required and involved in meeting community needs – namely, a "trained", "caring", "professional" and "specialized staff" which "agrees" with "collaborating agencies about program scope and focus". Knowing that their behavior and proposals will be scrutinized with these criteria in mind, SMLs are mindful of their actions and proposals. They are also mindful of their clients and goals and the reality of their relationships with other SMLs/CBOs, and so a tension results, productive of tactical subtleties and real conflict in the process of responding to RFP.[2]

Regardless of the desire the CDD has for a consensual process, they are legally obliged "to actively seek participation of its Community Action Board [representing a coalition of Community Improvement and Planning Areas, business, and government personnel], the clients, and non-profit and public agency staff in all stages of the planning, design, implementation, and evaluation processes for the delivery of human services" (Ibid., 1). In other words, the RFP cycle cannot *formally* exclude any CBO/SML no matter how they behave. Despite seeking unanimity, the CDD recognizes the inevitable conflict and, hence, politics of its RFP process and so implicitly admits the use of multiple leadership tools and techniques.

SMLs engage in the City sanctioned RFP process of identifying community needs by attending needs assessment functions. Usually attending these functions involves mobilizing their beneficiaries. By needs assessment functions, we mean those functions sponsored by or related to the City which consist of any of the following: CAB meetings, CDD hearings, town hall meetings, surveys, or focus group sessions. Each of these meetings has different purposes and SMLs recognize these permutations by mobilizing clients in different ways according to moment in the RFP process and the particulars of the circumstances.[3]

The clients of SMOs are a potent part of the LMS. They are sources of information and instruments the SML mobilizes in the RFP process. Whether responding to surveys or conducting a demonstration, clients are an important part of the identification of community needs. There is variation among SMLs about when and how to involve clients in the RFP process, but, broadly speaking, SMLs alternately engage their clients professionally or entrepreneurially.

Sometimes clients are organized professionally as a type of sub-committee of their CBO. Many SMLs make an official objective of organizing community members into the structure of their CBO for RFP purposes. For instance, one CBO's proposal reads, "The Violence Prevention program looks to find solutions at a grassroots level. A 4-year plan has been developed that includes; job training/placement, community organizing, and media advocacy" (*Reaching Out*, external documents). Other SMLs organize community members as part of the overall organization, but they do not explicitly make clients a part of their CBOs organization. Nick Smith stated in an interview with the press, "The parent is going to be the backbone of the program"; however, this CBO's (*Emergency Community Rescue's*) by-laws and program/proposal descriptions do not incorporate community members in the same way as *Reaching Out*. Yet, the leadership of *Emergency Community Rescue* makes sure that parents and youth attend needs-identification functions to informally express that *Emergency Community Rescue* understands their needs and is able to meet them effectively. Whether or not SMLs organize community members as sub-committees of CBO, there is a similar effect, the creation of a relationship of reciprocal loyalty.[4] On the one hand, community members pledge loyalty to a certain CBO, and in turn, the CBO pledges itself to a specific group of people and/or the needs of a specific part of a community. This *reciprocal* loyalty serves a critical function in stabilizing expectations and helping both sides meet each other's needs. Whether mobilized *ad hoc* or as part of a CBO, the resultant mutually orienting expectations become habitual and the subsequent behavior furthers the purposes of the CBO and of the community. Analytically these behaviors help us understand two things: first, they help us understand roles that community members play in the Leadership Meaning System, and secondly, they indicate that entrepreneurial or professional leadership is a choice, involving imperfect interpretation of others behavior and an effort at the orchestration of various players in the RFP game, not simply the result of being a particular point in the RFP process or reducible to a personality characteristic of some SMLs.

The creation of a relationship of reciprocal loyalty does not always guarantee that behaviors of community members will reciprocate the wishes of the SMLs or the CBOs or vise versa. It only points to the collaborative efforts used to secure funding. During the process of obtaining funding from participation in an RFP process, community members as well as SMLs behaviors are independent of each other. If funding is granted, those behaviors may change upon this economic contingency. What is true is the creation of a relationship between the community members and the CBOs, but what is unclear is the motives that propel community members and SMLs to act in collaboration with each other for the purpose of obtaining funding. Motives may be and are in fact multifaceted and contingent on each other's behaviors, promises, commitments, etc. and are not reducible to roles in a process. There are simply too many other factors in play at one time in an RFP process. What makes possible our understanding of these complex alliances is not our reliance on an analysis of motives, but an appreciation of mutually desirable outcomes. Motivations are not always clearly defined or communicated between the community members and CBOs, but both realize *some* benefits from working together.

On the other hand, similar dynamics are at work between SMLs and the City. SMLs are often called on from the City to participate in the identification of community needs, and they willingly participate as experts knowledgeable of community needs based on their working experience. They attend city organized focus-group sessions, fill-out city sponsored surveys, and attend CIPA meetings for CDDs. They attend City Council meetings to make suggestions, as well as receive recognition and recommendations. They also participate in City sponsored task forces and commissioned studies. SMLs participating in all these functions emphasize they know what the community needs are, and that their CBO provides the solution. Nick Smith stated at several CIPA meetings that there was a need for new programs to help gang members change their behavior, and he regularly argued that his CBO was well-placed in the community and well organized to meet that need. SMLs attend these City functions with their beneficiaries who legitimize their expertise and the effectiveness of their CBO. On those occasions, SMLs act professionally, directing their clients to behave appropriate with respect to a city organized function. Organizational legitimacy is at stake, but shepherding clients is only one way to secure that legitimacy. It is not uncommon for SMLs to coach their clients in how to respond to any situation. For instance, the same SML, Nick Smith, has shown his beneficiaries what to write in a letter-writing campaign and coached them on how to respond in public, such as on a radio or television talk show or at City Council meetings. As in the case of the community, SMLs co-create the LMS with City personnel. The possibilities and limits of City, SML and Client behavior is inscribed and incremental changes that behavior are described by enacting and accepting roles played in the RFP game.

Social Movement Leaders "bridge" levels and units of analysis. In the process of identifying community needs they talk to community members, establishing the idea of a program as well as providing a verbal sketch of the players of the funding game and the reason community members are needed and the different ways they can help. As they try to create a possible solution to a local problem, they "sell" the idea to community leaders and other SMLs, and so establish a shared sketch of concepts and relationships that will enable all the actors to understand the problem and form the same standpoint. Once the negotiation has taken place the SMLs and their confederates approach the fund-granting institution to negotiate the creation of a program or service to address the social need. In the process of seeking funding the SMLs approach the State, or fund-granting institution, and engage another negotiation with representatives of the "structural constraints" that SMLs must overcome. This interactive process can flow from the SMLs to the State and vice-versa, with negotiation occurring within each level. By negotiating and acting on relationships, and by establishing the "vocabulary of motive" SMLs and others represent "structure," and micro is linked to macro.

Occasionally SMLs want new or different community needs to be given special consideration by the City. It is then that they become activist or entrepreneurial. This does not mean that they radically change the Leadership Meaning System; instead change is secured by mobilizing alternative yet accepted meanings and behaviors in an entrepreneurial fashion. SMLs attend the same focus-group sessions, fill-out the same surveys for CDDs, attend the same CIPA meetings, attend the same City Council meetings, and also participate in the same City task forces and commissioned studies. The difference is not in what one does, it is in how one does it. SMLs will be more disruptive in order to bring attention to prevalent community's needs and absence of City attention in addressing those needs. Some of this riotous behavior is strategic. SMLs will stage events in a disruptive manner to expose the need for a service, but always by making the point that it is their organization which can fulfill the particular need. SMLs/CBOs will put on protest marches or rallies, they engage clients in letter writing campaigns, they (re)establish collaborations with other CBOs, they host television/radio talk shows criticizing governmental officials and sometimes those who collaborate with officials. They attend other CBOs sponsored functions (i.e. grand-openings) or City sponsored events to introduce the need for a service that their organization can fulfill. The tool-kit of ideas-in-practice for the LMS expands a great deal when SMLs become entrepreneurial by demanding special attention. The squeaky wheel gets the grease and the grease gotten by an SML legitimates both SMLs and CBOs.

Finally, SMLs have similar dynamics in their relationships with each other, this is to say they share purposes and create relationships with each other and vary in behavior toward each other, occasionally behaving professionally and entrepreneurially irrespective of collegiality.

Not all CBOs are always in competition for funds but typically some are in each RFP cycle and those engaged in a particular cycle are not all allied with or opposed to other CBOs. SMLs realize that they have broadly similar resources and broadly similar goals and needs. But within these similarities are important differences about how SMLs 'lead' their CBOs and respective 'communities' and how they respond to the RFP process.

Besides some of the tactics described above, SMLs have a few options in how they organize their relationships with other SMLs/CBOs. One of these is of particular interest; it is when a SML/CBO subordinates themselves to another SML/CBO, becoming a 'sub-agency' as part of a proposal to the CDD. This is an option exercised most often by small and/or more politically radical CBO. The choice to become a sub-agency offers particular opportunities and constraints. Constraints include foregoing independence and so being perceived as weak. Another constraint is foregoing direct experience and relationship with City political and bureaucratic processes. However by becoming a sub-agency the CBO operations are not monitored so closely and the organization need not comply so fully with government regulations. The absence of monitoring creates a temporary freedom to organize activities in a more experimental fashion, concerned with what personnel believe will 'work' instead of what will fulfill regulatory benchmarks (as described in the next section). Likewise, sub-agencies do not always agree with the goals and purposes of a lead agency, but this can be to mutual benefit as well. Pursuing an independent agenda can benefit a lead agency because some of the success rubs off on the lead agency and lead agency personnel benefit vicariously from indirectly participating in the sub-agencies activities.

In sum, SMLs, the community and City personnel enact a variety of ideas and behaviors that constitute the LMS in day-to-day practice. Occasionally SML behave disruptively, but recognizably so and, thus, are understandable as part of the LMS. This behavior may ruffle a few feathers, but it is almost always within expected limits. It is this mutually predictable behavior that SML (and the others) rely on in enacting the RFP process. Predictability does not imply ever harmonious or effortless interaction. It only means that everyone is oriented toward the same basic problem and can understand the reason in others' behavior. But needs identification is only part of the RFP process, a next, and key step is the transformation of those needs into plans responsive to communities, palatable to state and federal statutes and compatible to SML's politics.

The Transformation of Needs

Once needs are identified, the City government transforms them into "community action plans" (CAPs) otherwise known as "consolidated plans" (CPs). The transformation does not always retain the letter or spirit of the needs expressed in the identification process because the process of creating a CAP incorporates the interests, knowledge and associated assumptions about the community from the Community Action Board (CAB) members, university scholars, elected officials, City Community Development Department (CDD) personnel, and personnel from other City departments affected by the CAP. The CAB members provide recommendations about the community needs expressed in the CAP that pertain to the proposals produced as a result of the RFP. These suggestions incorporate the interests of CAB members into the plan process. For example, a CAB member told us that after the CDD submits its recommended CAPs and CPs and a draft of the RFP to which CBOs will respond then the CAB works to accept, reject or modify the CDD recommendations based on what the CAB thinks is in the best interest of the community. Considering this process, one low-income representative remarked:

> I reject most of the shit Gloria Clark (Director of Human Services and Family Development at the CDD) sends me because she wants to be in control and help only those that help her. Instead of helping those really concerned CBOs and the people in need. Since we (the CAB) will only see and deal with what is reccomended to us by the CDD then they (Gloria Clark and the CDD) are undermining us.

These sentiments are not uncommon and are echoed by the other competing interests. Since the CAB is required to have a tripartitite membership consisting of equal numbers of private and public sector members and representatives of low income communities then the CAPs, CPs and RFPs which emerge from those negotiations are complex reflections of those different interests.

The CAB is not the only sieve through which RFP's pass. Local university scholars are called upon to make recommendations to the CDD based on their disciplinary knowledge. For instance, one CDD administrator noted that the CDD regularly seeks assistance from well-known academics at the area universities to help interpret community needs and formulate CAPs, CPs and RFPs. For instance, one city planner noted his work with UCLA Professor of Urban Planning, Paul Ong. Elected officials also provide recommendations on CAPs, CPs and RFPs based on their fact-finding task forces and commissioned studies, constituent grievances, and/or the lobbying of a particular SML. The CDD also gathers the statistical information available for the City with the various external and internal recommendations, to formulate CAPs and RFPs to fulfill these CAPs. SMLs have some, but limited input into this transformative process because this part of the LMS is ruled by federal and state statute.

CAPs and the proposals CBO prepare as a response to RFPs must comply with state and federal government performance and measurement requirements. In order to comply with the federal Government Performance and Results Act of 1992, the state developed a "Family Development Matrix" to found benchmarks and measure progress. "Baseline data" identify the criteria of an individual or family experiencing certain kinds of needs. "Achievement indicators" illustrate if the individual or family has progressed from the baseline data. Objectives are projected completion dates and quantitative measures, which provide the means to judge successful programs. For example, the CAP might set forth the following goal in a RFP: "Enable 500 children to move from the Children's Education *In Crisis* benchmark of "non-enrollment in school" to *At Risk* benchmark of "high absenteeism" by 12/31/99". All parts of the CAP and resultant RFP must be in compliance with state and federal guidelines. When this is so, the CDD advertises the RFPs and SMLs, through their CBO, respond with proposals that incorporate this language and attempt to reconcile the formal language of the RFP with the needs of the community and the politics of the SMLs. In order to play the game, SML must either incorporate this language and the associated assumptions about their clients or identify allies in other CBO to subcontract from and so pursue multiple agendas simultaneously.

City requirements dispose CBOs towards bureaucratic organization. As stated earlier, the CDD calls for "professional" and "specialized staff". At a focus-group session, various SMLs recognize, "agencies have to spend approximately 20 percent of their time on grant compliance and paperwork" (Lyons et al., F-7). So, they have to devote significant time satisfying this call for a competent administration. But, one way to incorporate entrepreneurial and professional behavior in the RFP process is for SMLs/CBOs to seek out alliances with other SMLs/CBOs. CBOs who are sub-agencies under a lead-agency have some leeway to behave in a more activist/entrepreneurial fashion. This is because CBOs who are sub-agencies are contracted through a lead-agency to provide a service through a specific program, and so they avoid many constraints imposed on RFP in the transformation of needs process. These sub-agencies are accountable to the lead-agency for providing services through a designated program, but the sub-agencies' other programs are supported by the grant money or use it to leverage private funds that permit them to be more entrepreneurial in community organizing and mobilization.

Even when a CBO lead-agency has the administrative staff to comply with regulations, they do not require the same from their sub-agencies. Lead-agencies are directly accountable to CDD for overseeing their sub-agencies, and so the lead agency must be administratively viable. Consequently, they tend to be under more scrutiny to comply with CDD requirements. Engrid Milligan stated, "a lot of these sub-agencies are small non-profits, and they're struggling to survive. But, we're the lead agency and so we are contractually obligated to ensure that [these sub-agency] people fulfill their terms of the contract". However, sub-agency work is not scrutinized closely, and subcontracted work is a means to other ends for a sub-agency, and this is recognized by lead agencies whose formal agendas are superficially in line with those of the government, but who can foster relationships with sub-agencies to fulfill other goals or even the same goals but by non-standard means. Even as the city transforms the needs of a community, the CBO of a community seek alliances to address needs in their original form and in the form legitimized by the City.

Ultimately, despite the variety of ways in which to behave SML recognize each other's behavior as sensible and as part of a 'call/response' system of seeking the resources for survival for both community and CBO. All SMLs avail themselves of professional and entrepreneurial behaviors in the course of an RFP; they must in order to be effective SML. However, the *process* of leadership is more than the sum of professional/entrepreneurial behavior, and it is more than administering programs or finding funds from the RFP process. Leadership as a social process embraces all of these, and people become leaders by learning and modifying the living conventions of the local leadership meaning system. Jane Agee puts these matters plainly, "I was hired to supervise the eight directors and programs and also part of my other responsibility is organizing, community organizing that's actually what I, my strongest point, have been involved doing, but if we don't get funded and if we can't bring our community out in our support then how successful will I be? I may know what I need to do in a da' do the same things in the same way". Engrid Milligan puts it this way, "It's a constant tug of war, a kind of a struggle-battle, between what our contracts say and what's happening in our centers. We have to react to our community and to the City, but who we serve is our bread and butter". At a focus-group session one SML suggested, "The structure of the system itself is a barrier to service" (Lyond et al, F-6). SML must improvise *contingent processes* to meet the needs of their CBO and their beneficiaries. The RFP process is one of these. Ultimately, our research indicates that the behavior of SMLs cannot be categorized or understood by essentialist schemes. Instead, we can understand SML's behavior by using a process oriented and contingent approach which permits us to understand the ideas-in-use and how SMLs learn these in order to conform to City conventions while subverting the same.

Discussion

These data illustrate that SML's/CBO's behavior in East Los Angeles is not reducible to essentialist categories. Pragmatists account for behavior with reference to behavioral assumptions and the 'living' system of meaning/behavior which people, here SMLs/CBOs, co-create.

For example, SMLs choose from a variety of leadership techniques, but this choice is contingent. Time and place in the RFP process matters, as does the needs and orientation of the CBOs. SMLs continuously self-identify as leaders, seeking legitimacy from community and City. SMLs mobilize resources to legitimize themselves and their organizations by way of administrative expertise and their competency in marshaling their community in a number of ways, but always in an effort to select a strategy appropriate to circumstance. SMLs come to be identified as professionals, due in part to successfully mobilizing clients and because they are able to negotiate the difficulty City sponsored terrain of the RFP process. SMLs negotiate a complex terrain that grows more complex with the transformation of community needs into proposals acceptable to regulatory agencies. So, SML's expertise lies in identifying with the community and addressing its needs to the City during the initial phase of the political process and then developing alliances to implement proposals contingently within the constraints of government regulation. The permutations and apparent contradictions of SML's behavior are many, and it is most fruitful to understand the *context* that provokes behavior than to assume the behavior can be categorized by some abstract scheme.

Leadership is situational, and not reducible to solely individual characteristics.

Acknowledgement

I am grateful to Daniel Duran and Francisco Martinez for their useful comments.

Notes

1 This is a conservative estimate considering that SML/CBO continually engage throughout the year in some type of RFP process through various departments throughout the City, State, Federal, or possibly through private foundations. Somewhat similarly, Marcia Bok (1992: 77) notes federal funds have represented no less than 50 percent of CBO (CAAs) budgets in Connecticut since 1964 and "they receive funds from an average of nineteen sources in 1989".

2 Schorr discusses the reasons for a 'caring' staff and the difficulties of having such.

3 There are limits imposed on the actions of SML. But our claim is that the possibilities and limits are social in nature and found in the LMS. The legal opportunities and constraints to SML behavior in the RFP process come from the federally enacted Economic Opportunity Act which provides many CBOs with the opportunity to maintain many of their activist ties of grassroots participation and at the same time be regulated and monitored under institutional controls.

4 Sometimes sub-committees are organized ad hoc for the sole purpose of mobilizing informally on behalf of the CBO. SML entrepreneurially organize a sub-committee of parents or youth, or both as circumstances (a demonstration for instance) demand.

References

Aminzade, Ronald. (1995), "Between Movement and Party: The Transformation of Mid-Nineteenth-Century French Republicans". In *The Politics of Social Protest: Comparative Perspectives on States and Social Movements*, edited by Craig Jenkins and Bert Klandermans. Minneapolis: University of Minnesota Press.

Bok, Marcia. (1992), *Civil Rights and the Social Programs of the 1960s: The Social Justice Functions of Social Policy*. Westport: Praeger.

Bradley, David. (1995), *History of Community Action*. Washington D.C: National Community Action Foundation.

Edwards, Bob and Sam Marullo. (1995), "Organizational Mortality in a Declining Social : The Demise of Peace Movement Organizations in the End of the Cold War" *American Sociological Review*, vol. 60, pp. 908-927.

Gamson, William A. [1990] (1997), "The Success of the Unruly". In *Social Movements: Readings on Their Emergence, Mobilizations, and Dynamics,* edited by Doug McAdam and David Snow. Los Angeles: Roxbury Publishing Co.

Haines, Herbert H. [1984] (1997), "Black Radicalization and the Funding of Civil Rights: 1957-1970". In *Social Movements: Readings on Their Emergence, Mobilizations, and Dynamics*, edited by Doug McAdam and David Snow. Los Angeles: Roxbury Publishing Co.

Hutchinson, Richard N., et. al. Unpublished. "Local Mesomobilization: Informal Organization and Networks in the Accomplishment of Collective Action".

Jenkins, Craig J., and Bert Klandermans Eds. (1995), *The Politics of Social Protest: Comparative Perspectives on States and Social Movements*. Minneapolis: University of Minnesota Press.

Leaf, Murray J. (1979), *Man, Mind, and Science: A History of Anthropology*. New York: Columbia University Press.

McAdam, Doug, and David A. Snow. Eds. (1997), *Social Movements: Readings on Their Emergence, Mobilizations, and Dynamics*. Los Angeles: Roxbury Publishing Co.

McCarthy, John D and Mayer N. Zald. (1973), *The Trend of Social Movements in America: Professional and Resource Mobilization*. Morristown: General Learning Press.

_____. (1977), "Resource Mobilization and Social Movements", *American Journal of Sociology*, vol. 82, pp. 1212-41.

Meyer, David S., and Nancy Whittier. [1994] (1997), "Social Movement Spillover". In *Social Movements: Readings on Their Emergence, Mobilizations, and Dynamics*, edited by Doug McAdam and David Snow. Los Angeles: Roxbury Publishing Co.

Poster, Winifred. (1995), "The Challenges and Promises of Class and Racial Diversity in the Women's Movement: A Study of Two Women's Organizations", *Gender and Society*, vol. 9, pp. 659-679.

Staggenborg, Suzanne. [1988] (1997), "The Consequences of Professionalization and Formalization in the Pro-Choice Movement". In *Social Movements: Readings on Their Emergence, Mobilizations, and Dynamics*, edited by Doug McAdam and David Snow. Los Angeles: Roxbury Publishing Co.

Staggenborg, Suzanne. (1989), "Stability and Innovation in the Women's Movement: A Comparison of Two Movement Organization", *Social Problems*, vol. 36, pp. 75-92.

Taylor, Verta. [1989] (1997), "Social Movement Continuity: The Women's Movement in Abeyance". In *Social Movements: Readings on Their Emergence, Mobilizations, and Dynamics*, edited by Doug McAdam and David Snow. Los Angeles: Roxbury Publishing Co.

External and/or Internal Documents

Band Aid
Commission for Children, Youth, and Families
Community Aid
Community Outreach
Dove Services
Emergency Community Rescue
For Life
For The People
Helping Our Neighbors
Live Savers
Lucky Exchange
New Life
Onward Path
Opportunity Foundation
Reaching Out
Sol

STOP
Working Together
Youth Force
Youth Vanguard

Interviews

Agee, Jane. July 11, 1997 in Los Angeles, California (Reaching Out).
Bueno, Sam. July 9, 1997 in Los Angeles, California (Play Pen).
Delliger, Patricia. July 10, 1997 in Los Angeles, California (Working Together).
Flores, Luz. July 10, 1997 in Los Angeles, California (councilman's senior field deputy).
Frans, Larry. July 11, 1997 in Los Angeles, California (Onward Path).
Gold, Beth. May 30, 1997 in Los Angeles, California (Band Aid).
Goodman, Rachael. May 20, 1997 in Los Angeles, California (community member w/ ties to Helping Our Neighbors and Active Families).
Green, Paul. May 27, 1997 in Los Angeles, California (Community Aid).
Jackson, David. March 20, 1997 in Los Angeles, California (Helping Our Neighbors).
Millegan, Engrid. July 9, 1997 in Los Angeles, California (Community Outreach).
Montes, Sal. July 8, 1997 in Los Angeles, California (supervisor in the Commission for Children, Youth, and Families).
Nunez, Julie. June 2, 1997 in Los Angeles, California (Working Together).
Sterling, Gary. May 21, 1997 in Los Angeles, California (Dove Services).
Smith, Nick. On-going dialogue since 1993 (Emergency Community Rescue).
Valdez, Lucy and Mr. Right, May 29, 1997 in Los Angeles, California (Youth Force).

Observations-Participation of Activities

CIPA meeting March 20, 1997 in Los Angeles, California.
City Council and Committee meetings June 2, 1997 in Los Angeles, California.
Emergency Community Rescue "Parenting meetings", March 17–20, 1997 in Los Angeles, California.
For The People "Strategic Planning Meeting", May 29, 1997 in Los Angeles, California.
Grand opening May 29, 1997 in Los Angeles, California.
Lucky Services "Meeting", July 8, 1997 in Los Angeles, California.
Talk show May 29, 1997 in Los Angeles, California.

Periodicals

Alatorre, Richard. "Alatorre: Hit Piece Filled With Errors". *Northeast Sun*. 10 July 1997: Page 1. Approval of Scope of Services and Expenditure Plan for Program Year 1996 – Agreement No. 93236 – Youth Advocacy Program
Clark, Gloria S. 1996a. "1997 Community Action Plan – Draft". Los Angeles: Human Services and Neighborhood Development Division of the Community Development Department.

Clark, Gloria S. 1996b. "RFP POLICY and PLANNING ISSUES *COLLABORATIVES AND CONSORTIA*". Los Angeles: Human Services and Neighborhood Development Division of the Community Development Department.

_______.1996c. "1996 Community Service Block Grant Amendment No. 1". Los Angeles: Human Services and Neighborhood Development Division of the Community Development Department.

Cobo-Hanlon, Leila. "Youth Help Themselves by Helping Others". *Los Angeles Times.* 31 October 1995: B3.

Commission on Children, Youth, and Families. *LA4KIDS.* Community Aid. 1996. "Needs Assessment". Economic Opportunity Act of 1964.

Gold, Matea. "State Revives Schools for At-Risk Youths". *Los Angeles Times.* 11 July 1997: B10.

Government Performance and Result Act of 1992. L.A. Bridges RFP materials, application, proposal recommendations, etc.: Community Development Department.

Lopez, Robert J. and Rich Connell. "MTA Probes Charities Promoted by Alatorre". *Los Angeles Times.* 7 July 1997: A1.

Los Angeles Community Development Department. 1996. "1997 Community Action Plan".

Lyons, Morgan et al. 1993. "A Challenge to Service: An Assessment of the Needs of Lower Income Residents of The City of Los Angeles". Los Angeles: Community Development Department.

Quintanilla, Michael. "Bridge to a Life of Literacy". *Los Angeles Times.* 10 December 1995: E1.

Riordan, Richard J. (Mayor) *City of Los Angeles Budget Summary Fiscal Year 1996–1997. Wave Newspapers.*

10 Public Interest Lawyering and the Pragmatist Dilemma

Peter Margulies

Descriptions of pragmatism, like any accounts of political and legal action, often pose a tension between doing well in the world and doing well in relationships with individuals. Commentators such as Hannah Arendt have depicted pragmatism in the stark terms reflected in the familiar maxim, "The end justifies the means".[1] At its best, pragmatist thought transcends such reductive descriptions.[2] However, the best theory can be highly unstable in practice.

Instability stems from pragmatism's two central elements: dialogue and projectivity.[3] Dialogue speaks to the importance of participation, consultation, and shared experience. Projectivity refers to the human need to evaluate decisions not just in the present, but also through consideration of the "possible future trajectories of action".[4] An ideal mix of these elements would capture most of what is important in the normative and descriptive world. Unfortunately, as a good pragmatist would readily inform us, the world is rarely ideal. The mix of these elements in pragmatist practice is unstable. As a result, political action tends to careen between an unfeeling instrumentalism and a fixation with "authenticity". Constraining one tendency allows the other untrammeled rein. This is the pragmatist dilemma.

The pragmatist dilemma shapes the practice of public interest law.[5] Public interest lawyers risk becoming technocrats who dispense instrumental rationality without regard for their clients' human needs. Reacting to this threat, they also risk entrapment in a politics of authenticity that fails to take into account how clients' and others' identities evolve over time.

To integrate the dialogic and projective dimensions of pragmatism, this essay proposes a model of integrative advocacy.[6] The focus of integrative advocacy is the continued dialectic between the core pragmatist values of dialogue and projectivity. Legal practice under this model requires acknowledgment that both lawyer and client have effective material and ideological commitments that trigger the need for dialogue. The integrative model also recognizes that in a postmodern world people are in many different "places" — spiritual, material, racial, cultural, and economic — at once, and are frequently in transit.[7] Integrative advocacy reflects the understanding that the relationship of place to legal action requires considering not only where people are, but also where they aspire to be.

The essay is in three parts. Part I considers the promise of theory and the instability of practice in the work of the foremost American pragmatist, John Dewey. Part II considers how that instability plays out in public interest lawyering, particularly in the "impact lawyering" of civil rights class actions. Part III advances a model of integrative advocacy, considering lawyering for domestic violence survivors as a testing ground for the virtues and challenges of the integrative model.

I. Pragmatism in Theory and Practice

Pragmatism argues for the inextricable intertwining of theory and practice.[8] Furthermore, a profound strength of pragmatism is that the practice it contemplates is not solely the practice of theory in the academy, but also the interaction of theory with the practice of politics, law, and economics throughout the social landscape.[9] In light of the pragmatist emphasis on practice,[10] it seems particularly appropriate to consider not only the core elements of pragmatist theory, but how those elements play out in the world. I examine both with reference to John Dewey, the thinker most closely identified with American pragmatism.[11]

A. Pragmatist Theory

Pragmatist theory relies on two core values: dialogue and projectivity. Dialogue is crucial because of the nature of human beings and the logic of democracy. Pragmatism accepts the Aristotelian idea that human beings are inherently social and political.[12] Democracy cultivates this social dimension by requiring that persons make decisions collectively. Making decisions collectively requires dialogue: speaking and listening to others. Through dialogue, people learn to find mutuality in difference, and honor difference in mutuality. For a pragmatist, dialogue therefore is important both for its own sake[13] and as a pathway to sound decisions.[14]

The importance of dialogue is manifest in Dewey's thought. Dewey notes the importance of "consultation and discussion, which uncover social needs and troubles".[15] He confirms this point in a homely metaphor, observing, "[T]he man who wears the shoe knows best that it pinches and where it pinches".[16] A regime that substitutes so-called "expert judgment" for the opinion of the "man who wears the shoe" is merely an "oligarchy managed in the interests of the few".[17] Just as Dewey resists rule by the powerful few, he values the voices of the powerless. "It is true", he notes, "that all valuable as well as new ideas begin with minorities, perhaps a minority of one".[18]

Dewey's view of the value of dialogue encompasses justice, diversity, and connection. In an essay written between the world wars, Dewey's invocation of the plight of minorities in Europe, set to erupt into the Holocaust some 15 years after his writing, stresses the value of redress for oppression.[19] Yet diversity — the concept articulated by Justice Powell in Bakke that contact with other traditions, experiences, and perspectives enriches democratic dialogue and yields better ideas — is clearly also a vital part of Dewey's argument. Dewey emphasizes this point with his insistence that an idea originating with a "minority" — even a minority of one — must be provided the "opportunity ... to spread and to become the possession of the multitude".[20] In the key of connection, Dewey refers to the "face-to-face" relationships enabled in local communities.[21] Without a commitment to "enduring ties" to others,[22] organization becomes an end in itself, and anomie or tyranny follow.[23]

The projective element focuses on the intertemporal aspect of pragmatism. Pragmatists assert that human beings distinguish themselves from other forms of life through awareness of their place in the flow of time.[24] Human beings do not focus solely on the sensations of the present. They also consider the impact of the past, and implications for the future.[25] Projectivity captures the ability of human actors to exert agency by shaping possibilities.

Consideration of past commitments and future possibilities requires a conception of ends, means, and the relationship between them. A pragmatist views ends as open to revision in the light of experience.[26] Consider the end of promoting world "revolution". Leon Trotsky posited this goal in a telling exchange with Dewey.[27] Dewey objected, not to the indignation against injustice that fueled Trotsky's thought, but to the determinist trajectory that tamed it. For Trotsky, "revolution" was a product of laws of science and history.[28] Replying to Trotsky, Dewey rejected this mechanistic view of projectivity. He pointed out the role of contingency, noting that "revolution", just like the untrammeled private property, might create inequality and oppression.[29]

Viewing ends as contingent also means that the pragmatist rejects the rigid separation of ends and means. Ends like "revolution" or "property rights" are also means, bringing along the baggage of particular techniques and rhetoric. In addition, as Trotsky realized, means can subvert and shape ends. Using means that are objectionable will do nothing to make ends less contingent.[30] If there is a rule of revolutions, it is not Trotsky's but Peter Townshend's: "Meet the new boss/Same as the old boss".[31] The ruthless instrumentalist's credo that "the end justifies the means" is not a necessary conclusion for pragmatist theory. Indeed, a good pragmatist, while remaining reflexive about ends, will also be reflexive about means. Overcommitting to a particular means, whether the means be litigation or "taking it to the streets", is just as problematic as uncritical acceptance of ends. Developing a repertoire of strategies facilitates an effective response to the demands of particular situations.[32]

Sound decisions and democratic governance would be simple if society could bottle the optimal mixture of dialogue and projectivity. Such an ethereal blend would allow full dialogue and participation. Armed with insights from the dialogic process, society would proceed to an accurate projection of all possible future worlds, and select a package of strategies for getting to the world that appeared most appealing. Unfortunately, the dialogic and projective elements do not seem to mix together very well. The result is a tendency in practice for one element to dominate the other, to the detriment of both democracy and sound decision-making.

B. Pragmatism in Practice

In pragmatism's unstable mixture of elements, either projectivity or dialogue can predominate. Projectivity is perhaps the more prolific and conspicuous victor. Dialogue can seem like a luxury or an annoyance when the future is at stake. As a result, caveats about integration of means and ends go out the window. Instrumental rationality takes over, and with it, the maxim that "the end justifies the means". Yet, dialogue has its own distortions. Process can become not merely a good in and of itself, but a fetish. Two possible scenarios emerge from this reification of dialogue: 1) a static society where change is a threat to "authentic" identities and the status quo remains in force, or, 2) a volatile society where weak central authority gives way to an extreme and repressive faction.[33]

The dominion of instrumental rationality in which the ends justify the means has an extensive pedigree. The history of law, politics, and political theory is a history of beginnings emerging from interpersonal violence. Moses's killing of the Jews who worshiped the Golden Calf paved the way for the acceptance of the covenant with God embodied in the Ten Commandments.[34] Romulus' slaying of Remus was a crucial act in the founding of Rome.[35] More recently, the French and Russian Revolutions supply bloody illustrations, the latter featuring Trotsky as actor, commentator, and finally victim. The American Revolution involved significant violence, not only in the form of bloodletting against the British and their American sympathizers, but also in the form of the slavery of African-Americans that the American Constitution legitimated.

Pragmatist commentary on practical issues is not free from echoes of this lurid history. Consider again the relationship between experts and laypersons in Dewey's thought. While Dewey derides the arrogance of expert judgment and praises the insights of the ordinary "man who wears the shoe", his comments reveal a subtle separation of means from ends. Dewey notes that the "man who wears the shoe" is the best judge of the problems with the shoe. However, he notes further that "the expert ... is the best judge of how the trouble is to be remedied".[36] Dewey does not acknowledge that, 1) that the shoe's wearer might have some good ideas about solutions, or, 2) that the supposed experts, who clearly need enlightenment about the nature of the trouble, might also need help in formulating a remedy.[37] If the goal of finding a remedy justifies curbing expert consultation with the public, other instrumental moves also become permissible for pragmatists, after all.

This embrace of instrumentalism is manifest in one of the most troubling convergences of intellectuals and public policy in American history: Dewey's campaign for intellectuals' support of American entry into World War I. It is important to realize, despite the anger triggered by Germany's attacks on passenger ships such as the Lusitania, that World War I was to a significant degree a war between two camps of similar imperialist ambitions. This view of the warring camps as imperialists interested in mammon and dominion helped fuel pacifist sentiment in the early years of the war. Ultimately, events such as the German sinking of the Lusitania, with significant loss of life, helped turn the tide toward American entry. However, Dewey's support for American entry did not treat the particulars of the European conflict. His rationale was not one of self-defense, a rationale clearly applicable to the American response to aggression by the Axis powers in World War II. Instead, Dewey spoke of the good that the war could accomplish for the future of international governance, and derided the pacifists as being naive.[38]

What "reconciled America to war", for Dewey, was the desire for a "better ordered" international system.[39] For Dewey, the war had a clearly instrumental character, in "furthering whatever will bring into existence those new agencies of international control".[40] The virtue of the war what that it positioned the United States to "play a 'vitally energetic role' in a political reorganization of the world".[41] While the 20th century saw a gradual move in this direction, the move has been halting, and its results still unclear, as the bloody conflicts generated by the break-up of the Soviet empire have demonstrated. Certainly the Versailles Treaty that followed World War I was an imperialist land-grab that vindicated the pacifists' worst fears.[42]

Indeed, as Randolph Bourne pointed out in his incisive critique of Dewey's stance, Dewey's description of the pacifists as naive seems curiously misplaced. As Bourne notes, applying the instrumentalist theory of well-matched means and ends to war required Dewey "to ignore the fact that it is exactly in war that alternatives are rigorously limited"[43] (198, 198). War has its own logic and its own imperatives, as Bourne observes: "there is now but one end — victory; and but one means — the organization of all the resources of the nation into a conventional war technique".[44] The suppression of civil liberties at home after America's entry, and the Palmer raids on suspected Communists immediately afterward, demonstrated the truth of Bourne's observation.[45] One could also query whether the United States, with its history of slavery and genocide of native peoples, and its practice of eugenics which proved to be so influential to Fascists in the years immediately preceding World War II,[46] was the scintillating candidate for leadership of the new world order that Dewey envisioned.

II. Dialogue and Projectivity in Public Interest Law

Dewey's problematic descent into instrumentalism in World War I is more than an intriguing footnote in American intellectual history. It also reveals something about the down side of pragmatism in political practice. This section examines how the same drawbacks of pragmatism play out in a contemporary form of political practice with roots in the Progressive Era: public interest class action litigation.

A. Brandeis and the Marginalizing of Dialogue in Public Interest Law's Origins

From Brandeis forward, public interest lawyers have been a fixture on the American political and legal scene. They have contributed to extraordinary and overdue changes in American society, including the end of *de jure* desegregation and reform of public institutions such as prisons and psychiatric hospitals. Yet, the history of public interest law is also a history of tension between the objectives of elite lawyers and the aspirations of persons the lawyers purport to represent.

Starting with Brandeis, public interest lawyers adopted much of the rhetoric of technological progress that is also evident in Dewey's political writings[47] (discussing influence of William James and pragmatism on Brandeis); Farber, D.A. (1995), 'Reinventing Brandeis: Legal Pragmatism for the Twenty-First Century', University of Illinois Law Review, vol. 1995, pp. 163-190, 182-84 (discussing links between civic humanism, pragmatism, and Brandeis' thought). The characterization of public interest lawyers as "social engineers"[48] is one aspect of this technocratic identity. Emerging with this identity was a sharp turn toward the projective dimension, and a discounting of the importance of dialogue.

This tendency to discount dialogue is evident in Brandeis' own practice. One critic, while acknowledging Brandeis' intellect and integrity, nevertheless argued that Brandeis in his dealings with clients sometimes "overlooked the more human aspect ... after he has worked out the problem, he never consults anybody; he gives very little thought as to how it is going to affect the mind or minds of other men ... "[49] The difficulties caused by this disinterest in dialogue emerge in one of the defining moments of Progressive Era social advocacy: the efforts of Brandeis and an extraordinary group of women lawyer-activists to persuade the laissez-faire Supreme Court of the Lochner era to uphold maximum-hours laws for women.[50]

Brandeis and his allies believed that maximum hours regulation was a humane reform for all workers. However, their interest in implementing the reform for women was particularly acute. The crux of their concern was that long working hours interfered with women's role in child rearing. To support this argument, Brandeis and the women activists submitted an amicus brief in the case of Muller v. Oregon,[51] — the prototype of the "Brandeis brief" that has become a staple in public interest litigation. The brief assembled a mass of contemporary social science, purporting to study the effect of long working hours on women's physiology. The conclusion of the studies cited was that long working hours harmed women, whom the studies described as "often absent on account of slight indisposition" and — compared with men — liable to "break down sooner under strain".[52]

Brandeis and his allies did not engage in a broad dialogue before making this argument. To the extent that they considered whether their advocacy would reinforce images of women as inferior to men, they did not seem troubled by this possibility. Moreover, there was little acknowledgment from maximum hours advocates that enacting maximum hours legislation for women but not for men could place women at a competitive disadvantage in seeking employment. Women who needed to work to support their families, unlike the affluent women who worked with Brandeis, would experience negative effects. Indeed, subsequent research has suggested that women seeking entry into occupations dominated by men were pushed out by maximum hours legislation.[53]

B. Dialogue as an Endangered Species in the Modern Public Interest Class Action

The disfavoring of dialogue is also a feature of the modern public interest class action. Public interest class actions usually start with some kind of affective reaction to injustice. This sense of injustice can come from personal experience, or a vicarious source. It usually comes with a sense of calling — a sense that personal involvement in overcoming injustice is not so much a choice as a part of who one is.[54]

Animated by this sense of identity, public interest lawyers value the class action because it is more efficient than individual litigation in addressing policy issues. Defendants can moot out individual lawsuits, by offering plaintiffs attractive settlements that leave the existing policy in place. Since a class action survives such strategic behavior by defendants, it is a more powerful means for lasting change.

There is a thin line, however, between appreciating the uses of a tool and allowing the tool to dictate the framing of the problem. Means can take on a life of their own.[55] Unless lawyers and judges are exceptionally vigilant, the instrumental logic of class actions quickly overwhelms the human urge for dialogue. Class action lawyers and the trial courts that certify classes have virtually no connection with the great mass of individuals who comprise the class. Many class members and/or their allies and guardians either have no idea of what is transpiring on their behalf, or feel that the institutional workings of public interest class actions ignore, marginalize, or suppress their concerns.[56] Without dialogue, there is little to stop such distortion. America discovered this when, with cheerleading from Dewey, it entered World War I. The efficiency rationale of public interest class actions triggers a similar dynamic.

The "can do" rhetoric of pragmatism, displayed in Dewey's championing of the war effort, is prominent in public interest litigation. Advocates make decisions unilaterally, invoking their expertise as a surrogate for consultation. Dialogue becomes an indulgence, a distraction, or even a "trap". Examples are legion. Consider the views of a prominent public interest lawyer in a major child welfare class action that ultimately reached the United States Supreme Court. The lawyer took a position squarely against dialogue:

> [h]er thirty years experience told her what she believed she needed to know about foster children's needs in this setting and the position she should take ... she did not consult in advance with other groups or others likely to take a different position. Nor did she meet then — or later — with her seven named clients, deciding that it would be a 'trap' to become embroiled in arguing about the fates of a few children when the real issues at stake were so much broader.[57]

Similar rhetoric issues from the lead attorney in a groundbreaking class action suit on the rights of persons with mental disabilities: "I played God. I never met [the named class action plaintiff] or his aunt. And I never needed to do so. I knew what needed to be done".[58]

Individual named plaintiffs can suffer harm as a result of public interest lawyers' failure to communicate. One of the named plaintiffs in Roe v. Wade,[59] Norma McCorvey, recently alleged that her lawyer, Sarah Weddington, should have told her more about the possibility of getting an abortion in Mexico, which McCorvey said Weddington herself had done.[60] According to McCorvey, Weddington did not share this information because she was afraid an abortion for her client would moot out the case.[61] Weddington, in her remarks about the incident, did little to demonstrate that she had ever had any interest in dialogue with her client, asserting that, "The case was not about her ... the case was a class action".[62]

The absence of dialogue in public interest class actions can lead not only to betrayal of individuals, but also to more pervasive communal harms. Dialogue is important for pragmatist theory not merely as a process point, but also as a guide for sound decisions. Instrumentalism, with its focus on the "efficient" means for accomplishing a given end, has all the flaws of rational actor approaches. It sees problem solving as a straight line, while approaches that express skepticism about instrumentalism often rely on the decidedly non-linear metaphor of the "garbage can".[63]

Instrumentalism starts with the intentions of the actors, asking, "What do we want to do?". Often instrumentalism, as in Dewey's beating the drums for America's entry into World War I, also neglects who exactly constitutes the group referred to as "we". Discordant views, such as those of the pacifists prosecuted for sedition after America entered World War I or of African-Americans who did not see in their subordinated state a "beacon of freedom" for the world, are either suppressed or invisible. Thick local knowledge that might reveal factors not immediately in the purview of the instrumentalist is ignored. The result of this neglect of dialogue is that instrumentalist outlooks, like Dewey's confidence about the salutary outcome of World War I, are not very accurate projections of the future. By rejecting dialogue, an instrumentalist is making a strange kind of Ulysses contract, which in essence says, "Please prevent me from being confused by the facts".[64] That is an odd position for a pragmatist.

The result of this discounting of dialogue is that, along with the substantial victories wrought by public interest litigation, contingencies emerge that can undermine public interest goals. For example, mental health lawyers, including me, reasoned that improving conditions in psychiatric hospitals would not only be good for its own sake, but would also drive costs up, forcing the state to provide care for patients in the community. "Right to treatment" litigation produced significant gains in institutional conditions. The "community care" scenario of the mental health lawyers was not a golden moment in the history of prophecy. While patients ended up in the community, the same budgetary imperatives that reduced in-patient psychiatric admissions also produced a stripped-down model of community care.[65] Patients frequently became homeless, or were re-routed to more repressive institutions such as prisons and jails.

The desegregation lawyers, responsible for perhaps the greatest victory in American jurisprudence in Brown, offer another example of problems in prophecy. In desegregation litigation, advocates made strategic choices that failed to adequately address three kinds of exit: First, they decided that the best chance for African-Americans to get a quality public education was to pursue integration with white schools, as opposed to obtaining resources for education in predominantly African-American communities.[66] Second, they decided that the most effective rhetoric for accomplishing that goal was the rhetoric of color-blindness applied to children, rather than the rhetoric of citizenship applied to all African-Americans.[67] Third, they supported both arguments with social science evidence that pathologized the African-American community, implicitly discounting institutions such as historically Black schools as artifacts of self-hate.[68]

These strategic choices contributed to three important exits that adversely affected African-American interests over time: the flight of resources from African-American schools as a result of school districts' reallocation of resources to white schools; the flight of whites from central cities; and the flight of white support for "second-generation" remedies for racial subordination such as affirmative action.[69]

In sum, for litigation, as well as war, means construct ends. As Randolph Bourne observed about America's entry into World War I, war's internal logic makes certain interests appear less important, particularly "soft" concerns such as dialogue and self-expression. Controlling variables and achieving aims becomes difficult in the concatenation of interests, events, and personalities that results.[70] While litigation may have less of an ineluctable logic than war, disrupting that logic requires an abiding commitment to the interaction of dialogue and projectivity.

III. Integrative Advocacy as Pragmatist Practice

A. Overview

Addressing these problems requires a commitment to practice, not a paper plan. We can call these commitments and practices "integrative" advocacy. Integrative advocacy strives for a complementary approach between the dialogic and projective dimensions. Neither dimension should predominate. Instead, integrative advocacy requires recognition of the interaction of means and ends.[71]

Integrative advocacy acknowledges the process values embodied in dialogue. In integrative advocacy, the empathy, reciprocity, and participation promoted by dialogue are emblems of human identity, expressed in a shared search for core values.[72] This search may uncover differences within mutuality, as well as mutuality within differences.[73] The goal of an integrative institution is not homogeneity of perspectives, but instead an equitable regard for the importance of diverse points of view.[74] Moreover, an integrative approach recognizes the substantive virtues — the enhancement of deliberation, wisdom, and experience for sound decisions — served by dialogue. Dialogue can help ameliorate the failures of prophecy in pragmatist practice, whether the example is Dewey's cheerleading for World War I or the occasionally errant social engineering of public interest class action lawyers.

At the same time, integrative advocacy recognizes that human action occurs in time as well as space. As the projective dimension teaches us, change and contingency are inevitable parts of the human condition. Dialogue that enshrines present positions as "authentic" fails to reckon with projectivity. An integrative approach recognizes that lawyers should encourage clients to consider future as well as present selves and shape their advice and advocacy accordingly.

Integrative advocacy requires that lawyer and client collaborate in "imagining what the world would look like to me from another position, imagining how I would look to myself from within a different world, and coming to understand that I might define my principles differently if I did not stand where I am accustomed to".[75] Integrative advocacy considers both how another person feels in a difficult situation, taking into account the sources of both anxiety and support for that person, and how we would feel in that situation. Integrative advocacy requires this reciprocal focus. If we only ask ourselves the first question – how the other feels – we focus solely on perceived differences between others and ourselves, and make others more exotic than they need be. Because we do not risk our own beings within this perspective, we are not fully engaged. However, if we focus only on the second question – how we would feel – we homogenize everyone into ourselves. In doing so, we fail to engage with the experience of others, who may employ radically different assumptions about the world. It is the meeting of the two perspectives – self and others – that provides the integration required for both lawyer and client.[76]

B. A Test Case: Representing Survivors of Domestic Violence

To test the efficacy of an integrative approach, consider the case of advocacy for survivors of domestic violence. This kind of advocacy, which was a staple of traditional legal aid models, suffered a setback in the 1960s, as the technocratic tinge of public interest law made such lawyering seem unglamorous and ineffectual.[77] Domestic violence advocacy was often ignored or trivialized in poverty law practice as stressing affective concerns, but having little instrumental clout. Indeed, the standard Left line of the 1960s through early 1980s described domestic violence work, which in part might involve legal or social action by low-income women against low-income men, as an "intraclass transfer of resources".[78] This approach did two things: first, it downplayed dialogue and exalted instrumental calculation; second, it ignored differences within groups, treating particular groups and communities as monolithic.

Domestic violence advocacy initially was a reaction to this problem with poverty law theory.[79] However, the tendency to valorize harshness that is revealed in accounts of Moses, Romulus, and more contemporary theories of legal and political change also made its presence felt in the practice of domestic violence advocacy. Advocacy for survivors, as it turned out, had its own problems with instrumentalism.

By focusing on gender, domestic violence advocacy compensated for the marginalization of gender in Left poverty practice. However, this gender focus in turn marginalized class, race,[80] immigration status, and other crucial factors that a richer dialogue would have brought to the surface. More recent domestic violence advocacy has focused on these issues. One result has been the immigration provisions of the Violence Against Women Act (VAWA), which provide relief for immigrant survivors of domestic violence who formerly were held as virtual hostages by abusive citizen and resident spouses.[81] The efforts of feminist organizations were central to VAWA's passage and implementation. In addition, feminist organizations such as the NOW Legal Defense and Education Fund were effective advocates for provisions in welfare reform legislation allowing exemptions from benefit cut-offs in cases involving domestic violence.

Given the unstable nature of pragmatist practice, however, the turn toward dialogue creates its own problems. Domestic violence advocacy must be both dialogic and projective. While stressing dialogue, some visions of domestic violence lawyering have risked neglect of the projective dimension. Consider issues of mandatory arrest and prosecution of domestic violence offenders, or of the role of attorney-client deliberations in a survivor's decision on whether to vacate an injunction against an abuser. A dialogic approach might consider only one voice – the present voice – of a survivor as "authentic".[82] Such an approach would defer automatically to a survivor who tells authorities or attorneys not to arrest, prosecute, or continue to enjoin her spouse.

An integrative approach, in contrast, would allow more space for the projective dimension. It would recognize that guilt, denial, and the persistence of patriarchy influence the perceived limits of the possible in particular dialogic settings. Material and affective considerations, such as a survivor's lack of resources or her continued emotional ties to an abusive partner, are also relevant. Yet, at any given moment, as a survivor struggles with these issues, other survivors improvise or leverage support networks to protect their families from violence. While all cases have individual twists and turns, each of these survivors offers a scenario of a future self for the survivor struggling with violence in the present. Integrative advocacy must collaborate with the client in envisioning that future self.

Consider the story of a woman whom I will call Anna Novak, a former client of the Immigration Clinic at St. Thomas University School of Law that I co-direct with Professor Linda Kelly. Ms. Novak, who was from Thailand, had married a citizen. After prolonged psychological and physical abuse from her husband, Ms. Novak, a native of Thailand, left with the two children from the marriage. Many members of the Thai community, including potential employers, said she was the cause of the problem, because she "talked back" to her husband. Ms. Novak felt powerless in the face of this pervasive disapproval. The Immigration Clinic worked with Ms. Novak in 1994 to obtain an injunction against her husband, which among other relief barred him from committing further abuse, and awarded her custody of the children. On the way out of the courthouse, Ms. Novak turned to my students and me, and asserted, "Now, I have power".

Our subsequent contact with Ms. Novak matched the affirmation of that moment at the courthouse, but only at the conclusion of a convoluted and frightening route. On a positive note, Ms. Novak received a battered spouse waiver from the Immigration and Naturalization Service, which led to her obtaining lawful permanent resident status in the United States. But Ms. Novak, like many survivors of domestic violence, also asked us to vacate the injunction she had received against her husband. Her children missed their father, she said. Moreover, Ms. Novak's husband had told her that she had psychological problems, which could be the product of brain damage. The husband urged her to have an electro-encephalogram (EEG) to identify the cause of the problem. The apparent basis for the husband's "diagnosis" was that only a brain-damaged woman would leave him.

Ms. Novak returned to her husband. What she did not know was that while they were apart, her husband had obtained a divorce and legal custody of the couple's children through making fraudulent representations to a court in another state. Mr. Novak, who previously had been convicted of kidnaping children from a prior marriage, planned to take his and Anna's children to Costa Rica after changing their names. At the last moment, lawyers to whom we had referred Ms. Novak for help with her divorce and custody problems secured an injunction barring Mr. Novak from leaving the country. Mr. Novak was arrested, and Ms. Novak got her children back.

I do not regret taking steps on Ms. Novak's direction to vacate the injunction. In retrospect, however, Ms. Novak's view when she asked us to vacate the injunction does not wear well the mantle of "authenticity". If it is authentic, it is authentic as a product of the violence, both physical and psychological, that her spouse and her community had inflicted on her. Such violence contracts, rather than expands, the survivor's range of choices. The projective element embodied in choice – the ability, even within constraints, to shape the future – is exactly the element of humanity that violence seeks to extinguish. A lawyer practicing integrative advocacy should not give in readily to such violence in the name of "authenticity". An approach to lawyering that merely advises advocates to "accept battered women as they are"[83] does not pay enough attention to possibilities for change. Of course, the integrative advocate must consider the client's present situation.[84] However, the lawyer must also work with the client to shape an alternative vision closer to the way Ms. Novak felt as a later self, when she had thwarted her husband's attempt to abduct her children.

In addition to attorney-client deliberation, an integrative approach requires a repertoire of other strategies. Peering into the future, it is not hard to see that reliance on a single remedy, such as a restraining order, is insufficient. The lawyer should also assist the client in interfaces with providers of services such as transportation and employment training, as well as goods and cash assistance. Moreover, representation should extend to developing new spaces for dialogue where peers of the survivor can help shape alternative visions of the future. Groups such as Ayuda ("Help") in Washington, D.C. or La Lucha ("The Struggle") in Miami can extend the projective vision of a survivor in a more lasting and profound way than the lawyer's intervention.[85] Contrary to the logic of technocracy, the lawyer can fully realize the possibilities of the projective dimension only when she understands the limits of the lawyer's role.[86]

Conclusion

Dialogue and projectivity will always co-exist uneasily in pragmatist practice. The instability of the combination means that temptations to neglect one or the other dimension are omnipresent. In practice, dialogue will often seem expendable. The maxim, "You can't make an omelet without breaking eggs" will always have appeal whenever exigencies of institutions, states, and legal systems press home. Historical accounts of Moses, Romulus, and the modern public interest litigators, with their disregard for individual clients, amply demonstrate this point. However, projectivity can also become a casualty when concerns about instrumentalism or overreaching reach a critical mass. There are dangers, here, as well, as we are left with many voices but no exit from the status quo – or perhaps only a violent exit as one group asserts its voice over others.

The model of integrative advocacy advanced here in connection with representation of domestic violence survivors is a reaction to the instability of dialogue and projectivity. It will not resolve the pragmatist dilemma. However, it should highlight the importance of fulfilling commitments to both dialogue and projectivity. If it does this, it extends the hope that we can engage in a reflective, but still effective practice.

Acknowledgement

Thanks to Lydia Saenz for cite-checking this chapter.

Notes

1 See Arendt, H. (1958), *The Human Condition*, University of Chicago Press, Chicago and London, at p. 306 (arguing that "pragmatic trends of modern philosophy ... adopted the principle of utility as the key which would open all doors to the explanation of human motivation and behavior"); id. at 229 (discussing modernity's advice that "'he who wants an end must also want the means' and that 'you can't make an omelette without breaking eggs'"); cf. Canovan, M. (1994), *Hannah Arendt: A*

Reinterpretation of Her Political Thought, Cambridge University Press, Cambridge, at pp. 167-68 (discussing critique of instrumentalism in Arendt's work).

2 See Selznick, P. (1992), *The Moral Commonwealth: Social Theory and the Promise of Community*, University of California, Berkeley, at pp. 328-30 (distinguishing John Dewey's pragmatism from stark conception of instrumental rationality).

3 See Emirbayer, M. and Ann Mische, A. (1998), 'What Is Agency?', American Journal of Sociology, vol. 103, pp. 962-1023, at p. 971; cf. Tamanaha, B.Z. (1997), *Realistic Socio-Legal Theory: Pragmatism and a Social Theory of Law*, Oxford University Press, Oxford (outlining pragmatic theory of legal institutions).

4 Emirbayer and Mische, supra note 3, at 971.

5 I take as a premise here the point of all modern and post-modern legal theories, stemming from the pragmatist-inspired work of the Legal Realists, that there is no rigid dividing line between law and politics. See Gordon, R. (1990), 'New Developments in Legal Theory', in D. Kairys (ed), *The Politics of Law*, Pantheon Books, New York, pp. 413-35. I define public interest law broadly, to include any form of lawyering for subordinated groups or persons. This kind of practice can range from the "impact" litigation that led to the striking down of segregation in public education to the representation of a survivor of domestic violence.

6 I view my efforts here as supplementing new work on critical and community lawyering. See Gerald P. Lopez (1992), *Rebellious Lawyering*; Alfieri, Anthony V. (1993), 'Impoverished Practices', Georgetown Law Journal, vol. 81, pp. 2567-2663; Bell, Derrick (1976), 'Serving Two Masters: Integration Ideals and Client Interests in School Desegregation Litigation', Yale Law Journal, vol. 85, pp.470-516; Calmore, John O. (1999), 'A Call to Context: The Professional Challenges of Cause Lawyering at the Intersection of Race, Space, and Poverty', Fordham Law Review, vol. 67, pp. 1927-1957; Delgado, Richard (1996), 'Rodrigo's Eleventh Chronicle: Empathy and False Empathy', 84 California Law Review, vol. 84, pp.61-100; Margulies, Peter (1999), 'Multiple Communities or Monolithic Clients: Positional Conflicts of Interest and the Mission of the Legal Services Lawyer', Fordham Law Review, vol. 67, pp. 2339-2375; Margulies, Peter (1994), 'The Mother with Poor Judgment and Other Tales of the Unexpected: A Civic Republican View of Difference and Clinical Legal Education', Northwestern University Law Review, vol 88, pp. 695-732; Tremblay, Paul R. (1990), 'Toward a Community-Based Ethic for Legal Services Practice', 37 University of California at Los Angeles Law Review, vol. 37, pp. 1101-1156; White, Lucie E. (1990), 'Subordination, Rhetorical Survival Skills, and Sunday Shoes: Notes on the Hearing of Mrs. G.', Buffalo Law Review, vol. 38, pp. 1-58; cf. Ellmann, Stephen (1992), 'Client-Centredness Multiplied: Individual Autonomy and Collective Mobilization in Public Interest Lawyers' Representation of Groups', Virginia Law Review, vol. 78, pp. 1103-1173 (discussing dilemmas of group litigation); Rubenstein, William B. (1997), 'Divided We Litigate: Addressing Disputes Among Group Members and Lawyers in Civil Rights Campaigns', Yale Law Journal, vol. 106, 1623-1681 (same).

7 See, e.g., Calmore, supra note 6, at 1947-51 (discussing importance of conceptions of place in public interest law).

8 See Westbrook, Robert B. (1991), John Dewey and American Democracy, Cornell University Press, Ithaca, at ix-x.

9 This insistence on the link between theory and practice is also thoroughly American. While we can trace certain aspects of pragmatist thought to theorists from Aristotle to

Machiavelli, pragmatism has a special purchase on American thought and temperament. There are of course American thinkers who expressly or implicitly reject pragmatism. See, e.g., Dworkin, Ronald (1986), Law's Empire, Belknap Press, Cambridge, at 151-75 (critiquing pragmatism and offering conception of "law as integrity"); Rawls, John (1971), A Theory of Justice, Belknap Press, Cambridge (developing contractarian theory of justice based on what persons would agree to behind a "veil of ignorance" about their prospects and circumstances). While detailed discussion of these thinkers is beyond the scope of this essay, it is worth noting that their arguments would also be very different without the benefit of the American pragmatic tradition. Dworkin, for example, in his discussion of the Endangered Species Act, ultimately endorses the position that the jobs and physical plant involved in an almost-finished dam are more important than the survival of helpless and obscure species of animals such as the snail darter. Dworkin, supra, at 313-54. This position seems to embody a pragmatism of a particularly simplistic sort, one that this Essay rejects. Rawls in turn relies on Dewey in showing congruence between justice and the good life. See Rawls, supra, at 400 n., 408 n.

10 See Tamanaha, supra note 3.

11 My account here also reflects the influence of thinkers such as William James and George Herbert Mead, and dovetails in part with the work of Richard Rorty. See, e.g., Rorty, Richard (1989), Contingency, Irony, and Solidarity, Cambridge University Press, New York, at 57-58 (discussing Dewey); Tamanaha, supra note 3 (discussing James); Emirbayer and Mische, supra note 3 (discussing Mead's work).

12 Emirbayer and Mische, supra note 3, at 976-78, 996 (discussing continuum between Aristotle and more modern schools of thought such as the pragmatism of Dewey, the civic humanism of Hannah Arendt, the phenomenology of Alfred Schutz, the ethnomethodology of Harold Garfinkel, and the theoretics of practice of Bourdieu and Giddens).

13 See Selznick, Philip (1992), *The Moral Commonwealth: Social Theory and the Promise of Community,* University of California Press, Berkeley, at 330 (noting that for a pragmatist like John Dewey, "there is nothing wrong with valuing a means for its own sake ... [t]he experience of cooperation, for example, has intrinsic worth ...").

14 This process, rooted in human beings' connection to one another and to nature, may for a pragmatist have both moral and aesthetic significance. See Dewey, John (1981), 'Experience and Philosophic Method', in J.J. McDermott (ed), *The Philosophy of John Dewey*, University of Chicago Press, Chicago, at 249, 252.

15 Dewey, John (1993), 'The Problem of Method', in D. Morris and I. Shapiro (eds), *The Political Writings*, Hackett Publishing Company, Indianapolis, at 184, 186-87.

16 Dewey, *The Problem of Method*, supra note 15, at 187.

17 Id.

18 Id.

19 Id. This same conviction about the importance of redress is at least implied in Dewey's observation later in this passage that, "The world has suffered more from leaders and authorities than from the masses".

20 Id.

21 Id. at 189. Although Dewey focuses on "family" and "neighborhood" in his argument, id., he should be read to include certain kinds of virtual and verbal communities, such as those created through letters or cyberspace. Indeed, in Dewey's vision of a

community that is "alive and flexible as well as stable, responsive to the complex and world-wide scene in which it is enmeshed", id. at 191, we have a compelling precursor of some of the cyber-communities of today.

22 Id. at 189.

23 Cf. id. at 191 (critiquing "mechanical and external" role of organization).

24 See Emirbayer and Mische, supra note 3, at 984 ("an imaginative engagement of the future is also a crucial component of the effort of human actors").

25 See Emirbayer and Mische, supra note 3, at 985-88. Of course, the degree of projectivity will vary across persons, groups, and cultures. Id. at 985.

26 See Selznick, supra note 2, at 328. The pragmatist commitment to scientific method, see Tamanaha, supra note 3, is one illustration of this view.

27 See Selznick, supra note 13, at 46-48.

28 Id.

29 One could make the same pragmatic argument against contractarian thinkers who view preservation of property rights as the crucial goal of government. Id. at 48-49.

30 See Canovan, supra note 1, at 167-68 (noting Arendt's view that, "Given the inherent uncertainty of human affairs, the good that is supposed to come about in the end cannot be other than highly speculative: the only thing we can be sure about is the evil means").

31 The Who (1970), 'We Won't Get Fooled Again', on Who's Next, Decca Records, London; see also Hirschman, Albert O. (1982), Shifting Involvements: Private Interest and Public Action, Princeton University Press, Princeton, at 100 (commitments in politics "often develop a momentum of their own and take off in directions unanticipated by the original sponsors and often unwelcome to them... This is the story of most revolutions ..."); Margulies, P. (1999), 'Democratic Transitions and the Future of Asylum Law', University of Colorado Law Review, vol. 71, pp. 3-49, at 26 n. 74 (noting instances where "action against oppression consumed its own most prominent actors, or led to an even greater source of oppression").

32 See also Emirbayer and Mische, supra note 3, at 980 (discussing "maneuverability" of repertoires); cf. Benhabib, Seyla (1992), *Situating the Self*, Routledge, New York, at 42-43 (advocating for conception of "reflexivity" that entails a commitment to ongoing questioning of strategies, goals, and underlying assumptions).

33 See Morone, J.A. (1990), *The Democratic Wish: Popular Participation and the Limits of American Government*, Yale University Press, New Haven, at 332 ("a weak government is not just less competent; it is also more intrusive").

34 See Walzer, M. (1985), *Exodus and Revolution*, Basic Books, New York, at 55-66. Machiavelli provides a pithy explanation of this episode: "[I]n order that Moses might set about making laws and institutions, he had to kill a very great number of men ... " Id. at 59-60, citing Machiavelli, N. (1970), Richardson, B. (ed), *The Discourses*, at 486 (Book 3, Chap. 30).

35 See Berlin, I. (1982), 'The Originality of Machiavelli', in *Against the Current: Essays in the History of Ideas*, Viking Press, New York, at 25, 51 (discussing Machiavelli's account of the founding of Rome); Canovan, supra note 1, at 168 (discussing Arendt's analysis of Machiavelli's account).

36 Dewey, *The Problem of Method*, supra note 15, at 187.

37 Cf. Luban, D. (1996), 'What's Pragmatic About Legal Pragmatism?', Cardozo Law Review, vol. 20, pp. 43-73, 69 (arguing that Dewey believed erroneously that "law

should be reconstructed on a scientific basis, generating its principles by inductions from data").

38 Dewey, J. 'The Future of Pacifism', in Political Writings, supra, at 195, 195.

39 Id. (accusing the pacifists of "futile gesturings").

40 Id. at 197.

41 Id. at 196.

42 See Westbrook, supra note 8, at 238 (discussing Dewey's acknowledgment that the Versailles peace treaty had jettisoned Wilson's internationalist aspirations in favor of "unreconstructed" imperialism).

43 Randolph Bourne, 'Conscience and Intelligence in War', in Political Writings, supra.

44 Id.

45 See Abrams v. United States, 250 U.S. 616 (1919).

46 See Sturm, S. P. (1994), 'Sameness and Subordination: The Dangers of a Universal Solution', University of Pennsylvania Law Review, vol. 143, pp. 201-219.

47 See Strum, P. (1993), *Brandeis: Beyond Progressivism*, University Press of Kansas, Lawrence, at 5-6 (discussing influence of William James and pragmatism on Brandeis); Farber, D. A. (1995), 'Reinventing Brandeis: Legal Pragmatism for the Twenty-First Century', *University of Illinois Law Review*, vol. 1995, pp. 163-190, 182-84 (discussing links between civic humanism, pragmatism, and Brandeis thought).

48 See Wilkins, D.B. (1997), 'Social Engineers or Corporate Tools: Brown v. Board of Education and the Conscience of the Black Corporate Bar', in Sarat, A. (ed), *Race, Law, and Culture: Reflections on Brown v. Board of Education*, at 137.

49 See Spillenger, C. (1996), 'Elusive Advocate: Reconsidering Brandeis as People's Lawyer', Yale Law Journal, vol. 105, pp. 1445-1535, at 1510.

50 See Carle, S.D. (1999), 'Gender in the Construction of the Lawyer's Persona', Harvard. Women's Law Journal, vol. 22, pp. 239-273 (discussing legal identities of women reformers during Progressive Era); Lipschultz, S. (1989), 'Social Feminism and Legal Discourse, 1908-1923', Yale Journal of Law and Feminism, vol. 2, pp. 131-161 (same); cf. Gordon, L. (1994), *Pitied But Not Entitled: Single Mothers and the History of Welfare*, The Free Press, New York (discussing women reformers and welfare policy).

51 208 U.S. 412 (1908).

52 See Muller V. Oregon: A Brief History With Documents 109, 115 (1996).

53 Cf. Woloch, N. (1996), 'Legacy: Labor Law, Women's Politics, and Protective Policies', in *Muller v. Oregon: A Brief History with Documents*, Bedford Books of St. Martin's Press, Boston, pp. 58-90, at 61-62 (discussing mixed effects of maximum hours legislation for women). Lapses in dialogue in the early women's movement extended to race as well as class. See Gordon, supra note 5, at 117 (in the first decades of the 20th century, "the national network of white women reformers usually excluded black women").

54 See Ball, M.S. (1993), *The Word and the Law*, University of Chicago Press, Chicago, at 21 (discussing public interest attorney who started legal services program in Appalachia because he and his wife "wanted to settle into a community where they could invest themselves over the long term and help make life better for others"). This sense of identity is often reinforced by a sense of communal heritage. See id. (according to the lawyer just mentioned, his "commitment to justice and the service of others ... is a clear but hard-to-articulate function of his Jewish heritage").

55 This conception of how means influence ends is a hallmark of "new institutionalist" thought. See March, J.G. and Olsen, J.P. (1989), *Rediscovering Institutions: The Organizational Basis of Politics*, Free Press, New York, at 13 (noting that a "solution [in public policy terms]... is an answer actively looking for a question"). Massive problems of injustice and inequality clearly preceded emergence of the modern class action. However, a pragmatic analysis holds that the availability of class actions shaped how lawyers viewed those problems. The perspectives of lawyers also influenced wider public perceptions, as lawyers' images and narratives helped constitute the social world. See Margulies, P. (1998), 'Identity on Trial: Subordination, Social Science Evidence, and Criminal Defense', Rutgers Law Review, vol. 51, pp. 45-140 (discussing how images of subordinated groups advanced by lawyers in criminal trials help shape broader social perceptions); Umphrey, M. M. (1999), 'The Dialogics of Legal Meaning: Spectacular Trials, the Unwritten Law, and Narratives of Criminal Responsibility', Law and Society Review, vol. 33, pp. 393-420 (same); cf. Mosteller, R.P. (1996), 'Syndromes and Politics in Criminal Trials and Evidence Law', Duke Law Journal, vol. 46, pp. 461-516 (discussing interaction of substantive law, empirical investigation, and political meaning). The new critical lawyering literature has developed a similar analysis. See Lopez, supra note 6; Alfieri, supra note 6.

56 See Garth, Bryant G. (1992), 'Power and Legal Artifice: The Federal Class Action', *Law and Society Review*, vol. 26, pp. 237-71. at 257 (cases discussed in Article "provide a number of examples in which the class representatives do not get much from the class action litigation").

57 See Chambers, D. and Wald, M. (1985), 'Smith v. Offer', R. Mnookin (ed), in *In the Interests of Children*, PON Books, Cambridge, pp. 67-147, at 93.

58 See Herr, S.S. (1989-90), 'Representation of Clients with Disabilities: Issues of Ethics and Control', New York University Review of Law and Social Change, vol. 17, pp. 609-647, at 611.

59 410 U.S. 113 (1973).

60 See '"Jane Roe" Joins Anti-Abortion Group' (August 11, 1995), New York Times, A12, col. 4 (also noting that Ms. McCorvey had joined Operation Rescue, and now opposed abortions after the first trimester).

61 See ABC News Nightline, Aug. 10, 1995.

62 See Behrens, D. (August 11, 1995), 'Change of Heart; "Roe" of Roe vs. Wade Says Abortion Should Be Illegal', Newsday, A5 (emphasis added).

63 See March and Olsen, supra note 55, at 14.

64 As legend has it, Ulysses asked his crew to bind him to the mast, to avoid being seduced by the sirens' song. See Elster, J. (1990), *Nuts and Bolts for the Social Sciences*, Cambridge University Press, Cambridge.

65 See Margulies, P. (1990), '"Who Are You to Tell Me that?": Attorney-Client Deliberation Regarding Nonlegal Issues and the Interests of Nonclients', North Carolina Law Review, vol. 68, pp. 213-252 (discussing mental health litigation). Factors like gentrification of low-cost housing played a role here, too. But these phenomena were also interdependent consequences that an effective advocate would figure into her deliberations with her clients.

66 See Bell, D. (1976), 'Serving Two Masters: Integration Ideals and Client Interests in School Desegregation Litigation', 85 Yale Law Journal, vol. 85, pp. 470-516 (1976); Peller, G. (1990), 'Race Consciousness', Duke Law Journal, vol. 1990, pp. 758-847 at 767-71.

67 See Davis, P. (1997), 'Performing Interpretation: A Legacy of Civil Rights Lawyering in Brown v. Board of Education', in Race, Law, and Culture, Oxford University Press, New York, pp. 23-48.

68 See Scott, D.M. (1997), Contempt and Pity: Social Policy and the Images of the Damaged Black Psyche, 1880-1996, at pp. 82-83 (discussing research and theoretical perspective of social scientists working with the desegregation lawyers, particularly Kenneth and Mamie Clark, whose "doll experiments" purporting to show that black children subjected to discrimination preferred white dolls were central to the lawyers' arguments and relied on by the Brown Court).

69 Cf. Luban, D. (1988), Lawyers and Justice, Princeton University Press, Princeton, at pp. 349-51 (discussing "uncertainty" about effects of remedies in desegregation and other civil rights cases).

70 The new institutionalists describe this concatenation, not necessarily pejoratively, as the "garbage can" of public policy. See March and Olsen, supra note 55, at 14.

71 See Selznick, supra note 2, at 331; id. at 475 (discussing "institutional integration").

72 "New institutionalists" focus on the social nature of practices and institutions, as do pragmatists and civic humanists such as Hannah Arendt. See Emirbayer and Mische, supra note 3, at 983 ("Reacting to overly instrumental and purposive views of organizational life, [new institutionalist] researchers draw heavily upon ethnomethodological, phenomenological, and cognitive approaches, emphasizing the routinized, taken-for-granted (or 'scripted') quality of knowledge and action"); cf. March and Olsen, supra note 55, at 125 (noting that, in an integrative process, "rights express key aspects of the structure of social belief. They are metaphors of human unity, symbolizing the common destiny and humanity of those who share them".).

73 This focus on the interaction of mutuality and difference is a feature of critical race theory. See Crenshaw, K. (1991), 'Mapping the Margins: Intersectionality, Identity Politics, and Violence Against Women of Color', Stanford Law Review, vol. 43, pp. 1241-1299.

74 March and Olsen, supra note 55, at 126-27; cf. id. at 127 (rejecting use of integrative institutions to cloak social conflict or co-opt groups subjected to ongoing subordination).

75 See Disch, L.J. (1993), 'More Truth Than Fact: Storytelling as Critical Understanding in the Writings of Hannah Arendt', Political Theory, vol. 21, pp. 665-94, at 687 (1993). The discussion here stems from my exploration of "empathetic engagement" in Margulies, P. (1999), 'Re-Framing Empathy in Clinical Legal Education', Clinical Law Review, vol. 5, pp. 605-637.

76 This two-way inquiry bears some relation to the process of sympathy and detachment which Kronman identifies as central to lawyers' relationship with clients. Kronman, A. (1993), *The Lost Lawyer: Failing Ideals of the Legal Profession*, Belkanp Press of Harvard University Press, Cambridge.

77 See Margulies, P. (1995), 'Representation of Domestic Violence Survivors as a New Paradigm of Poverty Law: In Search of Access, Connection, and Voice', George Washington Law Review, vol. 64, pp. 1071-1104.

78 Abel, R.L. (1985), 'Law Without Politics: Legal Aid Under Advanced Capitalism', University of California, Los Angeles Law Review, vol. 32, 474-642, at 609, critiqued in Margulies, *Representation of Domestic Violence Survivors*, supra note 77.

79 See Schneider, E.M. (2000), *Battered Women and Feminist Lawmaking*, Yale University Press, New Haven; Cahn, N.R. (1992), 'The Looseness of Legal Language:

The Reasonable Woman Standard in Theory and Practice', *Cornell Law Review*, vol. 77, pp. 1398-1446 (1992); Martha R. Mahoney, M.R. (1990), 'Legal Images of Battered Women: Redefining the Issue of Separation', *Michigan Law Review*, vol. 90; pp. 1-94; Peter Margulies, *Representation of Domestic Violence Survivors*, supra note 77; Meier, J. (1993), 'Notes from the Underground: Integrating Psychological and Legal Perspectives on Domestic Violence in Theory and Practice', Hofstra Law Review, vol. 21, pp. 1295-1366; Mills, L.G. (1996), 'On the Other Side of Silence: Affective Lawyering for Intimate Abuse', Cornell Law Review, vol. 81, pp.1225-1263; Mills, L.G. (1999), 'Killing Her Softly: Intimate Abuse and the Violence of State Intervention', *Harvard Law Review*, vol. 113, pp. 550-613.

80 See Fenton, Z.E. (1998), 'Domestic Violence in Black and White: Racialized Gender Stereotypes in Gender Violence', *Columbia Journal Gender and Law*, vol. 8, pp. 1-65; Espinoza, L.G. (1997), 'Legal Narratives, Therapeutic Narratives: The Invisibility and Omnipresence of Race and Gender', *Michigan Law Review*, vol. 95, pp. 901; Allard, S.A. (1991), 'Rethinking Battered Woman Syndrome: A Black Feminist Perspective', University of California, *Los Angeles Women's Law Journal*, vol. 1, pp. 191-207; Ammons, L. (1995), *Mules, Madonnas, Babies, Bathwater, Racial Imagery and Stereotypes: The African-American Woman and the Battered Woman Syndrome*, 1995 Wis. L. Rev. 1003; Crenshaw, supra note 77; Harris, Angela (1990), 'Race and Essentialism in Feminist Legal Theory', *Stanford Law Review*, vol. 42, pp. 581-616, at 599-601 (1990).

81 See Kelly, L. (1998), 'Stories from the Front: Seeking Refuge for Battered Immigrants in the Violence Against Women Act', Northwestern University Law Review, vol. 92, pp. 665-705 (discussing strengths and pitfalls of immigration legislation on violence against women).

82 See Mills, Killing Her Softly, supra note 79, at 555 n. 25 (urging advocates to "accept battered women as they are"); cf. Balfour, L. (1998), ' "A Most Disagreeable Mirror": Race Consciousness as Double Consciousness', Political Theory, vol. 26, pp. 346-365 at 365 (asserting that struggles over a single "authentic" description of subordinated groups' experience "serve to dehumanize members of the very group in whose name the struggle is undertaken").

83 See Mills, supra note 79, at 555 n. 25. One can also read Mills as acknowledging that survivors "as they are" wish to change. Dialogue with a lawyer only occurs if the survivor has already done something affirmative to indicate a wish to change, such as call the police during or after an episode of abuse. A survivor intimidated by her abuser into discontinuing proceedings may therefore be suppressing her past as well as her future self. A competent and sensitive advocate will recognize this implicit projective dimension in Mills' approach, and explore the survivor's reasons for her reluctance to proceed. An inexperienced or uncommitted advocate adopting Mills' approach may, however, miss that projective dimension.

84 This does not mean that the lawyer can substitute her choices for the client's. Approaches to fighting domestic violence that pay no heed to the survivor's current situation exalt the projective dimension while neglecting dialogue. To the extent that Professor Hanna, in supporting mandatory arrest and prosecution, gives short shrift to dialogue, she restates the pragmatist dilemma, instead of resolving it. Cf. Hanna, at 1888 (arguing that mandated participation is justified pragmatically by "long-term benefits ... [that] outweigh short-term costs"). The dialogic dimension requires an effort by the lawyer to understand the context of the client's situation, and the extent to

which the projectivity that the lawyer possesses as a relatively well-compensated professional may be a perspective that the client's material and affective situation does not allow.

85 See Espinoza, supra note 80 (discussing partial perspective of attorney).

86 Integrative advocacy is also possible in the public interest class action context. Consider the federal litigation in New York State to reform the institution known as "Willowbrook" and create community placements for its residents, who were persons with mental retardation. See New York State Ass'n for Retarded Children, Inc. v. Rockefeller, 357 F. Supp. 752 (E.D.N.Y. 1973); 393 F. Supp. 715 (E.D.N.Y. 1975); cf. Minow, M. (1990), *Making All the Difference: Inclusion, Exclusion, and American Law*, Cornell University Press, Ithaca, at pp. 364-66 (discussing Willowbrook litigation); Burt, R. (1985), 'Pennhurst: A Parable', in R.N. Mnookin (ed), *In the Interest of Children: Advocacy, Law Reform, and Public Policy* PON Books, Cambridge, pp. 265, at 337-43 (same). Lawyers in the case had close ties with parents, high-functioning persons with mental retardation, and other constituencies. See Rothman, D.J. and Rothman, S.M. (1984), *The Willowbrook Wars: A Decade of Struggle for Social Justice*, Harper and Row, New York, at 359-60 (class counsel "made efforts to consult with the parents of the class members, especially when tough points of settlement arose during negotiations with the state"). Through building alliances with these constituencies, lawyers were able to foresee and address contingencies more effectively. This made the transition from institutions to community care for persons with mental retardation much more successful than it was in other cases, such as many of those involving persons with mental illness, that lacked such dialogue. See Margulies, P. (1990), '"Who Are You to Tell Me that?": Attorney-Client Deliberation Regarding Nonlegal Issues and the Interests of Nonclients', North Carolina Law Review, vol. 68, pp. 213-252 (discussing mental health litigation).

References

ABC News *Nightline*, Aug. 10, 1995.

Abel, R.L. (1985), "Law Without Politics: Legal Aid Under Advanced Capitalism", *University of California, Los Angeles Law Review*, vol. 32, 474-642, at 609.

Alfieri, Anthony V. (1993), "Impoverished Practices", *Georgetown Law Journal*, vol. 81, pp. 2567-2663.

Allard, S.A. (1991), "Rethinking Battered Woman Syndrome: A Black Feminist Perspective", *University of California, Los Angeles Women's Law Journal*, vol. 1, pp. 191-207.

Ammons, L. (1995), *Mules, Madonnas, Babies, Bathwater, Racial Imagery and Stereotypes: The African-American Woman and the Battered Woman Syndrome*, 1995 Wis. L. Rev. 1003; note 80.

Arendt, H. (1958), *The Human Condition*. Chicago – London: University of Chicago Press.

Balfour, L. (1998), "'A Most Disagreeable Mirror': Race Consciousness as Double Consciousness", *Political Theory*, vol. 26, pp. 346-365, at 365.

Ball, M.S. (1993), *The Word and the Law*. Chicago: University of Chicago Press.

Behrens, D. (August 11, 1995), "Change of Heart; 'Roe' of Roe vs. Wade Says Abortion Should Be Illegal", *Newsday*, A5 (emphasis added).

Bell, Derrick (1976), "Serving Two Masters: Integration Ideals and Client Interests in School Desegregation Litigation", *Yale Law Journal*, vol. 85, pp. 470-516.

Benhabib, Seyla (1992), *Situating the Self*. New York: Routledge.

Berlin, I. (1982), "The Originality of Machiavelli", in *Against the Current: Essays in the History of Ideas*, pp. 25-79, at 51. Cambridge: Viking Press.

Cahn, N.R. (1992), "The Looseness of Legal Language: The Reasonable Woman Standard in Theory and Practice", *Cornell Law Review*, vol. 77, pp. 1398-1446.

Calmore, John O. (1999), "A Call to Context: The Professional Challenges of Cause Lawyering at the Intersection of Race, Space, and Poverty", *Fordham Law Review*, vol. 67, pp. 1927-1957.

Canovan, M. (1994), *Hannah Arendt: A Reinterpretation of Her Political Thought*. Cambridge: Cambridge University Press.

Carle, S.D. (1999), "Gender in the Construction of the Lawyer's Persona", *Harvard. Women's Law Journal*, vol. 22, pp. 239-273 (discussing legal identities of women reformers during Progressive Era).

Chambers, D. and Wald, M. (1985), "Smith v. Offer", R. Mnookin (ed), *In the Interests of Children*, pp. 67-147, at 93. Cambridge: PON Books.

Crenshaw, K. (1991), "Mapping the Margins: Intersectionality, Identity Politics, and Violence Against Women of Color", *Stanford Law Review*, vol. 43, pp. 1241-1299.

Davis, P. (1997), "Performing Interpretation: A Legacy of Civil Rights Lawyering in Brown v. Board of Education", *Race, Law, and Culture*, pp. 3-229, at 23-48. New York: Oxford University Press.

Delgado, Richard (1996), "Rodrigo's Eleventh Chronicle: Empathy and False Empathy", *California Law Review*, vol. 84, pp. 61-100.

Dewey, John (1981), "Experience and Philosophic Method", in J.J. McDermott (ed), *The Philosophy of John Dewey*, at pp. 249, 252. Chicago: University of Chicago Press.

Dewey, John (1993), "The Problem of Method", in D. Morris and I. Shapiro (eds), *The Political Writings*, at pp. 184, 186-87. Indianapolis: Hackett Publishing Company.

Disch, L.J. (1993), "More Truth Than Fact: Storytelling as Critical Understanding in the Writings of Hannah Arendt", *Political Theory*, vol. 21, pp. 665-94, at 687.

Dworkin, R. (1986), *Law's Empire*, at pp. 151-75. Cambridge: Belknap Press (critiquing pragmatism and offering conception of "law as integrity").

Ellmann, Stephen (1992), "Client-Centredness Multiplied: Individual Autonomy and Collective Mobilization in Public Interest Lawyers' Representation of Groups", *Virginia Law Review*, vol. 78, pp. 1103-1173 (discussing dilemmas of group litigation).

Elster, J. (1990), *Nuts and Bolts for the Social Sciences*. Cambridge: Cambridge University Press.

Emirbayer, M. and Ann Mische, A. (1998), "What Is Agency?", *American Journal of Sociology*, vol. 103, pp. 962-1023.

Espinoza, L.G. (1997), "Legal Narratives, Therapeutic Narratives: The Invisibility and Omnipresence of Race and Gender", *Michigan Law Review*, vol. 95, pp. 901.

Farber, D.A. (1995), "Reinventing Brandeis: Legal Pragmatism for the Twenty-First Century", *University of Illinois Law Review*, vol. 1995, pp. 163-190, 182-84.

Fenton, Z.E. (1998), "Domestic Violence in Black and White: Racialized Gender Stereotypes in Gender Violence", *Columbia Journal Gender and Law*, vol. 8, pp. 1-65.

Garth, Bryant G. (1992), "Power and Legal Artifice: The Federal Class Action", *Law and Society Review*, vol. 26, pp. 237-71.

Gordon, L. (1994), *Pitied But Not Entitled: Single Mothers and the History of Welfare*. New York: The Free Press (discussing women reformers and welfare policy).

Gordon, R. (1990), "New Developments in Legal Theory", in D. Kairys (ed), *The Politics of Law*, pp. 413-35. New York: Pantheon Books.

Hanna, C. (1996), "No Right to Choose: Mandated Victim Participation in Domestic Violence Prosecutions", *Harvard Law Review*, vol. 109, pp. 1849-1910.

Harris, Angela (1990), "Race and Essentialism in Feminist Legal Theory", *Stanford Law Review*, vol. 42, pp. 581-616, at 599-601.

Herr, S.S. (1989-90), "Representation of Clients with Disabilities: Issues of Ethics and Control", *New York University Review of Law and Social Change*, vol. 17, pp. 609-647, at 611.

Hirschman, Albert O. (1982), *Shifting Involvements: Private Interest and Public Action*. Princeton: Princeton University Press.

Kelly, L. (1998), "Stories from the Front: Seeking Refuge for Battered Immigrants in the Violence Against Women Act", *Northwestern University Law Review*, vol. 92, pp. 665-705 (discussing strengths and pitfalls of immigration legislation on violence against women).

Kronman, A. (1993), *The Lost Lawyer: Failing Ideals of the Legal Profession*. Cambridge: Belknap Press of Harvard University Press,.

Lipschultz, S. (1989), "Social Feminism and Legal Discourse, 1908-1923", *Yale Journal of Law and Feminism*, vol. 2, pp. 131-161.

Lopez, G. (1992), *Rebellious Lawyering*. Boulder: Westview Press.

Luban, D. (1988), *Lawyers and Justice*, at pp. 349-351. Princeton: Princeton University Press.

Luban, D. (1996), "What's Pragmatic About Legal Pragmatism?", *Cardozo Law Review*, vol. 20, pp. 43-73.

Mahoney, M.R. (1990), "Legal Images of Battered Women: Redefining the Issue of Separation", *Michigan Law Review*, vol. 90, pp. 1-94.

March, J.G. and Olsen, J.P. (1989), *Rediscovering Institutions: The Organizational Basis of Politics*. New York: Free Press.

Margulies, P. (1990), '"Who Are You to Tell Me that?": Attorney-Client Deliberation Regarding Nonlegal Issues and the Interests of Nonclients', *North Carolina Law Review*, vol. 68, pp. 213-252.

Margulies, P. (1995), "Representation of Domestic Violence Survivors as a New Paradigm of Poverty Law: In Search of Access, Connection, and Voice", *George Washington Law Review*, vol. 64, pp. 1071-1104.

Margulies, P. (1998), "Identity on Trial: Subordination, Social Science Evidence, and Criminal Defense", *Rutgers Law Review*, vol. 51, pp. 45-140 (discussing how images of subordinated groups advanced by lawyers in criminal trials help shape broader social perceptions).

Margulies, P. (1999), "Democratic Transitions and the Future of Asylum Law", *University of Colorado Law Review*, vol. 71, pp. 3-49.

Margulies, P. (1999), "Re-Framing Empathy in Clinical Legal Education", *Clinical Law Review*, vol. 5, pp. 605-637.

Margulies, Peter (1994), "The Mother with Poor Judgment and Other Tales of the Unexpected: A Civic Republican View of Difference and Clinical Legal Education", *Northwestern University Law Review*, vol 88, pp. 695-732.

Margulies, Peter (1999), "Multiple Communities or Monolithic Clients: Positional Conflicts of Interest and the Mission of the Legal Services Lawyer", *Fordham Law Review*, vol. 67, pp. 2339-2375.

Meier, J. (1993), "Notes from the Underground: Integrating Psychological and Legal Perspectives on Domestic Violence in Theory and Practice", *Hofstra Law Review*, vol. 21, pp. 1295-1366.

Mills, L.G. (1996), "On the Other Side of Silence: Affective Lawyering for Intimate Abuse", *Cornell Law Review*, vol. 81, pp. 1225-1263.

Mills, L.G. (1999), "Killing Her Softly: Intimate Abuse and the Violence of State Intervention", *Harvard Law Review*, vol. 113, pp. 550-613.

Morone, J.A. (1990), *The Democratic Wish: Popular Participation and the Limits of American Government*. New Haven: Yale University Press.

Mosteller, R.P. (1996), "Syndromes and Politics in Criminal Trials and Evidence Law", *Duke Law Journal*, vol. 46, pp. 461-516.

Oregon, Muller V. (1996), "A Brief History With Documents 109, 115 'Jane Roe' Joins Anti-Abortion Group (August 11, 1995)", *New York Times*, A12, col. 4 (also noting that Ms. McCorvey had joined Operation Rescue, and now opposed abortions after the first trimester).

Peller, G. (1990), "Race Consciousness", *Duke Law Journal*, vol. 1990, pp. 758-847, at pp.767-71.

Rawls, J. (1971), *A Theory of Justice*. Cambridge: Belknap Press.

Rorty, Richard (1989), *Contingency, Irony, and Solidarity*. New York: Cambridge University Press.

Rubenstein, William B. (1997), "Divided We Litigate: Addressing Disputes Among Group Members and Lawyers in Civil Rights Campaigns", *Yale Law Journal*, vol. 106, pp.1623-1681 (same).

Schneider, E.M. (2000), *Battered Women and Feminist Lawmaking*. New Haven: Yale University Press,.

Scott, D.M. (1997), *Contempt and Pity: Social Policy and the Images of the Damaged Black Psyche, 1880-1996*, at pp. 82-83.

Selznick, P. (1992), *The Moral Commonwealth: Social Theory and the Promise of Community*. Berkeley: University of California.

Spillenger, C. (1996), "Elusive Advocate: Reconsidering Brandeis as People's Lawyer", *Yale Law Journal*, vol. 105, pp. 1445-1535, at 1510.

Strum, P. (1993), *Brandeis: Beyond Progressivism*, University Press of Kansas, Lawrence, at 5-6 (discussing influence of William James and pragmatism on Brandeis).

Sturm, S.P. (1994), "Sameness and Subordination: The Dangers of a Universal Solution", *University of Pennsylvania Law Review*, vol. 143, pp. 201-219.

Tamanaha, Brian Z. (1997), *Realistic Socio-Legal Theory: Pragmatism and a Social Theory of Law*. Oxford: Oxford University Press.

The Who (1970), "We Won't Get Fooled Again", in *Who's Next*. London: Decca Records.

Tremblay, Paul R. (1990), "Toward a Community-Based Ethic for Legal Services Practice", *University of California at Los Angeles Law Review*, vol. 37, pp. 1101-1156.

Umphrey, M.M. (1999), "The Dialogics of Legal Meaning: Spectacular Trials, the Unwritten Law, and Narratives of Criminal Responsibility", *Law and Society Review*, vol. 33, pp. 393-420.

Walzer, M. (1985), *Exodus and Revolution*. New York: Basic Books.

Westbrook, Robert B. (1991), *John Dewey and American Democracy*. Ithaca: Cornell University Pres.

White, Lucie E. (1990), "Subordination, Rhetorical Survival Skills, and Sunday Shoes: Notes on the Hearing of Mrs. G." *Buffalo Law Review*, vol. 38, pp. 1-58.

Wilkins, D.B. (1997). "Social Engineers or Corporate Tools: Brown v. Board of Education and the Conscience of the Black Corporate Bar", in Sarat, A. (ed), *Race, Law, and Culture: Reflections on Brown v. Board of Education*, at 137.

Woloch, N. (1996). "Legacy: Labor Law, Women's Politics, and Protective Policies", in *Muller v. Oregon: A Brief History with Documents*, Bedford Books of St. Martin's Press, Boston, pp. 58-90. Case Cited 'Abrams v. United States, 250 U.S. 616 (1919

Index